G-TELP

시험 직전 총정리
비법노트G

5. 관계사

* 쉼표 확인 후 that 오답 제거
* 선행사 유무 확인하기
* 사람 선행사(who, whom),
사물, 장소 선행사(which, where)
* 관계사절에서 완전한 문장인 경우
관계부사 where 확인하기

6. 조동사

* 90% 이상은 정확한 해석으로 풀리며, 시제 확인하기

7. 연결사

* 문장 구조 확인 후 문법 구조 확인하기
* 해석상 가장 자연스러운 것 고르기

청취 요약이G

* 난이도가 가장 높은 영역
* 미국 발음으로 진행됨
* 질문이 문제지에 적혀 있지 않음
* Note Taking 연습 무조건 많이 하기
- 질문이 나올 때, 대화를 나누는 남녀의 이름, 의문사 등의 여부를 파악하여 핵심 키워드를 Note Taking 하기
- 특히 숫자, 일 처리 과정 등의 정보, 문맥에서 긍정적, 부정적 힌트를 제시하는 형용사 등을 Note Taking 하기
- 영단어가 긴 경우는 한국어로 적을 것
* Part 1과 Part 3의 난이도가 낮은 편

Part	내용	Tip!
Part 1	Interesting story 남, 여 일상 주제로 2인 대화	· 문제 해결, 특정 장소 방문, 일정 및 계획 · 대화 주제에 대한 질문이 가장 먼저 나옴 · 주제 → 발생 이유 → 상대방의 반응 → 느낀 점 → 장단점 → 이후 할 일/선택
Part 2	Speech 1인 한 가지 주제로 담화	· 행사, 제품, 안내방송, 광고, 지시 사항 · 세부 정보 유형 다수 출제 경향 · 주제 → 청중 → 세부강연내용(기간, 특징 느낌 등) → 강연자 제안
Part 3	Conversation 서로 잘 아는 남녀 간의 격식 차리지 않은 2인 대화	· 두 가지의 선택 사항 중에 장단점을 구분해 하나를 선택하는 내용 · 주제 → 대상1에 대한 장단점 → 대상2에 대한 장단점 → 이후 할 일/선택
Part 4	Presentation 특정 주제에 대한 1인 담화	· 특정 주제에 대한 과정이나 방법 나열 · 추론(most likely) 문제의 난이도가 높은 편 · 강연 목적 → 강연 대상 → 세부강연내용(연구결과, 증명 사실, 과거 및 현재 사실) → 이후 할 일

독해 요약이G

* 대체로 꼬아서 내는 문제가 없음
* 단락 순차적으로 문제 풀기가 가능
* 지문의 흐름이 정형화 되어 있음
* 유사어구 반복에 주의하기
- 단어뿐만 아니라 구나 절, 문장 또한 그 형태를 바꾸어 같은 의미를 다시 표현한(Paraphrasing) 어구 반복에 유의할 것
* 6번, 7번 문제는 어휘 문제이며 뜻만 잘 외워도 풀기 수월한 문제임

Part	내용	특징
Part 1	Biography Article	· 역사적 위인, 유명인사 등 특정 인물의 일대기를 시간 순으로 서술한 지문 · 인물 소개 → 유년시절 → 주요활동 → 사망 or 근황
Part 2	Magazine Article	· 사회적 이슈(과학, 사회, 환경 등)에 관한 기사 형식의 지문 · 연구 결과 소개 → 연구하게 된 계기 → 특징 → 의의 및 추후 과제
Part 3	Encyclopedia Article	· 다양한 분야(동/식물, 환경, 기후, 역사, 현상 등) 내의 한 가지 소재를 설명하는 지문 · 정의 → 기원 → 특징
Part 4	Business or Formal Letter	· 구매 및 환불, 채용, 추천서, 이직, 서비스 홍보, 업무 요청 등의 비즈니스 편지 형식의 지문 · 편지의 목적 → 요청사항 및 답변 → 세부 설명 → 마무리 인사

비법노트G

문법 요약이G

1. 시제

시제	형태		정답 key point	의미
현재진행	am is are	Ving	(right)now currently	~하고 있다
과거진행	was were	Ving	last + 시간 at that time when + S + 과거시제	~하고 있었다
미래진행	will be	Ving	next + 시간 in + 미래연도 soon shortly when/if + S + 현재시제	~하고 있을 것이다
현재완료진행	has been have been	Ving	since for	~해오고 있는 중이다
과거완료진행	had been	Ving	when before + S + 과거시제	~해오고 있던 중이다
미래완료진행	will have been	Ving	by the time + S + 현재시제 by + 미래 연도 by the end of~	~해오고 있을 것이다

2. 가정법

가정법	문장 형태	의미
가정법 과거	If +S + 과거시제/were, S + 조동사과거(would, could, should, might) + V	만약 ~한다면, ~할텐데(현재 사실 반대의 상황)
가정법 과거완료	If +S + had p.p, S + 조동사과거 + have p.p~	만약 ~했었다면, ~했을 텐데(과거에 이미 벌어진 사실과 반대의 상황)

* 문장의 앞뒤로 if의 유무를 확인하기(가정법 도치) Should/Were/Had + S, ~

3. Should 생략

- 제안, 추천, 요구, 주장, 명령을 의미하는 동사의 that절에는 should 생략으로 **동사원형**만 사용
  suggest, recommend, demand, insist, order + that + S + (should) + **동사원형**

* 선택지 내에 동사원형이 있어야 하며, 밑줄 앞에 that과 S가 있는지 확인하기

4. 준동사

* 동명사와 to 부정사 동사 암기가 필수
* 문장 구조 확인 및 빈칸 위치 파악하기
- 주어, 전치사 목적어 : ing 정답
- 목적어 : 빈칸 바로 앞의 단어,
  숙어 표현 확인하기(보통 ing가 정답)
- 부사자리, 명사 후치수식 : to 부정사 정답

* 둘 다 가능한 동사는 해석으로 정답 찾기
- [try] + ing : 시도하다 / to 부정사 : 노력하다
- [remember/forget] + ing : 과거에 한 것
  + to 부정사 : 아직 안 한 것
- [regret] + ing : 후회하다 / to 부정사 : 유감이다

나만의 요약노트G

문법 | 핵심 POINT!

청취 | 핵심 POINT!

독해 | 핵심 POINT!

문법 점수 기록표

- 수험자 스스로 목표 시간을 설정하고 시간 분배를 조절할 수 있도록 도와주는 표를 통해 본인의 시간을 체크해볼 수 있도록 합시다.
- 문제를 풀어본 뒤, 본인이 각 영역 별로 점수를 매겨봅니다. 본인의 취약한 부분을 파악한 뒤 다시 한 번 복습하는 시간을 가지도록 해봅시다.

문법 채점 결과 : ____ /26

문항 번호 (a~d)	1	2	3	4	5	6	7	8	9	10
	11	12	13	14	15	16	17	18	19	20
	21	22	23	24	25	26				
채점 (O/X)	1	2	3	4	5	6	7	8	9	10
	11	12	13	14	15	16	17	18	19	20
	21	22	23	24	25	26				
복습	1	2	3	4	5	6	7	8	9	10
	11	12	13	14	15	16	17	18	19	20
	21	22	23	24	25	26				

채점 : 몰라서 틀린 문제는 X, 찍어서 맞혔거나 헷갈린 문제는 △ 표기
복습 : X, △ 문제는 꼭 다시 풀고 ✓ 표기

문법 채점 결과 : ____ /26

문항 번호 (a~d)	1	2	3	4	5	6	7	8	9	10
	11	12	13	14	15	16	17	18	19	20
	21	22	23	24	25	26				
채점 (O/X)	1	2	3	4	5	6	7	8	9	10
	11	12	13	14	15	16	17	18	19	20
	21	22	23	24	25	26				
복습	1	2	3	4	5	6	7	8	9	10
	11	12	13	14	15	16	17	18	19	20
	21	22	23	24	25	26				

채점 : 몰라서 틀린 문제는 X, 찍어서 맞혔거나 헷갈린 문제는 △ 표기
복습 : X, △ 문제는 꼭 다시 풀고 ✓ 표기

문법 채점 결과 : ____ /26

문항 번호 (a~d)	1	2	3	4	5	6	7	8	9	10
	11	12	13	14	15	16	17	18	19	20
	21	22	23	24	25	26				
채점 (O/X)	1	2	3	4	5	6	7	8	9	10
	11	12	13	14	15	16	17	18	19	20
	21	22	23	24	25	26				
복습	1	2	3	4	5	6	7	8	9	10
	11	12	13	14	15	16	17	18	19	20
	21	22	23	24	25	26				

채점 : 몰라서 틀린 문제는 X, 찍어서 맞혔거나 헷갈린 문제는 △ 표기
복습 : X, △ 문제는 꼭 다시 풀고 ✓ 표기

청취 점수 기록표

- 수험자 스스로 목표 시간을 설정하고 시간 분배를 조절할 수 있도록 도와주는 표를 통해 본인의 시간을 체크해볼 수 있도록 합시다.
- 문제를 풀어본 뒤, 본인이 각 영역 별로 점수를 매겨봅니다. 본인의 취약한 부분을 파악한 뒤 다시 한 번 복습하는 시간을 가지도록 해봅시다.

청취 채점 결과 : ____ /26

문항 번호 (a~d)	27	28	29	30	31	32	33	34	35	36
	37	38	39	40	41	42	43	44	45	46
	47	48	49	50	51	52				
채점 (O/X)	27	28	29	30	31	32	33	34	35	36
	37	38	39	40	41	42	43	44	45	46
	47	48	49	50	51	52				
복습	27	28	29	30	31	32	33	34	35	36
	37	38	39	40	41	42	43	44	45	46
	47	48	49	50	51	52				

채점 : 몰라서 틀린 문제는 X, 찍어서 맞혔거나 헷갈린 문제는 △ 표기
복습 : X, △ 문제는 꼭 다시 풀고 ✓ 표기

청취 채점 결과 : ____ /26

문항 번호 (a~d)	27	28	29	30	31	32	33	34	35	36
	37	38	39	40	41	42	43	44	45	46
	47	48	49	50	51	52				
채점 (O/X)	27	28	29	30	31	32	33	34	35	36
	37	38	39	40	41	42	43	44	45	46
	47	48	49	50	51	52				
복습	27	28	29	30	31	32	33	34	35	36
	37	38	39	40	41	42	43	44	45	46
	47	48	49	50	51	52				

채점 : 몰라서 틀린 문제는 X, 찍어서 맞혔거나 헷갈린 문제는 △ 표기
복습 : X, △ 문제는 꼭 다시 풀고 ✓ 표기

청취 채점 결과 : ____ /26

문항 번호 (a~d)	27	28	29	30	31	32	33	34	35	36
	37	38	39	40	41	42	43	44	45	46
	47	48	49	50	51	52				
채점 (O/X)	27	28	29	30	31	32	33	34	35	36
	37	38	39	40	41	42	43	44	45	46
	47	48	49	50	51	52				
복습	27	28	29	30	31	32	33	34	35	36
	37	38	39	40	41	42	43	44	45	46
	47	48	49	50	51	52				

채점 : 몰라서 틀린 문제는 X, 찍어서 맞혔거나 헷갈린 문제는 △ 표기
복습 : X, △ 문제는 꼭 다시 풀고 ✓ 표기

독해 점수 기록표

- 수험자 스스로 목표 시간을 설정하고 시간 분배를 조절할 수 있도록 도와주는 표를 통해 본인의 시간을 체크해볼 수 있도록 합시다.
- 문제를 풀어본 뒤, 본인이 각 영역 별로 점수를 매겨봅니다. 본인의 취약한 부분을 파악한 뒤 다시 한 번 복습하는 시간을 가지도록 해봅시다.

독해 채점 결과 : ____ /28

문항 번호 (a~d)	53	54	55	56	57	58	59	60	61	62
	63	64	65	66	67	68	69	70	71	72
	73	74	75	76	77	78	79	80		
채점 (O/X)	53	54	55	56	57	58	59	60	61	62
	63	64	65	66	67	68	69	70	71	72
	73	74	75	76	77	78	79	80		
복습	53	54	55	56	57	58	59	60	61	62
	63	64	65	66	67	68	69	70	71	72
	73	74	75	76	77	78	79	80		

채점 : 몰라서 틀린 문제는 X, 찍어서 맞혔거나 헷갈린 문제는 △ 표기
복습 : X, △ 문제는 꼭 다시 풀고 ✓ 표기

독해 채점 결과 : ____ /28

문항 번호 (a~d)	53	54	55	56	57	58	59	60	61	62
	63	64	65	66	67	68	69	70	71	72
	73	74	75	76	77	78	79	80		
채점 (O/X)	53	54	55	56	57	58	59	60	61	62
	63	64	65	66	67	68	69	70	71	72
	73	74	75	76	77	78	79	80		
복습	53	54	55	56	57	58	59	60	61	62
	63	64	65	66	67	68	69	70	71	72
	73	74	75	76	77	78	79	80		

채점 : 몰라서 틀린 문제는 X, 찍어서 맞혔거나 헷갈린 문제는 △ 표기
복습 : X, △ 문제는 꼭 다시 풀고 ✓ 표기

독해 채점 결과 : ____ /28

문항 번호 (a~d)	53	54	55	56	57	58	59	60	61	62
	63	64	65	66	67	68	69	70	71	72
	73	74	75	76	77	78	79	80		
채점 (O/X)	53	54	55	56	57	58	59	60	61	62
	63	64	65	66	67	68	69	70	71	72
	73	74	75	76	77	78	79	80		
복습	53	54	55	56	57	58	59	60	61	62
	63	64	65	66	67	68	69	70	71	72
	73	74	75	76	77	78	79	80		

채점 : 몰라서 틀린 문제는 X, 찍어서 맞혔거나 헷갈린 문제는 △ 표기
복습 : X, △ 문제는 꼭 다시 풀고 ✓ 표기

G-TELP | 공 | 식 | 주 | 관 | 사 |

G-TELP 영어연구소 저

퀵 지텔프

공식 모의고사

최신 출제 경향 반영

전면 개정판

Level 2

필수 어휘 800개 수록 | 문제 유형 표기 정확한 해설 | 비법노트 수록 | 청취 음원파일 QR코드 삽입 | OMR 답안지 수록

G-TELP KOREA 출판사업본부

G-TELP 영어연구소 소개

G-TELP 영어연구소는 국내외 영어 콘텐츠 전문 연구진들로 이루어진 조직으로서, G-TELP 시험들을 전문적으로 분석 및 연구해오고 있습니다. 다년간 쌓아온 디지털 데이터베이스와 정확한 데이터를 분석하는 도구를 기반으로 G-TELP의 모든 시험을 대비할 수 있는 수험서, 일반 영어, 비즈니스 영어, 전문 영어 등 다양한 분야의 영어학습서를 기획, 집필, 편집, 출간하고 있습니다.

퀵 지텔프 공식 모의고사 2급

개정판 3쇄 2023년 8월 10일

발행인 김현중
출판사 G-TELP KOREA 출판사업본부
저 자 G-TELP 영어연구소

ISBN 978-89-91164-56-7
정 가 18,000원

도서 문의 안내
PHONE 1577-3836
FAX 02-454-2137

PREFACE

안녕하세요. G-TELP 연구소입니다.

G-TELP는 1985년 ITSC 주관으로 개발 검증된 이래 세계 여러 나라 정부 기관과 기업에서 영어 활용능력 평가 도구로 활용되고 있는 국제 공인 영어 시험입니다.

G-TELP Level 2 시험은 국내 650여 개의 기업 채용 및 승진과 경찰, 군무원, 공무원뿐만 아니라 국가자격증 등에서 영어 능력 검정 자격시험으로 활용되며, 다수의 수험자들이 G-TELP 학습에 많은 시간을 투자하고 있습니다. G-TELP는 타 시험 대비 상대적으로 적은 문항 수와 짧은 시험 시간으로 시험에 대한 부담이 적고, 단기간에 원하는 목표 점수에 도달할 수 있기에 최근 응시자 수가 상당히 늘고 있습니다.

『퀵 지텔프 공식 모의고사 2급 개정판』은 수험자들이 보다 최신 경향을 반영한 문제들로 더 효과적으로, 그리고 영역별 구성으로 더 효율적으로 학습할 수 있도록 재구성 하였습니다.

☑ 최신 출제 경향 반영

최신 출제 경향에 따라 기존 문제 수정 및 지문 교체를 통해 최근 시험에 완벽히 대비할 수 있도록 준비하였습니다.

☑ 각 영역별 풀이 가능

수험자들이 보다 효율적으로 학습할 수 있도록 모의고사를 문법, 청취, 독해 각각의 영역별로 나누어 구성했습니다. 다시 말해, 모의고사 문제가 문법, 청취, 독해 각각의 영역별로 나누어져 있어, 수험자가 부족한 영역을 집중적으로 학습할 수 있습니다.

☑ 필수 어휘 800개

필수 어휘 800개를 부록으로 구성하였습니다. 고급 어휘를 포함하여 G-TELP 정기시험 대비에 필요한 단어들을 엄선하였고, 빈도수를 별도로 표시하여 단어의 중요도를 한눈에 파악할 수 있습니다.

『퀵 지텔프 공식 모의고사 2급』으로 G-TELP 입문자 부터 고득점을 목표로 하는 수험자까지, 모두가 원하는 바를 이룰 수 있길 기원합니다.

G-TELP 영어연구소 올림

시험 개요

■ 출제기관 소개

㈜한국지텔프는 신뢰성, 타당성, 실용성을 갖춘 종합적인 영어평가라는 신조 아래 ITSC's G-TELP Services의 글로벌 파트너로서 1985년부터 G-TELP 시험을 주관하는 어학 평가, 교육, 출판 전문 기업입니다. ㈜한국지텔프는 업무 협약을 통해 한국 내 G-TELP 시험의 시행, 마케팅, 홍보, 출판, 교육에 대한 운영을 담당하고 있습니다.

㈜한국지텔프는 지난 30여년 동안 영어학습자의 영어 능력을 보다 정확하고 세밀하게 분석할 수 있는 평가도구 개발에 끊임없이 노력을 기울여 왔습니다. 2006년부터 2019년 1월까지 12년 동안 국가 자격 시험인 항공 영어 구술증명시험(EPTA)을 시행하였으며, 평가 영역별, 레벨별, 목적별, 나이별 등으로 구분된 아래의 다양한 시험을 정기적으로 시행하고 있습니다.

- ☑ 문법과 듣기, 읽기 능력을 평가하는 5단계의 **G-TELP Level Test**
- ☑ 실생활과 관련된 영어 말하기/쓰기 능력을 평가하는 **G-TELP Speaking Test, G-TELP Writing Test**
- ☑ 비즈니스 말하기/쓰기 수행 능력 평가인 **G-TELP Business Speaking Test, G-TELP Business Writing Test**
- ☑ 영어 초급자 및 초등학생과 중학생의 영어 능력을 평가하는 **G-TELP Junior**

주니어부터 성인까지 영어를 종합적으로 평가할 수 있는 완성된 평가 교육 시스템을 갖추고, 전문 분야별 영어 활용 능력 평가도구 개발에 쏟아온 투자와 열정이 신뢰성과 타당성, 실용성을 갖춘 종합적인 평가 시스템 구축을 위한 밑거름이 되었으리라 믿으며, 단순히 우열을 가르는 평가가 아닌 학습자에게 개인의 능력을 분석 진단하여 학습 동기를 제공하고, 학습 과정으로써 진정한 평가가 될 수 있도록 최선의 노력을 다할 것입니다.

GLT(G-TELP Level Test 지텔프 등급 시험) 소개

G-TELP(General Tests of English Language Proficiency)는 미국 국제 테스트 연구원(ITSC, International Testing Services Center)에서 주관하여 University of California Los Angeles, Georgetown University, San Diego State University, Lado International College 등의 저명 교수진이 연구/개발하였고, 국내외 저명한 언어학자, 평가전문가들이 참여하여 국제적으로 시행하는 글로벌 영어 능력 평가 인증 시험입니다.

GLT는 Level 1부터 Level 5까지 다섯 등급으로 나누어진 등급 시험이며, 문제는 모두 4지 선다형의 객관식 형태로 출제됩니다. 문법/청취/독해 및 어휘로 이루어져 있으며, 각 영역에서 모두 75% 이상을 획득하였을 때 해당 응시 등급을 Mastery 한 것으로 인정됩니다.

■ 시험 특징

- ☑ 5단계(Level 1~5)의 수준별로 구분된 시험
- ☑ 문법/청취/독해 및 어휘 3가지 영역의 종합 영어 능력 평가 → 객관식 사지선다형
  (단, Level 1은 청취/독해 및 어휘 2가지 영역만 집중 평가)
- ☑ 절대 평가 방식
- ☑ 빠른 성적 확인 → 응시일로부터 일주일 이내 빠른 성적 발표
- ☑ 정기 시험: Level 2 시험 → **국가고시/국가자격시험/기업체 채용 시험에 주로 활용**
  수시 시험: Level 1~5 시험

■ 등급별 시험 구성

구분	출제 방식 및 시간	평가 기준	합격자의 영어 구사 능력	응시자격
Level 1	청취: 30문항/약 30분 독해 및 어휘: 70문항/70분 합계: 100문항/약 100분	Native Speaker에 준하는 영어 능력: 상담, 토론 가능	· 모국어로 하는 외국인과 거의 대등한 의사소통이 가능 · 국제회의 통역도 가능한 수준	Level 2 Mastery (영역별 75점 이상)
Level 2	문법: 26문항/20분 청취: 26문항/약 30분 독해 및 어휘: 28문항/40분 합계: 80문항/약 90분	다양한 상황에서 대화 가능: 업무 상담 및 해외연수 등이 가능한 수준	· 일상생활 및 업무 상담 등에서 어려움 없이 의사소통할 수 있는 수준 · 외국인과의 회의 및 세미나 참석, 해외 연수 등이 가능한 수준	제한 없음
Level 3	문법: 22문항/20분 청취: 24문항/약 20분 독해 및 어휘: 24문항/40분 합계: 70문항/약 80분	간단한 의사소통과 친숙한 상태에서의 단순 대화 가능	· 간단한 의사소통과 친숙한 상태에서의 단순한 대화가 가능한 수준 · 해외여행과 단순한 업무 출장을 할 수 있는 수준	제한 없음
Level 4	문법: 20문항/20분 청취: 20문항/약 15분 독해 및 어휘: 20문항/25분 합계: 60문항/약 60분	기본적인 문장을 통해 최소한의 의사소통이 가능한 수준	· 기본적인 어휘의 짧은 문장을 통해 최소한의 의사소통이 가능한 수준 · 외국인이 자주 반복하거나 부연설명을 해 주어야 이해할 수 있는 수준	제한 없음
Level 5	문법: 16문항/15분 청취: 16문항/약 15분 독해 및 어휘: 18문항/25분 합계: 50문항/약 55분	극히 초보적인 수준의 의사소통 가능	· 영어 초보자 · 일상의 인사/소개 등을 듣고, 이해할 수 있는 수준 · 말 또는 글을 통한 자기표현은 거의 불가능한 수준	제한 없음

G-TELP Level 2란?

■ 시험 구성

문법	+	청취	+	독해	=	총 80문항
26문항		26문항		28문항		약 90분
20분		약 30분		40분		

영역	내용	지문 수 (개)	문항 수 (개)	배점 (점)	시간 (분)
Grammar (총 26문항)	가정법, 시제, 조동사, to부정사, 동명사, 연결어, 관계사	-	26	100	20분
Listening (총 26문항)	Part 1. Interesting story	1	7	100	약 30분
	Part 2. Speech	1	6		
	Part 3. Conversation	1	6		
	Part 4. Presentation	1	7		
Reading & Vocabulary (총 28문항)	Part 1. Biography Article	1	7	100	40분
	Part 2. Magazine Article	1	7		
	Part 3. Encyclopedia Article	1	7		
	Part 4. Business or Formal Letter	1	7		
Total			80	300	약 90분

* 시험 시간을 특정 영역에 제한을 두지는 않으므로, 주어진 시간 내에 다른 영역의 문제풀이 가능
* 각 영역 100점 만점으로 총 300점이며, 세 개 영역의 평균 값으로 성적 산출

■ 점수 비율

Section	점수 비율	Mastery 기준
문법	100점 만점	**Mastery:** 세 가지 영역(문법, 청취, 독해 및 어휘) 모두 75% 이상 획득한 경우 **Near Mastery:** 세 가지 영역(문법, 청취, 독해 및 어휘) 중 두 개 영역에서 75% 이상 획득한 경우 **No Mastery:** 세 가지 영역(문법, 청취, 독해 및 어휘) 중 두 개 이상의 영역에서 75% 미만을 획득한 경우
청취	100점 만점	
독해 및 어휘	100점 만점	
총점	총 300점 만점	
평균	100점 (성적표상 You have answered 100% of all the question in the test correctly 부분)	** 국내에서는 대개 Level 2시험의 특정 평균 점수 이상을 획득하면 영어 대체 시험 합격점으로 인정

성적표

G-TELP의 개인성적표는 그 등급의 Mastery(합격) 여부를 표시하는 Overall Proficiency(전체 등급 능숙도)와 Skill Area Score(문법, 청취, 독해 및 어휘 점수) 그리고 Task/Structure Score(각 기능의 세분화된 부분의 점수 및 문제 형태)에 대한 정보를 알려줍니다.

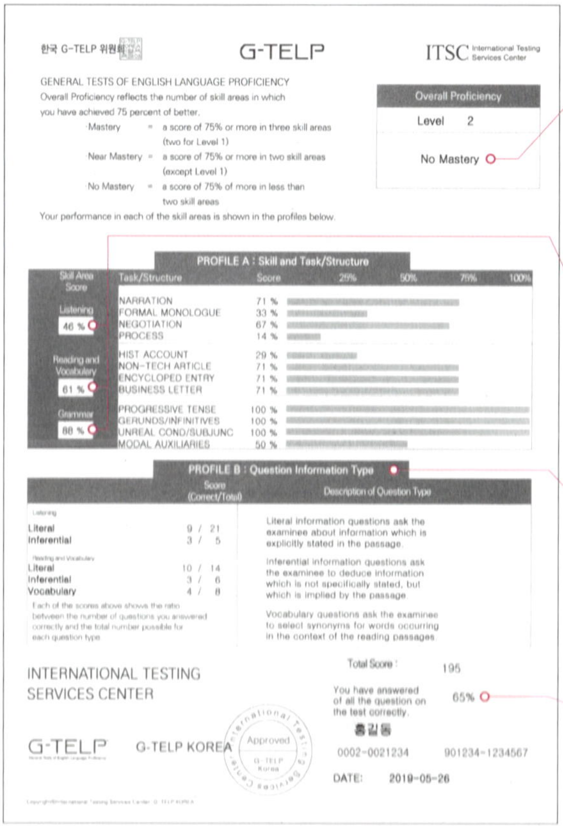

한국 G-TELP 위원회 G-TELP ITSC International Testing Services Center

GENERAL TESTS OF ENGLISH LANGUAGE PROFICIENCY
Overall Proficiency reflects the number of skill areas in which you have achieved 75 percent of better.
Mastery = a score of 75% or more in three skill areas (two for Level 1)
Near Mastery = a score of 75% or more in two skill areas (except Level 1)
No Mastery = a score of 75% of more in less than two skill areas
Your performance in each of the skill areas is shown in the profiles below.

Overall Proficiency
Level 2
No Mastery

PROFILE A : Skill and Task/Structure

Skill Area Score	Task/Structure	Score
Listening 46 %	NARRATION	71 %
	FORMAL MONOLOGUE	33 %
	NEGOTIATION	67 %
	PROCESS	14 %
Reading and Vocabulary 61 %	HIST ACCOUNT	29 %
	NON-TECH ARTICLE	71 %
	ENCYCLOPED ENTRY	71 %
	BUSINESS LETTER	71 %
Grammar 88 %	PROGRESSIVE TENSE	100 %
	GERUNDS/INFINITIVES	100 %
	UNREAL COND/SUBJUNC	100 %
	MODAL AUXILIARIES	50 %

PROFILE B : Question Information Type

	Score (Correct/Total)	Description of Question Type
Listening		
Literal	9 / 21	Literal information questions ask the examinee about information which is explicitly stated in the passage.
Inferential	3 / 5	
Reading and Vocabulary		
Literal	10 / 14	Inferential information questions ask the examinee to deduce information which is not specifically stated, but which is implied by the passage.
Inferential	3 / 6	
Vocabulary	4 / 8	Vocabulary questions ask the examinee to select synonyms for words occurring in the context of the reading passages.

Each of the scores above shows the ratio between the number of questions you answered correctly and the total number possible for each question type.

INTERNATIONAL TESTING SERVICES CENTER

Total Score : 195
You have answered of all the question on the test correctly. 65%
홍길동
0002-0021234 901234-1234567
DATE: 2019-05-26

G-TELP G-TELP KOREA
International Testing Services Center Approved G-TELP Korea

Copyright©International Testing Services Center G-TELP KOREA

해당 등급의 합격 여부를 알려주는 항목

Mastery
- 세 가지 영역(문법, 청취, 독해 및 어휘) 모두 75% 이상 획득한 경우

Near Mastery
- 세 가지 영역(문법, 청취, 독해 및 어휘) 중 두 개 영역에서 75% 이상 획득한 경우

No Mastery
- 세 가지 영역(문법, 청취, 독해 및 어휘) 중 두 개 이상의 영역에서 75% 미만을 획득한 경우

Skill Area Score
- 각 Section별 맞은 문제에 대한 백분율(점수)

PROFILE B
- 청취·독해 파트의 정답 분석
- 응시자의 정답 타입을 용이하게 파악

Percent
- 세가지 기능분야의 평균 백분율(총점)
- 실제 취득한 지텔프 점수

■ 성적 발표

- 시험일로부터 5일 후 G-TELP KOREA 공식 홈페이지 (www.g-telp.co.kr)에서 성적 확인이 가능합니다.
- 원본 성적표는 온라인 성적표를 바로 인쇄하거나 시험일로부터 2주 이내에 기재하신 주소로 우편 발송됩니다.

■ 성적 유효 기간

시험일로부터 2년간 유효

최신 출제 경향

■ 문법 영역

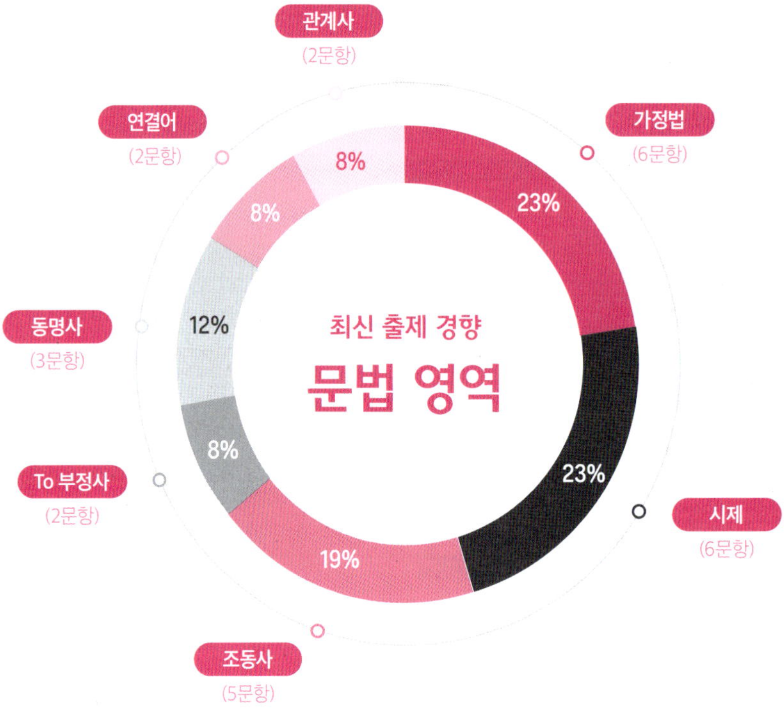

- 주요 문법 영역 중 시제와 가정법이 전체 출제의 약 46%를 차지할 정도로 높은 비중으로 출제됩니다.
- 나머지 영역은 고루 출제되기 때문에 고득점을 목표로 하는 수험자는 8가지 영역 모두 학습하는 것이 필수입니다.
- 모의고사 3회분의 해설집에 표기된 각 문항별 문법 유형을 통해, 스스로 강점과 취약점을 파악하고 취약한 문법 영역을 집중적으로 학습해야 합니다.

가장 출제 비중이 높은 시제와 가정법 지문에서는 시간 표현(시간 부사구) 단서를 찾는 것이 중요합니다.
특히, 최근에는 시제 중 진행형과 완료 진행형이 정답 보기로 자주 출제되는 경향이 있습니다.

최신 출제 경향

■ 청취 영역

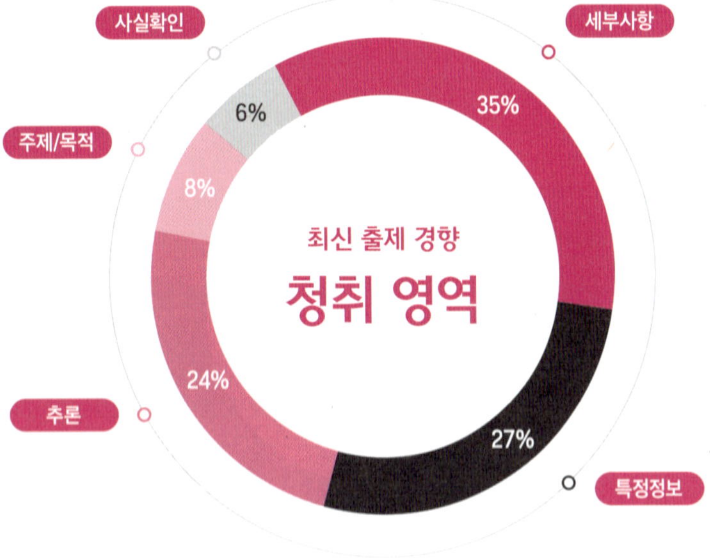

- 청취 영역의 문제 유형은 크게 나누면 5가지로, 주제, 세부사항, 특정정보, 사실확인, 추론이 있습니다.
- 가장 출제 비중이 큰 유형은 세부사항이며, 그 다음으로는 특정정보, 추론이 있으며, 각각 전체 문항 수의 35%, 27%, 24%를 차지합니다.
- 청취 영역 역시 해설지에 표기된 유형과 질문을 통해 취약한 문제 유형을 파악하여 사전에 철저히 학습해야합니다.
- 아래 표를 통해, 더욱 자세하고 명확한 문제 유형 파악이 가능합니다. (출제 비중 순서)

유형	특징
세부사항	wh-questions(why, how, where, when 등)으로 시작하는 질문으로, 화자의 특정 이유(why)를 찾는 질문이 꼭 출제됩니다.
특정정보	주로 what으로 시작하는 질문으로, 특정 키워드와 함께 열거된 특징, 장점, 단계(feature, benefit, step) 등을 잘 듣고 메모하는 것이 중요합니다.
추론	'most likely, probably 등'의 표현이 포함된 질문으로, 주로 각 파트의 마지막 부분에 등장합니다. 대화 중 화자(들)의 다음 행동을 예측하는 질문이 꼭 출제됩니다.
주제/목적	화자가 무엇을 이야기하는지 그 주제나 목적에 관해 질문하는 것으로, 각 파트의 처음 부분에 주로 등장합니다.
사실확인	질문에 직접적으로 true/not true라는 표현이 있으며, 전체적인 흐름을 파악하여야 정답 보기를 찾을 수 있습니다. 역시 특정 키워드 메모가 필수입니다.

처음 질문을 들려줄 때 질문의 키워드를 시험지에 빠르게 메모하는 것이 중요하며,
지문 내용이 패러프레이즈(바꾸어 표현)된 정답 보기를 찾는 연습으로 고득점을 획득할 수 있습니다

최신 출제 경향

■ 독해 및 어휘 영역

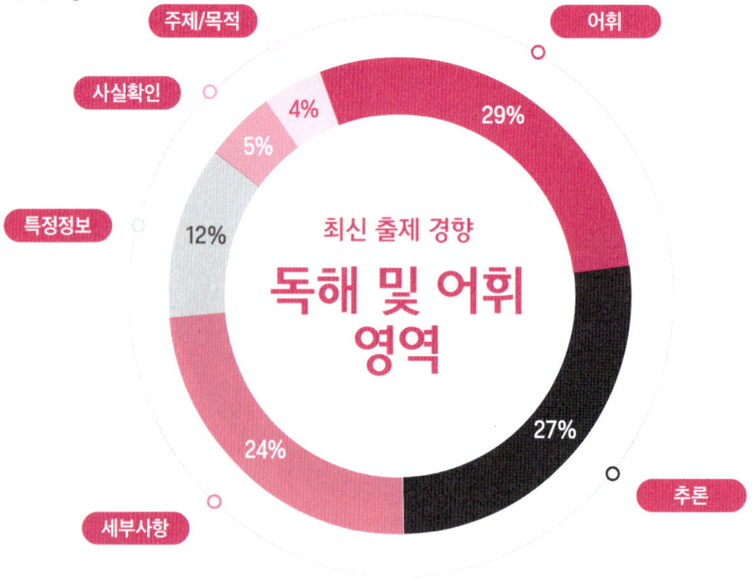

- 독해 및 어휘 영역의 문제 유형을 크게 나누면 6가지로, 주제, 세부사항, 특정정보, 사실확인, 추론, 어휘가 있습니다. 청취와 다르게 각 파트별로 어휘 문제가 2개씩 출제된다는 점이 특징입니다.
- 어휘를 제외하고 가장 출제 비중이 높은 유형은 추론으로, 전체 문항 수의 27%를 차지합니다.
- 문제와 지문의 키워드(학명, 지역, 이름, 년도 등)를 빠르게 찾아 작게 표시할 뿐만 아니라, 지문 내용과 패러프레이즈(바꾸어 표현) 된 정답 보기를 일치시키는 연습을 통해 고득점을 획득할 수 있습니다.

어휘 유형은 단순히 동의어를 찾는 능력보다 어휘의 여러 가지 뜻과 문맥을 파악하는 능력을 필요로 하는 문제가 출제됩니다.
폭넓은 어휘력과 정확한 해석을 필요로 하는 어휘 유형은 뒤에 수록된 필수 고급 어휘들을 암기하여 대비하도록 합니다.

문제 유형 예시(출제 비중 순서)

유형	예시
어휘	In the context of the passage, X means ________.
추론	How can X most likely be described?
세부사항	Why(When, How, etc.) did X do Y?
특정 정보	According to the article, what is a characteristic of X?
사실확인	Which of the following is true(not true) about X?
주제/목적	What is the purpose of X?

지텔프 Level 2 활용현황

대한민국정부 국가 공무원 5,7급 **지텔프 65점**	대한민국정부 외교관 후보자 **지텔프 88점**	대한민국정부 국가 공무원 7급(외무영사직영) **지텔프 77점**	대한민국정부 국가 공무원 7급(지역인재) **지텔프 65점**
경찰청 경찰공무원(순경) **지텔프 43점**	대법원 법원 행정고시 **지텔프 65점**	대한민국국회 NATIONAL ASSEMBLY 입법고시 **지텔프 65점**	병무청 카투사 지텔프 **지텔프 73점**
국민안전처 소방간부 후보생 **지텔프 50점**	경찰청 경찰간부 후보생 **지텔프 50점**	대한민국 국방부 Ministry of National Defense 군무원 5, 7, 9급 **지텔프 65, 47, 32점**	금융감독원 FINANCIAL SUPERVISORY SERVICE 공인회계사 **지텔프 65점**
HRDK 한국산업인력공단 공인노무사 **지텔프 65점**	HRDK 한국산업인력공단 변리사 **지텔프 77점**	HRDK 한국산업인력공단 세무사 **지텔프 65점**	HRDK 한국산업인력공단 외국어번역 행정사 **지텔프 라이팅 3급**
HRDK 한국산업인력공단 관광통역 안내사 **지텔프 74점**	HRDK 한국산업인력공단 호텔경영사 **지텔프 79점**	HRDK 한국산업인력공단 호텔관리사 **지텔프 66점**	HRDK 한국산업인력공단 호텔서비스사 **지텔프 39점**
HRDK 한국산업인력공단 감정평가사 **지텔프 65점**	HRDK 한국산업인력공단 박물관 및 미술관 준학예사 **지텔프 50점**	HRDK 한국산업인력공단 국제의료관광코디네이터 **지텔프 65점**	공공기관, 공기업, 일반기업 채용, 승진, 대학교 신입선발, 졸업인증, 중고등학교 영어 경시대회 등에 활용

G-TELP

교재 구성 및 특징

01 지텔프 개요

지텔프 소개, 시험 소개, 성적 및 활용 현황 등을 간결하게 정리하여 수험자가 지텔프 시험에 대한 이해를 통해 체계적인 시험 대비를 할 수 있도록 구성하였습니다.

02 최신 출제 경향

모의고사를 풀기 전에 기출 모의고사를 체계적으로 분석한 영역별 정보를 제공하여 수험자가 실전 준비를 용이하게 할 수 있습니다.

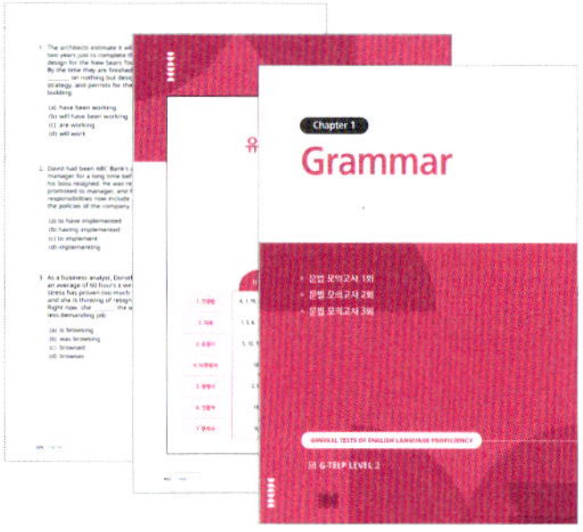

03 영역별 유형 연습

정기시험 난이도의 영역별 실전 대비 문제로 구성되어 있으며, 수험자 스스로가 부족하다고 느끼는 영역을 집중적으로 학습할 수 있습니다.

04 해석 및 해설

문제에 대한 정답과 해석, 그리고 해설을 제공합니다. 문제를 풀어 본 후, 문제 유형과 단서를 통해 자신의 강점과 취약점을 분석할 수 있으며, 해설에 제시된 풀이 방식과 수험자 자신의 풀이 방식과의 차이점을 분석하며 문제 풀이 능력을 향상할 수 있습니다.

05 필수 어휘 800

빈출 어휘를 알파벳순으로 정리하여, 시험 직전에 어휘 부록만 복습하여도 점수 상승이 가능하도록 구성했습니다.

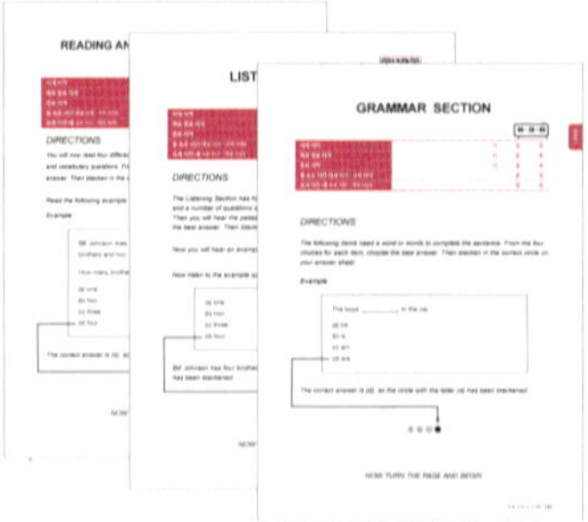

06 시간 분배 기록표

수험자 스스로 목표 시간을 설정하고 시간 분배를 연습할 수 있도록 도와주는 표가 수록되어 있습니다.

07 한 장으로 보는 정답

수험자의 편의를 위하여 한 번에 채점할 수 있도록 정답지를 따로 제공하였습니다.

08 OMR 연습

매회 연습할 수 있는 OMR카드가 수록되어 있어 실전 감각을 키울 수 있습니다.

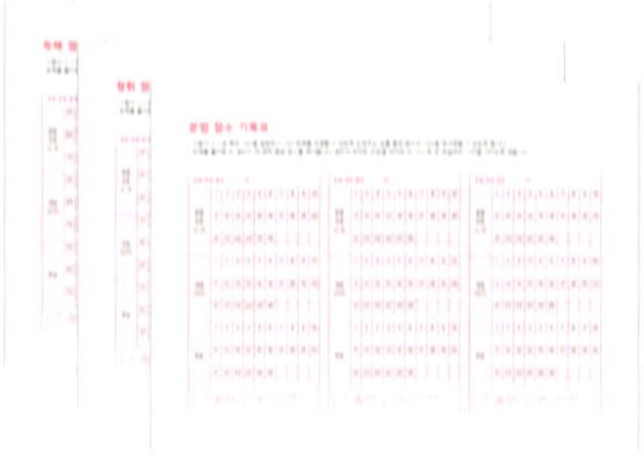

09 점수 기록표 (부록)

문제를 풀어보면서 유형별로 점수를 기록할 수 있는 표를 제공합니다. 취약한 영역을 파악하고, 틀린 문제를 다시 한번 복습해볼 수 있는 기회를 제공합니다.

시험 전 확인하기!

시험장으로 가기 전 준비물 Check!

☐ 규정 신분증 ☐ 컴퓨터용 사인펜 ☐ 수정 테이프 ☐ 아날로그 시계

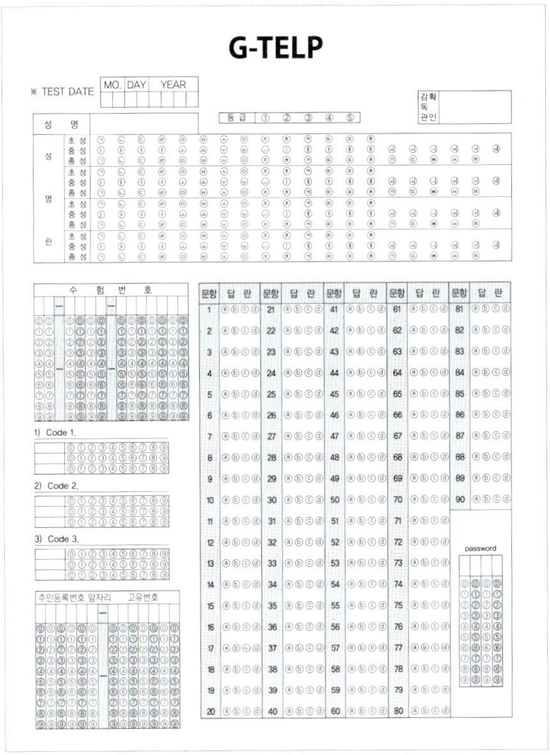

OMR 작성법 예습하기!

01 TEST DATE란에 월, 일, 년 순으로 기재합니다.

02 성명란에 초성, 중성, 종성에 맞게 기재합니다.

03 수험번호는 책상 위에 비치된 이름표를 참고하여 기재합니다.

04 Code 1과 Code 2는 OMR카드 뒷면에서 해당하는 코드를 찾아 마킹합니다.
(대학생이 아닌 일반인의 경우 Code 1은 098, Code 2는 090을 기재하시면 됩니다.)

05 Code 3은 수험번호 마지막 7자리 숫자의 앞 3자리 숫자를 마킹합니다.

06 개인 정보 보호를 위해 주민등록번호는 앞자리만 마킹한 후, 뒷자리는 이름표에 기재된 고유 번호로 마킹합니다.

07 답안지는 총 90번까지 있으나 Level 2 시험은 80번까지 출제되므로 80번까지 마킹합니다.

08 Password는 인터넷 성적 출력 시 필요한 번호로 본인이 기억할 수 있는 번호로 마킹합니다.

시험 시간에는 별도의 답안지 마킹 시간이 주어지지 않습니다

G-TELP | 공 | 식 | 주 | 관 | 사 |

G-TELP 영어연구소 저

퀵 지텔프

공식 모의고사

문제집

Level 2

G-TELP KOREA 출판사업본부

퀵지텔프

목차

Chapter 1

Grammar

- 문법 모의고사 1회
- 문법 모의고사 2회
- 문법 모의고사 3회

GENERAL TESTS OF ENGLISH LANGUAGE PROFICIENCY

☑ G-TELP LEVEL 2

GENERAL TESTS OF ENGLISH LANGUAGE PROFICIENCY

G-TELP™

LEVEL 2

유형별 분류표

	TEST 1	TEST 2	TEST 3
1. 가정법	4, 7, 15, 19, 22, 25	1, 5, 14, 16, 18, 23	2, 8, 12, 17, 22, 26
2. 시제	1, 3, 6, 10, 14, 24	4, 8, 10, 11, 15, 20	1, 4, 7, 11, 15, 20
3. 조동사	5, 12, 16, 20, 26	2, 6, 9, 12, 22	3, 5, 19, 24, 25
4. to부정사	13, 21	19, 26	14, 21
5. 동명사	2, 8, 23	7, 21, 25	6, 9, 16
6. 연결어	11, 18	3, 13	13, 23
7. 관계사	9, 17	17, 24	10, 18

Grammar Answer Sheet

TEST 1

문항	답란	문항	답란
1	ⓐ ⓑ ⓒ ⓓ	14	ⓐ ⓑ ⓒ ⓓ
2	ⓐ ⓑ ⓒ ⓓ	15	ⓐ ⓑ ⓒ ⓓ
3	ⓐ ⓑ ⓒ ⓓ	16	ⓐ ⓑ ⓒ ⓓ
4	ⓐ ⓑ ⓒ ⓓ	17	ⓐ ⓑ ⓒ ⓓ
5	ⓐ ⓑ ⓒ ⓓ	18	ⓐ ⓑ ⓒ ⓓ
6	ⓐ ⓑ ⓒ ⓓ	19	ⓐ ⓑ ⓒ ⓓ
7	ⓐ ⓑ ⓒ ⓓ	20	ⓐ ⓑ ⓒ ⓓ
8	ⓐ ⓑ ⓒ ⓓ	21	ⓐ ⓑ ⓒ ⓓ
9	ⓐ ⓑ ⓒ ⓓ	22	ⓐ ⓑ ⓒ ⓓ
10	ⓐ ⓑ ⓒ ⓓ	23	ⓐ ⓑ ⓒ ⓓ
11	ⓐ ⓑ ⓒ ⓓ	24	ⓐ ⓑ ⓒ ⓓ
12	ⓐ ⓑ ⓒ ⓓ	25	ⓐ ⓑ ⓒ ⓓ
13	ⓐ ⓑ ⓒ ⓓ	26	ⓐ ⓑ ⓒ ⓓ

TEST 2

문항	답란	문항	답란
1	ⓐ ⓑ ⓒ ⓓ	14	ⓐ ⓑ ⓒ ⓓ
2	ⓐ ⓑ ⓒ ⓓ	15	ⓐ ⓑ ⓒ ⓓ
3	ⓐ ⓑ ⓒ ⓓ	16	ⓐ ⓑ ⓒ ⓓ
4	ⓐ ⓑ ⓒ ⓓ	17	ⓐ ⓑ ⓒ ⓓ
5	ⓐ ⓑ ⓒ ⓓ	18	ⓐ ⓑ ⓒ ⓓ
6	ⓐ ⓑ ⓒ ⓓ	19	ⓐ ⓑ ⓒ ⓓ
7	ⓐ ⓑ ⓒ ⓓ	20	ⓐ ⓑ ⓒ ⓓ
8	ⓐ ⓑ ⓒ ⓓ	21	ⓐ ⓑ ⓒ ⓓ
9	ⓐ ⓑ ⓒ ⓓ	22	ⓐ ⓑ ⓒ ⓓ
10	ⓐ ⓑ ⓒ ⓓ	23	ⓐ ⓑ ⓒ ⓓ
11	ⓐ ⓑ ⓒ ⓓ	24	ⓐ ⓑ ⓒ ⓓ
12	ⓐ ⓑ ⓒ ⓓ	25	ⓐ ⓑ ⓒ ⓓ
13	ⓐ ⓑ ⓒ ⓓ	26	ⓐ ⓑ ⓒ ⓓ

TEST 3

문항	답란	문항	답란
1	ⓐ ⓑ ⓒ ⓓ	14	ⓐ ⓑ ⓒ ⓓ
2	ⓐ ⓑ ⓒ ⓓ	15	ⓐ ⓑ ⓒ ⓓ
3	ⓐ ⓑ ⓒ ⓓ	16	ⓐ ⓑ ⓒ ⓓ
4	ⓐ ⓑ ⓒ ⓓ	17	ⓐ ⓑ ⓒ ⓓ
5	ⓐ ⓑ ⓒ ⓓ	18	ⓐ ⓑ ⓒ ⓓ
6	ⓐ ⓑ ⓒ ⓓ	19	ⓐ ⓑ ⓒ ⓓ
7	ⓐ ⓑ ⓒ ⓓ	20	ⓐ ⓑ ⓒ ⓓ
8	ⓐ ⓑ ⓒ ⓓ	21	ⓐ ⓑ ⓒ ⓓ
9	ⓐ ⓑ ⓒ ⓓ	22	ⓐ ⓑ ⓒ ⓓ
10	ⓐ ⓑ ⓒ ⓓ	23	ⓐ ⓑ ⓒ ⓓ
11	ⓐ ⓑ ⓒ ⓓ	24	ⓐ ⓑ ⓒ ⓓ
12	ⓐ ⓑ ⓒ ⓓ	25	ⓐ ⓑ ⓒ ⓓ
13	ⓐ ⓑ ⓒ ⓓ	26	ⓐ ⓑ ⓒ ⓓ

GRAMMAR SECTION

00 : 20 : 00

TEST 1

시작 시각	시	분	초
목표 종료 시각	시	분	초
종료 시각	시	분	초
총 소요 시간 (종료 시각 - 시작 시각)		분	초
초과 시간 (총 소요 시간 - 목표 시간)		분	초

DIRECTIONS:

The following items need a word or words to complete the sentence. From the four choices for each item, choose the best answer. Then blacken in the correct circle on your answer sheet.

Example:

The boys ____________ in the car.

(a) be
(b) is
(c) am
(d) are

The correct answer is (d), so the circle with the letter (d) has been blackened.

ⓐ ⓑ ⓒ ●

NOW TURN THE PAGE AND BEGIN

1. The architects estimate it will take two years just to complete the design for the New Sears Tower. By the time they are finished, they ________ on nothing but design, strategy, and permits for the building.

   (a) have been working
   (b) will have been working
   (c) are working
   (d) will work

2. David had been ABC Bank's assistant manager for a long time before his boss resigned. He was recently promoted to manager, and his responsibilities now include ________ the policies of the company.

   (a) to have implemented
   (b) having implemented
   (c) to implement
   (d) implementing

3. As a business analyst, Dorothy works an average of 60 hours a week. The stress has proven too much for her, and she is thinking of resigning. Right now, she ________ the web for a less demanding job.

   (a) is browsing
   (b) was browsing
   (c) browsed
   (d) browses

4. Alan doesn't often visit his girlfriend. She lives on the other side of town, and the bus going to her place is very uncomfortable. If he were to buy a car, he ________ her more often.

   (a) would have visited
   (b) will visit
   (c) would visit
   (d) has visited

5. Sara's car broke down an hour before she had an important meeting. I told her she ________ use my car if she wanted to. I didn't have anywhere to go that day anyway.

   (a) could
   (b) must
   (c) might
   (d) would

6. Jerry can't stop talking about the girl he met at the supermarket yesterday. He said that he ________ which cereal to buy when he accidentally bumped into the lovely lady.

   (a) would choose
   (b) was choosing
   (c) has been choosing
   (d) chooses

7. Paul was trying to leave for an important business trip yesterday when he got caught in a traffic jam. If he had taken another route to the station, he ________ his train.

   (a) does not miss
   (b) would not miss
   (c) had not been missing
   (d) would not have missed

8. The tiled area near a swimming pool can get extremely slippery when wet, creating hazardous conditions. This is why most swimming facilities make rules that forbid ________, especially for small children.

   (a) having run
   (b) to have run
   (c) running
   (d) to run

9. Martha was intrigued by the man who was escorting Lucy at her birthday party. When Martha asked who he was, Lucy replied, "The man ________ is my cousin."

   (a) who was with me
   (b) which was with me
   (c) what was with me
   (d) that he was with me

10. Janet finally closed her small bookstore due to declining sales and growing competition from online book sellers. A lot of people were saddened by her decision. She ________ books in our area for over fifteen years.

    (a) will be selling
    (b) had been selling
    (c) would have sold
    (d) is selling

11. Scientists have confirmed that working long hours every day can eventually cause stress, fatigue, and heart problems. ________ this finding, many people are putting in long hours at work just to make ends meet.

    (a) Despite
    (b) Because of
    (c) Aside from
    (d) Otherwise

12. After receiving detention last week for misbehaving in class, Tom was called to the principal's office again for the same reason. Concerned for the boy, the principal demanded that Tom ________ some serious counseling.

    (a) is getting
    (b) will get
    (c) get
    (d) gets

13. The world population has been increasing so rapidly that food supplies are becoming strained. In response, scientists are splicing and manipulating seeds hoping ________ plants that are resistant to diseases, thus, boosting crop yields.

(a) breeding
(b) to breed
(c) having bred
(d) to have bred

14. To increase its market share, a famous mobile phone maker plans to launch a series of innovative smart phones. The company ________ these phones on the fourth of July.

(a) introduces
(b) introduced
(c) has been introducing
(d) will be introducing

15. Cristina is attending evening classes after work for a master's degree. This routine is making her exhausted. If she had more time to rest, she ________ a lot better about her well-being.

(a) would feel
(b) is feeling
(c) would have felt
(d) will feel

16. Henry is so busy doing his end-of-the-month reports that he cannot attend a business conference next Friday. His supervisor told Henry that he ________ assign one of his subordinates to attend the conference on his behalf.

(a) shall
(b) should
(c) would
(d) will

17. My friend has asked me three times if I am going to his wedding, and I keep answering "Yes." For almost a year, he has been preparing for the big event ________ at the end of this month.

(a) who will be held
(b) what will be held
(c) which it will be held
(d) that will be held

18. Mary has a tendency to say one thing and then do the exact opposite afterwards. ________ many are turned off by her behavior, she still has quite a lot of friends.

(a) Therefore
(b) Whenever
(c) Although
(d) Unless

19. I told my cousin to minimize his expenses so he could pay his hundred-dollar debt. Unfortunately, he did not listen. If he had taken my advice, the debt ________ to the $2,000 it is now.

(a) would not grow
(b) would not have grown
(c) has not grown
(d) did not grow

20. Many professional basketball players are now engaging in unsportsmanlike conduct. To address this issue, the league now insists that new players ________ a seminar on good behavior both before and after being drafted.

(a) attend
(b) attended
(c) were attending
(d) will attend

21. Many now consider English to be the universal language. This is why people not proficient with the language are trying to improve their skills. The first things ________ when studying English are the parts of speech.

(a) to have learned
(b) having learned
(c) to learn
(d) learning

22. Tina had wanted to be the class valedictorian, but the results of her final exams only won her the salutatory spot. If she had performed better on the tests, she ________ the top spot.

(a) has earned
(b) would earn
(c) will be earning
(d) would have earned

23. Karl may have lost in the national science competition, but his teachers are still very proud of him. Karl feels good, too. A year ago, he couldn't have even imagined ________ such a prestigious contest.

(a) to enter
(b) entering
(c) having entered
(d) to have entered

24. The James Michener novel I'm reading, *The Source*, must be his longest yet. I ________ it for two months now, and I'm still not even halfway through the book.

(a) have read
(b) am reading
(c) have been reading
(d) will have read

25. Every time Alice passes by 23rd Street, she looks longingly at the designer bags displayed in a shop window. She likes collecting bags, and if the ones on display were to go on sale, she ________ one.

(a) would buy
(b) would have bought
(c) has bought
(d) will have bought

26. Dave Edwards has been accused of a crime, but his lawyer says there is a lack of direct evidence against him. The lawyer therefore says it is important that Dave ________ "not guilty" to the charges.

(a) will plead
(b) is pleading
(c) pleads
(d) plead

THIS IS THE END OF THE GRAMMAR SECTION
DO NOT GO ON UNTIL TOLD TO DO SO

GRAMMAR SECTION

00 : 20 : 00

시작 시각	시	분	초
목표 종료 시각	시	분	초
종료 시각	시	분	초
총 소요 시간 (종료 시각 - 시작 시각)		분	초
초과 시간 (총 소요 시간 - 목표 시간)		분	초

TEST 2

DIRECTIONS:

The following items need a word or words to complete the sentence. From the four choices for each item, choose the best answer. Then blacken in the correct circle on your answer sheet.

Example:

The boys __________ in the car.

(a) be
(b) is
(c) am
(d) are

The correct answer is (d), so the circle with the letter (d) has been blackened.

ⓐ ⓑ ⓒ ●

NOW TURN THE PAGE AND BEGIN

1. Frank couldn't play golf with his friends last weekend because he was in the office working on a report for his client. If only he had finished it earlier, he _______ his friends at the golf course.

   (a) will have joined
   (b) would have joined
   (c) had joined
   (d) would join

2. The traffic was so bad last night that it took me four hours instead of two to reach my home. It ________ have been ten o'clock by the time I finally pulled into my driveway.

   (a) must
   (b) should
   (c) could
   (d) would

3. Jean finds her smartphone to be a most essential device for communicating with people. _________, she is addicted to surfing the Internet with it whenever there is a Wi-Fi connection.

   (a) As a result
   (b) In contrast
   (c) Afterward
   (d) Furthermore

4. Harold's mother called to inform him that she will be in town and would like to stay at his apartment next week. Hence, he _______ the place now to prepare for her visit.

   (a) had been cleaning
   (b) will have been cleaning
   (c) was cleaning
   (d) is cleaning

5. Karl started reading John Grisham's *A Painted House*, but has found it only mildly interesting. If the best-selling author _________ another legal thriller instead of a new coming-of-age novel, Karl would have enjoyed it better.

   (a) wrote
   (b) had written
   (c) was writing
   (d) would write

6. A boy was separated from his parents in a shopping mall. A woman who took pity on the lost boy insisted to the security guard that he _______ to the information desk to notify his parents.

   (a) be taken
   (b) was taken
   (c) will be taken
   (d) is taken

7. Alex started getting poor grades after he joined his school's basketball team. He enjoyed ________ basketball so much that he could not focus on his studies as much as he should have.

(a) to have played
(b) having played
(c) to play
(d) playing

8. I hope the new bathroom sink is ready to use by now. The plumber ________ the wastewater pipe coupling when I last saw him, and that was more than an hour ago.

(a) has been tightening
(b) was tightening
(c) would tighten
(d) tightened

9. My eight-year-old niece was very excited to show off the latest magic trick she had just learned. "Watch me, Uncle! I ________ turn this ordinary handkerchief into a flower," she declared.

(a) could
(b) might
(c) must
(d) will

10. Claire wants to get a higher grade in Professor Smith's history class. Since she ________ in the class lately, she plans to spend every weekend in the library researching upcoming discussion topics.

(a) has not been doing well
(b) will not have done well
(c) was not doing well
(d) will not have been doing well

11. You won't find Jeremy in his old apartment. He moved to San Francisco a long time ago when he accepted a teaching job at one of the local universities. By April, he ________ there for five years.

(a) is living
(b) has lived
(c) will have been living
(d) has been living

12. Chris would really like to travel around the world if he were ever to win the lottery. I suggested that he ________ more tickets to increase his chances of winning.

(a) bought
(b) buy
(c) buys
(d) will buy

13. Bill loves car racing despite the dangers it involves. He has been doing it since even before he got married. In fact, he refuses to give up car racing ________ his wife constantly begs him to.

(a) even though
(b) after
(c) unless
(d) since

14. Cynthia is so bright that she could be at the top of her class. However, she spends most nights playing video games, leaving her assignments untouched. If I were her, I _________ video games only on weekends.

(a) am playing
(b) would play
(c) will play
(d) would have played

15. Mary will not have any difficulty spotting Todd at the crowded airport when she picks him up by car tomorrow. He says he _________ an orange Hawaiian shirt, neon green shorts, and a large straw hat.

(a) is wearing
(b) wears
(c) will be wearing
(d) will have worn

16. Jenny is disappointed about not having a piano at home. She says if she were to get her very own piano, she ________ every day until she could play all her favorite songs.

(a) will practice
(b) would practice
(c) has practiced
(d) would have practiced

17. Ernest Cline is an American novelist best known for his award-winning book *Ready Player One*. The book, ________, was adapted into a film that was quite successful at the box office.

(a) that revolves around a virtual society
(b) who revolves around a virtual society
(c) what revolves around a virtual society
(d) which revolves around a virtual society

18. It's fortunate that the sun is positioned so ideally in relation to Earth. Scientists say that if it had been any closer or farther from the planet, life on Earth ________ billions of years ago.

(a) could not have begun
(b) did not begin
(c) could not begin
(d) had not begun

19. Sarah has to forgo reading *To Kill a Mockingbird* by Harper Lee to work on her physics assignment. She hopes ________ her assignment quickly so she can return to reading the novel.

(a) to have finished
(b) finishing
(c) having finished
(d) to finish

20. After receiving the results of the math test, Betty was not surprised at all to see her low score. Prior to taking the test, she ________ as much as she should have.

(a) will not have been studying
(b) had not been studying
(c) is not studying
(d) has not studied

21. Ms. Finley announced that she only had a few rules in her class. She made it very clear, however, that she would not tolerate ________ in any form.

(a) having cheated
(b) to be cheating
(c) cheating
(d) to cheat

22. Samantha is seriously considering accepting the position Glamour Publishing is offering her. However, I suggested that she ________ her salary before accepting the job. It should at least be higher than her current salary.

(a) negotiate
(b) will negotiate
(c) negotiated
(d) negotiates

23. Bernard thinks his teacher made a mistake in making him enter the essay writing contest, which he subsequently failed. He believes that if he had entered the math contest instead, he ________ a lot better.

(a) would perform
(b) will perform
(c) had performed
(d) would have performed

24. You had better be wary of the hiring department head during your panel interview; she asks pointed questions. You can recognize her as the panelist ________ in a bun.

(a) who has her hair tied up
(b) whom she has her hair tied up
(c) which has her hair tied up
(d) that she has her hair tied up

25. Ms. Hill is very confident that the choir she is leading will win the gold medal in the group vocal competition. To prepare, her group has practiced ________ their piece for several weeks now.

(a) to sing
(b) having sung
(c) singing
(d) to have sung

26. The sales representatives of a pharmaceutical company succeeded in reaching, and even exceeding, their quota for this quarter. To reward their good work, the company president decided ________ everyone a hefty bonus.

(a) giving
(b) to have given
(c) to give
(d) having give

THIS IS THE END OF THE GRAMMAR SECTION
DO NOT GO ON UNTIL TOLD TO DO SO

GRAMMAR SECTION

00 : 20 : 00

시작 시각	시	분	초
목표 종료 시각	시	분	초
종료 시각	시	분	초
총 소요 시간 (종료 시각 - 시작 시각)		분	초
초과 시간 (총 소요 시간 - 목표 시간)		분	초

DIRECTIONS:

The following items need a word or words to complete the sentence. From the four choices for each item, choose the best answer. Then blacken in the correct circle on your answer sheet.

Example:

The boys ___________ in the car.

(a) be
(b) is
(c) am
(d) are

The correct answer is (d), so the circle with the letter (d) has been blackened.

ⓐ ⓑ ⓒ ●

NOW TURN THE PAGE AND BEGIN

1. Earlier today, I dropped by Alicia's house to invite her to a football game. However, she could barely stand when I saw her. Apparently, she ________ from a leg injury she got last week.

   (a) had still recovered
   (b) is still recovering
   (c) still recovered
   (d) will still have been recovering

2. Ryan nearly went to his friend's wedding in a T-shirt and blue jeans. If I had not reminded him about the black tie dress code before he left, he ________ appropriately for the formal event.

   (a) would not have been dressed
   (b) will not have been dressed
   (c) had not been dressed
   (d) would not be dressed

3. Many children are becoming obese due to physical inactivity. To avoid this problem, experts recommend that kids ________ in active sports instead of spending their time playing computer games.

   (a) will engage
   (b) are engaging
   (c) engage
   (d) engaged

4. Peggy is hosting a dinner party and has been cooking since noon. By the time her guests arrive, she ________ the food for five hours straight. Hopefully, she'll still have time to change before they come.

   (a) is preparing
   (b) has prepared
   (c) has been preparing
   (d) will have been preparing

5. Emilia's apartment caught fire the other day and was badly damaged. She is now looking for a place to stay. Being her longtime friend, I told her that she ________ live with me in the meantime.

   (a) would
   (b) might
   (c) could
   (d) will

6. Kate Winslet is one of the world's finest actresses. Being raised in a family of performers proved to be advantageous. She recalls ________ exposure to stage plays and television shows at an early age.

   (a) gaining
   (b) having gained
   (c) to have gained
   (d) to gain

7. Many parents in Canada are upset about rising college tuition fees. A report states that in Canada, tuition ________ at a rate that's nearly double that of white-collar wages since 1980.

(a) had been increasing
(b) was increasing
(c) will have increased
(d) has been increasing

8. A magazine in New York City wanted to hire me as a graphic artist, but I declined the offer. If they had agreed to my desired salary, I ________ the job without hesitation.

(a) will accept
(b) would have accepted
(c) had accepted
(d) would accept

9. Warming up before any kind of workout is important because it helps reduce the chance of injury. Experts advise ________ as a warm-up exercise. It prevents muscle strain by improving the flexibility of the muscles.

(a) stretching
(b) to stretch
(c) to be stretching
(d) having stretched

10. Thomas Jefferson, the third president of the United States, was homeschooled until the age of 14. His tutor was a clergyman named William Douglas, from ________ Greek, Italian, and French.

(a) that he learned
(b) who he learned
(c) whom he learned
(d) which he is learning

11. Luke was recently granted a full graduate scholarship by the University of Melbourne. He ________ the next two years in Australia completing his master's degree in business management.

(a) will be spending
(b) has spent
(c) will have been spending
(d) spends

12. Katherine is fond of her aunt's cats, but tends to sneeze a lot when she's around them. If she were not allergic to cat fur, she ________ about next week's visit to her aunt's house.

(a) would have felt more excited
(b) has felt more excited
(c) would feel more excited
(d) will feel more excited

13. When Anthony put his Ford Focus up for sale for $10,000, he had a hard time finding a buyer. ________, he lowered the price to $8,000, and soon enough, the car was sold.

(a) Nevertheless
(b) Despite that
(c) Meanwhile
(d) Eventually

14. Physics is Jeremy's least favorite subject. He has a hard time following most lessons in class. Whenever the professor gives a problem to solve, Jeremy spends too much time trying ________ it out.

(a) figuring
(b) to figure
(c) to have figured
(d) having figured

15. Brian and his wife finally went fishing at the nearby Cedar Creek Lake. They ________ to go on the trip for the past several weeks, but kept postponing it due to rainy weather.

(a) would plan
(b) have been planning
(c) planned
(d) had been planning

16. Emma is very enthusiastic about her new job as a wedding planner. Right now, she's in a meeting. After she finishes ________ with her first client, she will head downtown to talk to a supplier.

(a) to talk
(b) having talked
(c) talking
(d) to have talked

17. Though an account executive by profession, Lisa volunteers as a ballet teacher for kids every Saturday. She says if she were to have the time and money, she ________ her own ballet school.

(a) is opening
(b) would open
(c) will open
(d) would have opened

18. Reports say that more than 100 million animals are killed in US laboratories each year for research and experiments. In response, animal rights activists are campaigning against companies ________ for their products.

(a) that use animal testing
(b) who use animal testing
(c) what use animal testing
(d) which they use animal testing

19. Our final project in history class is to give a creative presentation about the French Revolution. One member of my group proposed that we ________ our presentation with a historical reenactment.

(a) are beginning
(b) have begun
(c) begin
(d) will begin

20. The boss just told Leonard to take the rest of the day off. Leonard ________ of a headache since he arrived at the office. If it doesn't go away soon, he'll have to see a doctor.

(a) complains
(b) is complaining
(c) had complained
(d) has been complaining

21. One of Wendy's goals is to have her picture taken in front of every famous landmark in America. Last week, she asked me ________ her to the Lincoln Memorial in Washington for her tenth photo.

(a) to accompany
(b) accompanying
(c) to have accompanied
(d) having accompanied

22. The electric company announced that there will be an 8-hour power outage starting at 6 p.m. tonight. If I had not reminded my dad about it, he ________ to recharge our emergency flashlights earlier today.

(a) will forget
(b) would have forgotten
(c) had forgotten
(d) would forget

23. Contrary to what many people believe, whales are not fish but mammals. They differ from fish in many ways. ________, whales do not have gills like fish. Instead, they use blowholes to breathe in air.

(a) For example
(b) In conclusion
(c) However
(d) Furthermore

24. Samantha will be going to a concert with her friends tonight. Based on the forecast, it seems like there ________ be a storm today. I hope she doesn't forget to bring an umbrella when she leaves.

(a) should
(b) would
(c) might
(d) can

25. Benedict often fails his tests because he doesn't review the instructions carefully enough. I suggested that he ________ each question at least twice before answering it; otherwise, he'll just continue failing his exams.

(a) is reading
(b) will read
(c) reads
(d) read

26. Tiffany agreed to attend Warren's party. If she had not told him that she was a vegetarian, though, Warren ________ forward with an all-meat menu. In the end, everyone enjoyed the additional dish: artichoke mushroom lasagna.

(a) would go
(b) had gone
(c) would have gone
(d) will be going

THIS IS THE END OF THE GRAMMAR SECTION
DO NOT GO ON UNTIL TOLD TO DO SO

TEST 3

Chapter 2

Listening

- 청취 모의고사 1회
- 청취 모의고사 2회
- 청취 모의고사 3회

GENERAL TESTS OF ENGLISH LANGUAGE PROFICIENCY

☑ G-TELP LEVEL 2

GENERAL TESTS OF ENGLISH LANGUAGE PROFICIENCY
G-TELP™

LEVEL 2

Listening Answer Sheet

TEST 1

문항	답란	문항	답란
27	ⓐ ⓑ ⓒ ⓓ	40	ⓐ ⓑ ⓒ ⓓ
28	ⓐ ⓑ ⓒ ⓓ	41	ⓐ ⓑ ⓒ ⓓ
29	ⓐ ⓑ ⓒ ⓓ	42	ⓐ ⓑ ⓒ ⓓ
30	ⓐ ⓑ ⓒ ⓓ	43	ⓐ ⓑ ⓒ ⓓ
31	ⓐ ⓑ ⓒ ⓓ	44	ⓐ ⓑ ⓒ ⓓ
32	ⓐ ⓑ ⓒ ⓓ	45	ⓐ ⓑ ⓒ ⓓ
33	ⓐ ⓑ ⓒ ⓓ	46	ⓐ ⓑ ⓒ ⓓ
34	ⓐ ⓑ ⓒ ⓓ	47	ⓐ ⓑ ⓒ ⓓ
35	ⓐ ⓑ ⓒ ⓓ	48	ⓐ ⓑ ⓒ ⓓ
36	ⓐ ⓑ ⓒ ⓓ	49	ⓐ ⓑ ⓒ ⓓ
37	ⓐ ⓑ ⓒ ⓓ	50	ⓐ ⓑ ⓒ ⓓ
38	ⓐ ⓑ ⓒ ⓓ	51	ⓐ ⓑ ⓒ ⓓ
39	ⓐ ⓑ ⓒ ⓓ	52	ⓐ ⓑ ⓒ ⓓ

TEST 2

문항	답란	문항	답란
27	ⓐ ⓑ ⓒ ⓓ	40	ⓐ ⓑ ⓒ ⓓ
28	ⓐ ⓑ ⓒ ⓓ	41	ⓐ ⓑ ⓒ ⓓ
29	ⓐ ⓑ ⓒ ⓓ	42	ⓐ ⓑ ⓒ ⓓ
30	ⓐ ⓑ ⓒ ⓓ	43	ⓐ ⓑ ⓒ ⓓ
31	ⓐ ⓑ ⓒ ⓓ	44	ⓐ ⓑ ⓒ ⓓ
32	ⓐ ⓑ ⓒ ⓓ	45	ⓐ ⓑ ⓒ ⓓ
33	ⓐ ⓑ ⓒ ⓓ	46	ⓐ ⓑ ⓒ ⓓ
34	ⓐ ⓑ ⓒ ⓓ	47	ⓐ ⓑ ⓒ ⓓ
35	ⓐ ⓑ ⓒ ⓓ	48	ⓐ ⓑ ⓒ ⓓ
36	ⓐ ⓑ ⓒ ⓓ	49	ⓐ ⓑ ⓒ ⓓ
37	ⓐ ⓑ ⓒ ⓓ	50	ⓐ ⓑ ⓒ ⓓ
38	ⓐ ⓑ ⓒ ⓓ	51	ⓐ ⓑ ⓒ ⓓ
39	ⓐ ⓑ ⓒ ⓓ	52	ⓐ ⓑ ⓒ ⓓ

TEST 3

문항	답란	문항	답란
27	ⓐ ⓑ ⓒ ⓓ	40	ⓐ ⓑ ⓒ ⓓ
28	ⓐ ⓑ ⓒ ⓓ	41	ⓐ ⓑ ⓒ ⓓ
29	ⓐ ⓑ ⓒ ⓓ	42	ⓐ ⓑ ⓒ ⓓ
30	ⓐ ⓑ ⓒ ⓓ	43	ⓐ ⓑ ⓒ ⓓ
31	ⓐ ⓑ ⓒ ⓓ	44	ⓐ ⓑ ⓒ ⓓ
32	ⓐ ⓑ ⓒ ⓓ	45	ⓐ ⓑ ⓒ ⓓ
33	ⓐ ⓑ ⓒ ⓓ	46	ⓐ ⓑ ⓒ ⓓ
34	ⓐ ⓑ ⓒ ⓓ	47	ⓐ ⓑ ⓒ ⓓ
35	ⓐ ⓑ ⓒ ⓓ	48	ⓐ ⓑ ⓒ ⓓ
36	ⓐ ⓑ ⓒ ⓓ	49	ⓐ ⓑ ⓒ ⓓ
37	ⓐ ⓑ ⓒ ⓓ	50	ⓐ ⓑ ⓒ ⓓ
38	ⓐ ⓑ ⓒ ⓓ	51	ⓐ ⓑ ⓒ ⓓ
39	ⓐ ⓑ ⓒ ⓓ	52	ⓐ ⓑ ⓒ ⓓ

LISTENING SECTION

시작 시각	시	분	초
목표 종료 시각	시	분	초
종료 시각	시	분	초
총 소요 시간 (종료 시각 - 시작 시각)		분	초
초과 시간 (총 소요 시간 - 목표 시간)		분	초

DIRECTIONS:

The Listening Section has four parts. In each part you will hear a spoken passage and a number of questions about the passage. First you will hear the questions. Then you will hear the passage. From the four choices for each question, choose the best answer. Then blacken in the correct circle on your answer sheet.

Now you will hear an example question. Then you will hear an example passage.

Now listen to the example question.

(a) one
(b) two
(c) three
(d) four

Bill Johnson has four brothers, so the best answer is (d). The circle with the letter (d) has been blackened.

ⓐ ⓑ ⓒ ●

NOW TURN THE PAGE AND BEGIN

PART 1. *You will hear a conversation between two people. First you will hear questions 27 through 33. Then you will hear the conversation. Choose the best answer to each question in the time provided.*

27. (a) to tell her about winning a contest
    (b) to give her two free tickets
    (c) to invite her to a theatrical event
    (d) to tell her about a play that he saw

28. (a) by watching a movie version
    (b) by being a fan of the composer
    (c) by reading critics' reviews
    (d) by seeing a live performance

29. (a) It ran on Broadway for a long time.
    (b) Its romantic storyline is well-known.
    (c) It had a song that was released as a single.
    (d) It was adapted into a best-selling novel.

30. (a) He had forgotten to join the raffle.
    (b) He thought they were too expensive.
    (c) He thought the tickets were all sold out.
    (d) He didn't remember entering the raffle.

31. (a) because he wants her to see the musical with him
    (b) because there are plenty of tickets available
    (c) because the musical is running for only two days
    (d) because he is selling her one of his tickets

32. (a) to overcome financial loss on Broadway
    (b) to increase the production's ticket sales
    (c) to support affiliated department stores
    (d) to support local theater companies

33. (a) He thinks first performances are always better.
    (b) He only has tickets for the first showing.
    (c) He knows that night is better for Rose.
    (d) He wants to see it as soon as possible.

PART 2. *You will hear a presentation by one person to a group of people. First you will hear questions 34 through 39. Then you will hear the talk. Choose the best answer to each question in the time provided.*

34. (a) its latest smart phone
    (b) an advanced digital camera
    (c) an improved operating system
    (d) its new electronic gadget

35. (a) because the market lacks affordable tablets
    (b) because they discontinued their line of phones
    (c) because the way people use technology is changing
    (d) because consumers are getting tired of desktops

36. (a) its screen's considerable size
    (b) its in-depth camera technology
    (c) its speedy processing ability
    (d) its impressive storage capacity

37. (a) by selling it with a special carrying case
    (b) by giving it an extended battery life
    (c) by creating it with built-in earphones
    (d) by making it more difficult to damage

38. (a) It was done within a year.
    (b) It involved a lot of preparation.
    (c) It presents a great risk for the company.
    (d) It was based on another company's technology.

39. (a) getting some accessories at a lower cost
    (b) having all of one's friends be jealous
    (c) getting a large discount on the tablet's price
    (d) having exclusive access to a limited release

PART 3. *You will hear a conversation between two people. First, you will hear questions 40 through 45. Then you will hear the conversation. Choose the best answer to each question in the time provided.*

40. (a) to help her choose between two types of businesses
    (b) to help her decide what services to offer
    (c) to ask him about professional requirements
    (d) to tell him about her new business venture

41. (a) higher chance of succeeding
    (b) fewer complex legal disputes
    (c) more ease in hiring workers
    (d) full control of the business

42. (a) It has special tax exemptions.
    (b) It requires less work to succeed.
    (c) The partners can share obligations.
    (d) The partners can take trips together.

43. (a) They always lead to misunderstandings.
    (b) They often cause the business to falter.
    (c) They are better addressed by individuals.
    (d) They can cause tension even for sensible partners.

44. (a) lacking full control of the business
    (b) having to possibly assume a partner's debts
    (c) running the business alone when a partner is away
    (d) sharing the profits with the partner

45. (a) start a business as the sole owner
    (b) apply for a partnership
    (c) seek a reliable business partner
    (d) think of ways to earn more funds

PART 4. *You will hear an explanation of a process. First, you will hear questions 46 through 52. Then you will hear the explanation. Choose the best answer to each question in the time provided.*

46. (a) how to support a charity
(b) the steps to plan a concert
(c) the ways to be a good leader
(d) how to promote an event

47. (a) because other members can catch their passion
(b) because they can convince people better
(c) because they will not be motivated by pay
(d) because they can work longer hours

48. (a) by convincing active members not to leave
(b) by dealing only with reliable people
(c) by signing up a surplus of sponsors
(d) by adapting to disappointing situations

49. (a) by skipping leisure time
(b) by working all the time
(c) by spending as little as possible
(d) by hiring a budget manager

50. (a) Advertise on only the biggest channels
(b) Contact all of one's friends aggressively
(c) Use a variety of promotional methods
(d) Hire only famous bands for the concert

51. (a) It can let one completely avoid the problem.
(b) It can give one time to think about solutions.
(c) It guarantees that the problem will be solved.
(d) It allows the problem to go away on its own.

52. (a) It makes the work seem easier.
(b) It inspires sponsors to donate more.
(c) It secures the completion of the task.
(d) It presents fresh solutions to problems.

THIS IS THE END OF THE LISTENING SECTION
DO NOT GO ON UNTIL TOLD TO DO SO

LISTENING SECTION

시작 시각	시	분	초
목표 종료 시각	시	분	초
종료 시각	시	분	초
총 소요 시간 (종료 시각 - 시작 시각)		분	초
초과 시간 (총 소요 시간 - 목표 시간)		분	초

DIRECTIONS:

The Listening Section has four parts. In each part you will hear a spoken passage and a number of questions about the passage. First you will hear the questions. Then you will hear the passage. From the four choices for each question, choose the best answer. Then blacken in the correct circle on your answer sheet.

Now you will hear an example question. Then you will hear an example passage.

Now listen to the example question.

(a) one
(b) two
(c) three
(d) four

Bill Johnson has four brothers, so the best answer is (d). The circle with the letter (d) has been blackened.

ⓐ ⓑ ⓒ ●

NOW TURN THE PAGE AND BEGIN

TEST 2

PART 1. *You will hear a conversation between two people. First you will hear questions 27 through 33. Then you will hear the conversation. Choose the best answer to each question in the time provided.*

27. (a) She wanted to visit Paris.
    (b) She was an exchange student.
    (c) She was there visiting her friend Jason.
    (d) She was working as a fashion designer.

28. (a) learning the French language
    (b) adjusting to her sponsor family
    (c) accepting the patriotism of the French
    (d) adjusting to school life

29. (a) Having the most landmarks in Europe
    (b) Being home to the most romantic people
    (c) Having decent weather most of the time
    (d) Being a very family-oriented country

30. (a) to find work in the fashion industry
    (b) to communicate with her sponsor family
    (c) to impress people in the fashion industry
    (d) to follow the customs of the country

31. (a) someone who designs and creates fashion wear
    (b) someone who markets clothing and accessories
    (c) someone who has a keen interest in fashion
    (d) someone who has considerable experience in fashion

32. (a) She will start her own business very soon.
    (b) She will be a successful French fashion designer.
    (c) She might become well known in the fashion world someday.
    (d) She will work for famous designers in the future.

33. (a) research the history of France
    (b) read up on famous French designers
    (c) visit the school's exchange program department
    (d) consult with Carol for fashion advice

PART 2. *You will hear a presentation by one person to a group of people. First you will hear questions 34 through 39. Then you will hear the talk. Choose the best answer to each question in the time provided.*

34. (a) to update the public on advances in technology
    (b) to launch a new company
    (c) to predict future trends
    (d) to introduce a new product

35. (a) It wanted to find a use for a new system it developed.
    (b) It aimed to test its technology on humanoid robotics.
    (c) It needed a symbol for the company.
    (d) It wanted to enrich people's lives through the robot.

36. (a) in an old building in New York
    (b) in an industrial complex
    (c) in a garage in Mexico
    (d) in George Driscoll's barn in Ohio

37. (a) Its human-like appearance
    (b) Its ability to make choices
    (c) Its pre-programmed tasks
    (d) Its ability to walk around

38. (a) for the robots to function exactly like humans
    (b) for the robots to run Driscoll Robotics
    (c) to give the robots keener electronic sensors
    (d) to program the robots to communicate with other robots

39. (a) Humanoid robots will replace humans in all activities.
    (b) They can be designed to do almost any human task.
    (c) They can conduct their own research and development.
    (d) Future robots will be indistinguishable from humans.

PART 3. *You will hear a conversation between two people. First, you will hear questions 40 through 45 Then you will hear the conversation. Choose the best answer to each question in the time provided.*

40. (a) an autographed book
    (b) money to buy books
    (c) an electronic book reader
    (d) a collection of e-books

41. (a) It fits well in a backpack.
    (b) It is readily available in bookstores.
    (c) It can be easily borrowed by friends.
    (d) It has text that is easier to view.

42. (a) It doesn't stop working unexpectedly.
    (b) It doesn't run out of print.
    (c) It can be bought in large text.
    (d) It has its own light.

43. (a) Most textbooks are available as e-books.
    (b) It is easy to download textbooks online.
    (c) Multiple textbooks can be contained in a single reader.
    (d) Most teachers require students to bring e-books to school.

44. (a) E-books can neither be lent nor borrowed without a reader.
    (b) E-books are too expensive to download and share.
    (c) E-books are not compatible with all e-book readers.
    (d) Owners cannot mark their e-books with their names.

45. (a) read the latest Divine Stuart book
    (b) lend John one of her books
    (c) check if the bookstore has Stuart's books
    (d) thank her father for the gift

PART 4. *You will hear an explanation of a process. First you will hear questions 46 through 52. Then you will hear the talk. Choose the best answer to each question in the time provided.*

46. (a) people who would like to start a business
(b) people who are fond of baked products
(c) people with unused baking equipment
(d) people who want a part-time job

47. (a) find a good location to start the business
(b) learn the basic skills of baking
(c) be advanced in baking all types of baked goods
(d) find a good supplier for ingredients

48. (a) because you can borrow larger sums of money
(b) because they will not ask for interest
(c) because you will not have to repay them
(d) because they will give you more time to repay

49. (a) Most restaurants do business only with reliable suppliers.
(b) Most people buy baked goods from restaurants.
(c) Restaurants sell high-quality breads and pastries.
(d) Restaurants are the main buyers of baked products.

50. (a) by selling products at low prices
(b) by choosing a supplier that offers expensive supplies
(c) by buying supplies in large volumes
(d) by producing baked products in large amounts

51. (a) When the products are too expensive
(b) When the workplace is not secure
(c) When the ingredients cause allergic reactions
(d) When the food quality is unsafe

52. (a) They can develop new types of baking.
(b) They can merge with other businesses.
(c) They can learn up-to-date information.
(d) They can start their own websites.

THIS IS THE END OF THE LISTENING SECTION
DO NOT GO ON UNTIL TOLD TO DO SO

LISTENING SECTION

시작 시각	시	분	초
목표 종료 시각	시	분	초
종료 시각	시	분	초
총 소요 시간 (종료 시각 - 시작 시각)		분	초
초과 시간 (총 소요 시간 - 목표 시간)		분	초

DIRECTIONS:

The Listening Section has four parts. In each part you will hear a spoken passage and a number of questions about the passage. First you will hear the questions. Then you will hear the passage. From the four choices for each question, choose the best answer. Then blacken in the correct circle on your answer sheet.

Now you will hear an example question. Then you will hear an example passage.

Now listen to the example question.

(a) one
(b) two
(c) three
(d) four

Bill Johnson has four brothers, so the best answer is (d). The circle with the letter (d) has been blackened.

ⓐ ⓑ ⓒ ●

NOW TURN THE PAGE AND BEGIN

TEST 3

PART 1. *You will hear a conversation between two people. First you will hear questions 27 through 33. Then you will hear the conversation. Choose the best answer to each question in the time provided.*

27. (a) the effects of too much fast food
    (b) the importance of counting calories
    (c) Raymond's dislike for fast food
    (d) Marie's hectic work schedule

28. (a) because it is packed with enough daily calories
    (b) because it is convenient for her to do so
    (c) because it is more filling than healthy food
    (d) because it tastes better than home-cooked meals

29. (a) They are converted into body fat.
    (b) They lead to an inactive lifestyle.
    (c) They block the absorption of nutrients.
    (d) They provide extra energy.

30. (a) by serving better-tasting meals
    (b) by providing more nutrition
    (c) by serving larger portions
    (d) by improving their service

31. (a) Nutrition information on the menu
    (b) Healthy ingredients in the food
    (c) Meals that taste really good
    (d) People who enjoy natural flavors

32. (a) It gets rid of minerals in the body.
    (b) It lacks vitamins.
    (c) It has artificial additives.
    (d) It contains too much salt.

33. (a) avoid upgrading her fast food meals
    (b) start working out to burn calories
    (c) cut down on her fast food consumption
    (d) start monitoring her daily calorie intake

PART 2. *You will hear a presentation by one person to a group of people. First you will hear questions 34 through 39. Then you will hear the talk. Choose the best answer to each question in the time provided.*

34. (a) the importance of proper babysitting
    (b) the services of a childcare provider
    (c) the difficulties of parenthood
    (d) the benefits of art exploration

35. (a) because they do not trust babysitters
    (b) because they cannot afford a babysitter
    (c) because they have to care for their kids
    (d) because they usually work long hours

36. (a) their rigid training in the arts
    (b) their years of real-life experience in childcare
    (c) their carefully screened personal histories before hiring
    (d) their advanced knowledge of first aid

37. (a) fewer than four children in the household
    (b) a child who needs special attention
    (c) a session that goes beyond 10:00 p.m.
    (d) more than two kids below the age of three

38. (a) By expressing some concerns about the service
    (b) By choosing to sign up for the service
    (c) By deciding to break their contract agreement
    (d) By paying an extra consultation cost

39. (a) working parents
    (b) aspiring babysitters
    (c) professional artists
    (d) nursing students

TEST 3

PART 3. *You will hear a conversation between two people. First, you will hear questions 40 through 45 Then you will hear the conversation. Choose the best answer to each question in the time provided.*

40. (a) Jesse's experiences in a traditional college
    (b) Jesse's interest in getting a master's degree
    (c) Kim's plan to enroll in an online university
    (d) Kim's budget for her graduate education

41. (a) They have many hidden charges.
    (b) They are higher than that of traditional schools.
    (c) Students cannot apply for scholarships to cover fees.
    (d) The costs of training materials are part of the fees.

42. (a) because it offers more flexible schedules
    (b) because they can afford it compared to regular students
    (c) because it allows them to apply for student funds
    (d) because it assigns them less schoolwork

43. (a) It saves her from having to work with other people.
    (b) It allows her to focus on her lessons.
    (c) She can skip lectures at any time.
    (d) She enjoys interacting online.

44. (a) Face-to-face education is more direct than online training
    (b) A traditional classroom is a better environment for learning.
    (c) Students need to see each other to learn well.
    (d) Traditional classroom teachers are smarter.

45. (a) complete her bachelor's degree
    (b) prepare to enroll in an online university
    (c) enroll in a traditional graduate school program
    (d) learn more about online university courses

PART 4. *You will hear an explanation of a process. First you will hear questions 46 through 52. Then you will hear the talk. Choose the best answer to each question in the time provided.*

46. (a) to invite them to join a photography club
    (b) to give advice on choosing a photograph's subject
    (c) to talk about composing a photograph
    (d) to give tips on buying a camera

47. (a) because it is similar to painting a picture
    (b) because cameras can be bought cheaply
    (c) because photographs are easy to edit
    (d) because it does not require intensive study

48. (a) using only one subject
    (b) choosing a plain subject
    (c) adding different elements to the picture
    (d) emphasizing the different subjects equally

49. (a) by ensuring an odd number of elements
    (b) by giving the image a sense of balance
    (c) by placing the subject in the center
    (d) by providing space for more than one subject

50. (a) To make the subjects look unusual
    (b) To change the viewer's feelings
    (c) To hide the most unique features
    (d) To show a different perspective

51. (a) They can choose subjects with authority.
    (b) They can put the camera at an elevation.
    (c) They can shoot the subject from below.
    (d) They can focus on personal relationships.

52. (a) It helps one create high-quality pictures.
    (b) It allows one to shoot from all angles.
    (c) It develops one's interest in photography.
    (d) It inspires one to become a professional photographer.

THIS IS THE END OF THE LISTENING SECTION
DO NOT GO ON UNTIL TOLD TO DO SO

Chapter 3

Reading & Vocabulary

- 독해 모의고사 1회
- 독해 모의고사 2회
- 독해 모의고사 3회

GENERAL TESTS OF ENGLISH LANGUAGE PROFICIENCY

☑ G-TELP LEVEL 2

GENERAL TESTS OF ENGLISH LANGUAGE PROFICIENCY
G-TELP™

LEVEL 2

Reading & Vocabulary Answer Sheet

TEST 1

문항	답란	문항	답란
53	ⓐ ⓑ ⓒ ⓓ	67	ⓐ ⓑ ⓒ ⓓ
54	ⓐ ⓑ ⓒ ⓓ	68	ⓐ ⓑ ⓒ ⓓ
55	ⓐ ⓑ ⓒ ⓓ	69	ⓐ ⓑ ⓒ ⓓ
56	ⓐ ⓑ ⓒ ⓓ	70	ⓐ ⓑ ⓒ ⓓ
57	ⓐ ⓑ ⓒ ⓓ	71	ⓐ ⓑ ⓒ ⓓ
58	ⓐ ⓑ ⓒ ⓓ	72	ⓐ ⓑ ⓒ ⓓ
59	ⓐ ⓑ ⓒ ⓓ	73	ⓐ ⓑ ⓒ ⓓ
60	ⓐ ⓑ ⓒ ⓓ	74	ⓐ ⓑ ⓒ ⓓ
61	ⓐ ⓑ ⓒ ⓓ	75	ⓐ ⓑ ⓒ ⓓ
62	ⓐ ⓑ ⓒ ⓓ	76	ⓐ ⓑ ⓒ ⓓ
63	ⓐ ⓑ ⓒ ⓓ	77	ⓐ ⓑ ⓒ ⓓ
64	ⓐ ⓑ ⓒ ⓓ	78	ⓐ ⓑ ⓒ ⓓ
65	ⓐ ⓑ ⓒ ⓓ	79	ⓐ ⓑ ⓒ ⓓ
66	ⓐ ⓑ ⓒ ⓓ	80	ⓐ ⓑ ⓒ ⓓ

TEST 2

문항	답란	문항	답란
53	ⓐ ⓑ ⓒ ⓓ	67	ⓐ ⓑ ⓒ ⓓ
54	ⓐ ⓑ ⓒ ⓓ	68	ⓐ ⓑ ⓒ ⓓ
55	ⓐ ⓑ ⓒ ⓓ	69	ⓐ ⓑ ⓒ ⓓ
56	ⓐ ⓑ ⓒ ⓓ	70	ⓐ ⓑ ⓒ ⓓ
57	ⓐ ⓑ ⓒ ⓓ	71	ⓐ ⓑ ⓒ ⓓ
58	ⓐ ⓑ ⓒ ⓓ	72	ⓐ ⓑ ⓒ ⓓ
59	ⓐ ⓑ ⓒ ⓓ	73	ⓐ ⓑ ⓒ ⓓ
60	ⓐ ⓑ ⓒ ⓓ	74	ⓐ ⓑ ⓒ ⓓ
61	ⓐ ⓑ ⓒ ⓓ	75	ⓐ ⓑ ⓒ ⓓ
62	ⓐ ⓑ ⓒ ⓓ	76	ⓐ ⓑ ⓒ ⓓ
63	ⓐ ⓑ ⓒ ⓓ	77	ⓐ ⓑ ⓒ ⓓ
64	ⓐ ⓑ ⓒ ⓓ	78	ⓐ ⓑ ⓒ ⓓ
65	ⓐ ⓑ ⓒ ⓓ	79	ⓐ ⓑ ⓒ ⓓ
66	ⓐ ⓑ ⓒ ⓓ	80	ⓐ ⓑ ⓒ ⓓ

TEST 3

문항	답란	문항	답란
53	ⓐ ⓑ ⓒ ⓓ	67	ⓐ ⓑ ⓒ ⓓ
54	ⓐ ⓑ ⓒ ⓓ	68	ⓐ ⓑ ⓒ ⓓ
55	ⓐ ⓑ ⓒ ⓓ	69	ⓐ ⓑ ⓒ ⓓ
56	ⓐ ⓑ ⓒ ⓓ	70	ⓐ ⓑ ⓒ ⓓ
57	ⓐ ⓑ ⓒ ⓓ	71	ⓐ ⓑ ⓒ ⓓ
58	ⓐ ⓑ ⓒ ⓓ	72	ⓐ ⓑ ⓒ ⓓ
59	ⓐ ⓑ ⓒ ⓓ	73	ⓐ ⓑ ⓒ ⓓ
60	ⓐ ⓑ ⓒ ⓓ	74	ⓐ ⓑ ⓒ ⓓ
61	ⓐ ⓑ ⓒ ⓓ	75	ⓐ ⓑ ⓒ ⓓ
62	ⓐ ⓑ ⓒ ⓓ	76	ⓐ ⓑ ⓒ ⓓ
63	ⓐ ⓑ ⓒ ⓓ	77	ⓐ ⓑ ⓒ ⓓ
64	ⓐ ⓑ ⓒ ⓓ	78	ⓐ ⓑ ⓒ ⓓ
65	ⓐ ⓑ ⓒ ⓓ	79	ⓐ ⓑ ⓒ ⓓ
66	ⓐ ⓑ ⓒ ⓓ	80	ⓐ ⓑ ⓒ ⓓ

READING AND VOCABULARY SECTION

00 : 40 : 00

시작 시각	시	분	초
목표 종료 시각	시	분	초
종료 시각	시	분	초
총 소요 시간 (종료 시각 - 시작 시각)		분	초
초과 시간 (총 소요 시간 - 목표 시간)		분	초

DIRECTIONS:

You will now read four different passages. Each passage is followed by comprehension and vocabulary questions. From the four choices for each item, choose the best answer. Then blacken in the correct circle on your answer sheet.

Read the following example passage and example question.

Example :

Bill Johnson lives in New York. He is 25 years old. He has four brothers and two sisters.

How many brothers does Bill Johnson have?

(a) one
(b) two
(c) three
(d) four

The correct answer is (d), so the circle with the letter (d) has been blackened.

ⓐ ⓑ ⓒ ●

NOW TURN THE PAGE AND BEGIN

PART 1. *Read the following biography article and answer the questions. The underlined words in the article are for vocabulary questions.*

H.G. WELLS

Herbert George Wells was an English historian and novelist who gained worldwide acclaim for his science fiction novels. He is perhaps best known for his novel *The War of the Worlds*, which was adapted for the radio in 1938 and then twice for film, first in 1953 and again in 2005. For his important contributions to the genre, Wells is often called the "Father of Science Fiction."

Herbert George Wells was born in Kent, England on September 21, 1866. His parents were Joseph Wells and Sarah Neal. At eight years old, Wells suffered from an accident that confined him to bed for many months. He spent his time reading books, which started his interest in other worlds and lives and developed his passion for writing. He received basic education at a local school and became a pupil-teacher at Midhurst Grammar School in 1879. Wells won a scholarship to the Normal School of Science at Midhurst. His biology teacher was the famous English biologist, T. H. Huxley.

Wells moved to London and earned money by writing for weekly newspapers. While studying at London University, he became a science master at the Henley House School where he taught the future renowned poet, A. A. Milne. He received his degree in zoology in 1890.

In 1895, Wells came out with his first successful science fiction novel, *The Time Machine.* This was followed by three more successful science fiction stories: *The Island of Dr. Moreau, The Invisible Man,* and *The War of the Worlds.* He also began writing non-fiction books and commentaries about society, politics, and technology. His first non-fiction work, subtitled *An Experiment in Prophecy,* was a collection of his predictions for the future.

Wells advocated a utopian world where society is better organized and people live more contentedly. This ideal was at the center of his 1905 novel, *A Modern Utopia,* which depicts a "world state" where people live in happiness. In his utopian novels, Wells also predicted catastrophic events like the Second World War in *The Shape of Things to Come*, and the rise of dictators in *The Holy Terror.*

H.G. Wells traveled to France between the first and second world wars. He moved back to London in 1933 and, refusing to flee the German attacks on the city, continued to live there throughout the war. He died of complications from diabetes in 1946.

53. What is H.G. Wells known for?

(a) his range of talent as a film director
(b) his work in the science fiction genre
(c) his storytelling skills on a radio show
(d) his extensive knowledge of history

54. When did Wells start to develop an interest in writing?

(a) when he took to reading as a child
(b) when he was attending the local school
(c) while he was teaching at the grammar school
(d) while he was attending London University

55. What did Wells do while he was at London University?

(a) He became a resident assistant.
(b) He published a newspaper.
(c) He taught a soon-to-be great literary figure.
(d) He joined the faculty of the zoology department.

56. Which of the following is NOT one of Wells' science fiction novels?

(a) *The War of the Worlds*
(b) *The Time Machine*
(c) *The Invisible Man*
(d) *An Experiment in Prophecy*

57. Based on the article, how can H.G. Wells' utopian novels most accurately be described?

(a) They were partly visionary.
(b) They promoted discontent.
(c) They were published before the 20th century.
(d) They were written between the wars.

58. In the context of the passage, confined means _________.

(a) captured
(b) trapped
(c) limited
(d) imprisoned

59. In the context of the passage, utopian means _________.

(a) fictional
(b) realistic
(c) romantic
(d) idealistic

PART 2. *Read the following magazine article and answer the questions. The underlined words in the article are for vocabulary questions.*

SCIENTISTS DISCOVER REMAINS OF ANCIENT FRESHWATER "MONSTER"

A team of paleontologists have discovered the fossils of an 84-million-year-old freshwater "sea monster." The creature belongs to a family of ancient marine reptiles known as "mosasaurs." Not technically dinosaurs, the mosasaurs were related to monitor lizards and snakes, and most of them looked like a cross between a whale and a crocodile.

The fossils were discovered in the waste dump of a coal mine in the Bakony Hills of Western Hungary. Named *Pannoniasaurus inexpectatus*, the newly discovered species is the first that is assumed to have adapted to and lived entirely in fresh water. Previous species of mosasaurs are known to have lived exclusively in salt water.

The researchers uncovered thousands of *Pannoniasaurus* fossils in the area. The concentration of so many specimens at one site suggests that the creature was a true freshwater dweller and not just a saltwater animal that swam into rivers the way some sharks do. The area was part of a chain of islands in the middle of a big freshwater seaway that <u>separated</u> Africa and Southern Europe. Its small sharp teeth suggest that *Pannoniasaurus* probably preyed on the other forms of life that dwelled in the rivers running through the islands.

The fossils range from three feet to thirteen feet in length and are representative of specimens of varying ages. According to Michael Caldwell, a mosasaur expert at the University of Alberta, scientists usually discover big mosasaurs and rarely find young ones. The research also showed that, unlike other mosasaurs that swam with flippers, the *Pannoniasaurus* had limbs that resemble legs, suggesting that they occasionally traveled on land. Paleontologists believe that they may have <u>behaved</u> like crocodiles, spending a lot of time in cold water, but sometimes crawling inland to regulate their body temperature.

Caldwell believes that *Pannoniasaurus* is not the only ancient marine reptile to successfully adapt to fresh water. He is certain that there are other ancient marine species that were also able to make the same transition. These species just have yet to be discovered.

60. How can the *Pannoniasaurus* be classified?

(a) It is related to other species of reptiles.
(b) It is a cross between two aquatic animals.
(c) It is native to Eastern Hungary.
(d) It is a newly evolved dinosaur.

61. What makes the *Pannoniasaurus* unique from other mosasaurs?

(a) its fondness for other sea creatures
(b) its successful adaptation to fresh water
(c) its tendency to imitate the behavior of sharks
(d) its ability to live both in fresh and salt water

62. What does the concentration of fossils in the area most likely suggest?

(a) that they fed collectively
(b) that they had previously lived in the sea
(c) that they had moved to land
(d) that they didn't live outside of fresh water

63. Which is NOT true about the way the newly discovered mosasaur lived?

(a) They inhabited island territory.
(b) They fed on other river creatures.
(c) They lived in the ocean in Southern Europe.
(d) Their population converged in one area.

64. Based on the passage, why did the *Pannoniasaurus* most likely crawl inland using its limbs?

(a) to increase its body heat
(b) to travel from island to island
(c) to hunt for land animals
(d) to evolve into a land-dweller

65. In the context of the passage, separated means __________.

(a) departed
(b) alienated
(c) divided
(d) united

66. In the context of the passage, behaved means __________.

(a) worked
(b) acted
(c) differed
(d) seemed

PART 3. *Read the following encyclopedia article and answer the questions. The underlined words in the article are for vocabulary questions.*

THE GREAT BARRIER REEF

The Great Barrier Reef is the largest coral reef system in the world. This natural structure is located off the coast of Queensland, Australia, and consists of 2,900 individual reefs and 900 islands. Covering an area of 133,000 square miles, it is the largest structure on earth to have been made by living organisms, and can be seen from outer space.

The reefs are composed of billions of tiny organisms known as "coral polyps" that have built up over time. The formation stretches more than 1,600 miles from the Torres Strait in the north to the area between Lady Elliot and Fraser Islands in the south.

The reef was formed through a long and complex process. It began to take shape between 58 and 48 million years ago when the Coral Sea Basin was developing. When the Australian continent reached its present location, sea levels began to change, and the coral reefs grew more quickly. They began to <u>flourish</u> in the favorable sea temperatures and levels of sunlight that resulted from the shift. However, changing climate cycles and the resulting changes in sea levels caused the reefs to grow in spurts and then periodically lie dormant and even decline. Scientists believe that the present Great Barrier Reef was formed about 20,000 years ago when new coral polyps started growing over the remains of the old reef.

Today, the Great Barrier Reef <u>harbors</u> a wide variety of species, many of which are endemic to the reef system and currently endangered. The reef has 30 species of whales, dolphins, and porpoises. Six species of endangered sea turtles breed in the reef, including two which have developed into distinct populations in the northern and southern parts.

Around two million people visit the Great Barrier Reef yearly. The site is protected by an Australian national park that regulates human activities such as fishing and tourism in the area. While the government attempts to control the impact of tourism, the reef's rich biodiversity remains under constant threat from illegal fishing and other harmful human activities.

67. What is the main topic of the article?

(a) how coastal islands are formed
(b) how organisms create natural structures
(c) one of the world's natural wonders
(d) Australia's unique endemic wildlife

68. How are coral reefs formed?

(a) by the buildup of tiny organisms
(b) by controlling human activities
(c) through changes in the climate
(d) through the formation of the seas

69. What did NOT help in the formation of the Great Barrier Reef millions of years ago?

(a) the conducive water temperatures
(b) the decrease in the number of coral polyps
(c) the movement of the Australian continent
(d) the formation of the Coral Sea Basin

70. What is probably true about the present reef's development?

(a) It has been growing for millions of years.
(b) It is constantly moving seaward.
(c) It has stopped developing.
(d) It is a relatively new formation.

71. Based on the passage, why most likely should the Great Barrier Reef be protected?

(a) It is the home to many animals native to the area.
(b) It is an income-generating tourist destination.
(c) It provides fishermen with a source of livelihood.
(d) It helps in controlling climate change.

72. In the context of the passage, flourish means __________.

(a) bloom
(b) thrive
(c) form
(d) decline

73. In the context of the passage, harbors means __________.

(a) breeds
(b) expels
(c) anchors
(d) shelters

PART 4. *Read the following business letter and answer the questions. The underlined words in the letter are for vocabulary questions.*

February 12, 2018

Mr. Edward Palmer
Hotel Manager
Blue Sapphire Hotel

Dear Mr. Palmer:

Please be reminded of your <u>outstanding</u> balance for the landscaping work we completed for Blue Sapphire Hotel. When you asked for a discounted "cash price" for the work, we agreed provided that full payment would be made the day it was completed. However, since you were out of the office on the day of completion, we could not collect payment on that day, and as you requested by telephone, we left the invoice with your assistant, hoping that the payment would be made the next day. More than a week has passed, and our office hasn't received your payment as of this writing.

We are happy to offer a variety of payment plans to our clients, including a discounted cash price. However, we do ask our clients to honor the terms of their contracts punctually so we can continue to offer all clients excellent service. Unfortunately, the delay in your payment is affecting our cash flow and preventing us from completing a commission for another valued client. I'm sure you understand how failing to meet the expectations of our other customers could be detrimental to our business.

We would like to make a request for the immediate payment of the completed work mentioned above. I have attached an invoice for $80,500.00 for the service completed on February 4, 2018. As a sign of good faith, we are <u>waiving</u> applicable late payment penalties if you comply with our request no later than Wednesday, February 24th.

If you have any questions regarding this matter, please contact me at 312-752-3489 or e-mail me at staten@diamond_landscaping.com. We thank you in advance for your kind cooperation.

Sincerely,

Abigail Staten

Abigail Staten
Finance Officer
Diamond Landscaping Co.

74. Why did Abigail Staten write Edward Palmer a letter?

(a) to promote her company's services
(b) to tell him about her company's financial problem
(c) to remind him about an obligation
(d) to ask him for an advanced payment for a job

75. When was Palmer supposed to submit his payment?

(a) before the agreement was reached
(b) a week after the work was completed
(c) the day following the project's conclusion
(d) on the day the work was finished

76. How is Palmer's failure to fulfill the agreement affecting Staten's company?

(a) It is interfering with the company's other commitments.
(b) Clients are canceling their contacts with the company.
(c) It caused the company to lose a new client.
(d) The company can no longer give discounts.

77. Why probably does Diamond Landscaping offer a cash payment plan?

(a) to be able to charge late payment penalties
(b) to have ready funds for other projects
(c) to avoid being paid in installments
(d) to prevent the company from running out of cash

78. Based on the letter, what will most likely happen if the balance is still not settled quickly?

(a) Staten will write another letter.
(b) Staten's firm will close down.
(c) A penalty fee will be added to it.
(d) The payment period will be extended.

79. In the context of the passage, outstanding means ________.

(a) unpaid
(b) settled
(c) excellent
(d) excessive

80. In the context of the passage, waiving means ________.

(a) enforcing
(b) forgoing
(c) volunteering
(d) expecting

THIS IS THE END OF THE TEST

READING AND VOCABULARY SECTION

00 : 40 : 00

시작 시각	시	분	초
목표 종료 시각	시	분	초
종료 시각	시	분	초
총 소요 시간 (종료 시각 - 시작 시각)		분	초
초과 시간 (총 소요 시간 - 목표 시간)		분	초

DIRECTIONS:

You will now read four different passages. Each passage is followed by comprehension and vocabulary questions. From the four choices for each item, choose the best answer. Then blacken in the correct circle on your answer sheet.

Read the following example passage and example question.

Example :

Bill Johnson lives in New York. He is 25 years old. He has four brothers and two sisters.

How many brothers does Bill Johnson have?

(a) one
(b) two
(c) three
(d) four

The correct answer is (d), so the circle with the letter (d) has been blackened.

ⓐ ⓑ ⓒ ●

NOW TURN THE PAGE AND BEGIN

TEST 2

PART 1. *Read the following biography article and answer the questions. The underlined words in the article are for vocabulary questions.*

HANS CHRISTIAN ANDERSEN

Hans Christian Andersen was a Danish writer and poet who is best known for his children's stories. These include the popular stories "The Little Mermaid," "The Emperor's New Clothes," and "The Snow Queen." Many of his stories and poems have been translated into several languages and adapted into films, plays, ballets, and animated movies.

Born on April 2, 1805, in Odense, Denmark, Andersen was the only child of Hans Andersen, a shoemaker, and Anne Marie Anders, a laundry worker. Despite being poor, his father made sure to take Andersen to the local playhouse. After his father's death, the 14-year-old Andersen traveled to Copenhagen to pursue an acting career in the Royal Danish Theater. Under the patronage of Jonas Collin, the theater's director, he attended grammar school in Slagelse, then a school in Elsinore until 1827, and finally the University of Copenhagen in 1828.

In 1829, Andersen earned some success when he published a short story titled "A Journey on Foot from Holmen's Canal to the East Point of Amager," an account of a character's walking trip. He received a grant from King Frederick VI for travel expenses and went on a 16-month tour through Germany, Switzerland, Italy, and France. This trip started Andersen's lifelong fondness for travel. In 1835, he published his first successful novel, *The Improvisatore*, which was largely based on his experiences in Italy.

1835 was also the year that Andersen published his first book of fairy tales, *Tales, Told for Children*, which included "The Tinderbox" and "The Princess and the Pea." More children's stories were published in 1836 and 1837, completing his first volume. He completed his second volume in 1842 and newer collections appeared in the succeeding years.

His appeal across cultures was so strong that his stories began to be translated into English as early as 1846. His books have become timeless favorites and are still being published around the world. In recent decades, Hollywood songs and a Disney cartoon have helped to ensure that Andersen's stories remain popular.

In 1872, Andersen fell from his bed, incurring an injury from which he never fully recovered. He died on August 4, 1875, in Copenhagen. The Danish government had recognized Hans Christian Andersen as a national treasure even before his death. And in Denmark, International Children's Book Day is celebrated on his birthday.

53. What is Hans Christian Andersen best known for?

(a) his cultural appeal
(b) his travels
(c) his unfortunate death
(d) his fairy tales

54. When did Andersen decide to travel to Copenhagen to pursue acting?

(a) after finishing college
(b) after his father passed away
(c) after being recognized by the Danish government
(d) after visiting Italy

55. According to the article, how was Andersen able to fund some of his travels?

(a) by using his mother's money
(b) by selling some of his works
(c) by receiving a grant
(d) by getting a gift from his father

56. Aside from his first novel, what other works did he publish in 1835?

(a) He published his first collection of children's stories.
(b) He published a book of his poetry.
(c) He published his travel memoirs.
(d) He published a compilation of children's songs.

57. How did Andersen probably spend most of his adult life?

(a) He spent most of it acting in the Royal Danish Theater.
(b) He spent most of it exploring places and writing.
(c) He spent most of it hosting extravagant parties.
(d) He spent most of it struggling to earn a living.

58. In the context of the passage, patronage means ________.

(a) sponsorship
(b) leadership
(c) friendship
(d) protection

59. In the context of the passage, timeless means ________.

(a) constant
(b) forgettable
(c) persistent
(d) deathless

PART 2. *Read the following magazine article and answer the questions. The underlined words in the article are for vocabulary questions.*

HITLER'S PAINTING COLLECTION DISCOVERED IN A CONVENT

A collection of paintings belonging to Adolf Hitler was discovered in a convent in the town of Doskany, north of Prague. *The Telegraph* reported that Jiri Kuchar, a historian from Czechoslovakia, unearthed the collection. The body of artistic works includes a massive canvas called *Memories of Stalingrad* that shows wounded German soldiers taking shelter in a trench. The painting is said to have been one of Hitler's favorites, which experts see as surprising because Hitler suffered one of his greatest defeats in the battle of Stalingrad during World War II.

Adolf Hitler was known for ordering German forces to <u>plunder</u> museums and other art establishments for expensive works of art and to hide them. Robert M. Edsel, author of *"Rescuing da Vinci"*, tells of how American soldiers recovered thousands of lost artworks during the Second World War. Some of the artworks Hitler's forces stole were priceless paintings and sculptures by masters such as Michelangelo, Edgar Degas, Paul Cézanne, and Vincent Van Gogh. The German dictator himself was known to be a frustrated artist and architect.

Hitler was reported to have ordered the collection discovered by Kuchar to be hidden in a monastery in southern Bohemia. This collection was found by American forces during the war. However, nobody knows how exactly the paintings later disappeared and ended up in the convent in Prague. The Czech historian has only discovered seven of the paintings in the collection and reports that nine more paintings are still missing.

Art experts predict that the collection could be auctioned for about $2.6 million, but historians believe that the collection's historical value is a lot more. The convent in Doskany, however, has declared that it is not willing to auction off the collection and intends to keep it. Meanwhile, Kuchar is still searching for the remaining paintings, but said it will be difficult to find them. Some institutions, whose artworks may have belonged to the original collection, may not want to be associated with Hitler's <u>notorious</u> acts during World War II, and presumably might wish to remain silent about them.

60. What was discovered by Jiri Kuchar?

(a) a collection of stolen paintings
(b) a famous Michelangelo sculpture
(c) a priceless Van Gogh masterpiece
(d) da Vinci's *Mona Lisa*

61. Why is it most likely "surprising" that Hitler should favor *Memories of Stalingrad*?

(a) It would remind him of his defeat during World War I.
(b) It would frustrate him more as a failed artist.
(c) It would remind him of a lost battle during the war.
(d) It would remind him of his wartime looting crimes.

62. What motivated the German soldiers to gather up precious works of art?

(a) having a strong interest in artwork
(b) being commanded by their dictator
(c) wanting to sell them for their personal wealth
(d) needing to take something from the Americans

63. Who recovered many of the stolen artworks during the war?

(a) Jiri Kuchar
(b) Robert M. Edsel
(c) Russian soldiers
(d) American soldiers

64. Based on the article, why will it be difficult for Kuchar to find the missing paintings?

(a) The owners might be ashamed of the paintings' origins.
(b) The paintings are hidden well.
(c) The Germans refuse to surrender their loot.
(d) The convent intends to keep the collection.

65. In the context of the passage, plunder means ______.

(a) search
(b) give
(c) destroy
(d) rob

66. In the context of the passage, notorious means ______.

(a) renowned
(b) infamous
(c) guilty
(d) unpopular

PART 3. *Read the following encyclopedia article and answer the questions. The underlined words in the article are for vocabulary questions.*

THE TASMANIAN DEVIL

The Tasmanian devil, commonly called a "devil," is a fierce, meat-eating animal that lives on the Australian island of Tasmania. Being a marsupial like the kangaroo, the Tasmanian devil gives birth very early, and the underdeveloped young continue growing in the mother's pouch. The animal is known for its bad temper after which it was named. It will go into an uncontrollable rage when threatened by a predator, fighting for a mate, or defending its food.

The Tasmanian devil is about the same size as a small dog and has a muscular build, large head, and black fur. It also has long front legs and short back legs, giving it an unusual gait. Other traits that contribute to the animal being called a devil include its unpleasant odor and the loud screeching sound it makes. It is also known for its keen smell, sharp teeth, and muscular jaw that can deliver a very powerful bite.

Tasmanian devils typically feed on smaller animals such as snakes, birds, and insects, while ignoring fruits and vegetation. They are at their most <u>rowdy</u> and temperamental when fighting for the right to feed on a large carcass. Devils mostly hunt at night and spend their days alone in hollow logs, caves, or burrows. They use their long whiskers, strong sense of smell, and excellent sight to avoid predators and find food. They will eat almost anything they can catch and consume everything—even hair, organs, and bones.

Tasmanian devils are not monogamous animals, and males mate with more than one female. Males compete violently for females and then guard their partners from other male devils. The annual mating period lasts about three weeks and the female devil gives birth 18 days later. A female gives birth to 20 to 30 young devils during each mating season. However, the mother has only four nipples in its pouch, so only a few babies survive.

Once <u>plentiful</u> throughout Australia, Tasmanian devils are now found only on the island state of Tasmania. Biologists believe their extinction on mainland Australia was caused by the introduction of Asian dogs.

67. Which of the following is NOT a characteristic of the Tasmanian devil?

(a) It has long front legs.
(b) It makes a loud unpleasant sound.
(c) It has a foul odor.
(d) It has brown fur.

68. What kind of food do they normally eat?

(a) They usually eat fish.
(b) They usually eat small animals.
(c) They usually eat fruits.
(d) They usually feed on young Tasmanian devils.

69. Why do the males become more aggressive during certain times of the year?

(a) to win the attention of female devils
(b) to get food for their mates
(c) to protect their offspring
(d) to defend against larger predators

70. What is said to have caused their extinction on mainland Australia?

(a) the destruction of their habitat
(b) the increasing number of people
(c) the introduction of dogs
(d) their fierce behavior towards one another

71. Why would Tasmanian devils most likely not make good pets?

(a) because they are very big
(b) because they demand a lot of attention
(c) because they tend to eat a lot
(d) because they are very aggressive animals

72. In the context of the passage, rowdy means ________.

(a) disorderly
(b) delicate
(c) rude
(d) peaceful

73. In the context of the passage, plentiful means ________.

(a) overpopulated
(b) lacking
(c) abundant
(d) ample

PART 4. *Read the following business letter and answer the questions. The underlined words in the letter are for vocabulary questions.*

Ms. Mary Modest
Financial Manager
Saundex Financial

Dear Ms. Modest:

First, let me start by saying that I'm very happy to work for Saundex Financial and eager to continue contributing to its profitability under your management. I have learned and grown so much under your guidance that I've come up with new ideas for the company. Please allow me then to mention an opportunity for greater profits.

I'm confident that you will agree that my efforts as your salesman have been effective in bringing in greater profits for Saundex. My sales in the past year more or less came in at $425,000, surpassing the $250,000 goal we had <u>anticipated</u> at our year-end meeting twelve months ago. I believe, however, that I can be even more productive for the company as your Sales Manager.

Having had four years of experience selling our financial portfolio, I've gained a clear idea about our customers' needs and how to meet them. I know ways to increase sales dramatically and gear our sales team to do precisely that. As Sales Manager, I truly believe that we can <u>procure</u> an excess of $10,000,000 in sales by the end of a two-year period, generating a level of profits we have never attained before.

I know you are a very busy person, but you also have a reputation for being fair and approachable. If you can find the time to meet with me at your convenience, I would be very happy to discuss this matter in whole and share my ideas with you. I would very much appreciate your thoughts on this professional proposal.

Cordially,

Richard Felt

Richard Felt
Sales Associate
Saundex Financial

74. What is the purpose of Richard Felt's letter to Mary Modest?

(a) to apologize for his lack of performance
(b) to inform Ms. Modest about the increase in sales
(c) to discuss his proposal to be promoted to Sales Manager
(d) to resign as the company's Sales Manager

75. What can be said about Felt's sales performance?

(a) It took him four years to meet his sales quota.
(b) He has brought in profits above and beyond what was required.
(c) He has not met his quota since last year.
(d) He is setting a higher quota since he has been doing well.

76. By how much did Felt exceed his quota in the past year, approximately?

(a) $250,000
(b) $175,000
(c) $425,000
(d) $10,000,000

77. Which of the following statements is NOT true?

(a) Felt feels he can motivate the sales team to perform better.
(b) Felt has had four years of experience in the company.
(c) Felt thinks greater productivity will occur if his suggestions are considered.
(d) Felt believes he can achieve an excess of $10,000,000 in one year.

78. How will the letter most likely affect Modest?

(a) She will most likely consider Felt's proposal.
(b) She will most likely ignore Felt's letter.
(c) She will most likely retain Felt in his present position.
(d) She will most likely ask Felt to wait for another year.

79. In the context of the passage, anticipated means _________.

(a) expected
(b) awaited
(c) guessed
(d) realized

80. In the context of the passage, procure means _________.

(a) purchase
(b) earn
(c) manage
(d) fulfil

THIS IS THE END OF THE TEST

READING AND VOCABULARY SECTION

00 : 40 : 00

시작 시각	시	분	초
목표 종료 시각	시	분	초
종료 시각	시	분	초
총 소요 시간 (종료 시각 - 시작 시각)		분	초
초과 시간 (총 소요 시간 - 목표 시간)		분	초

DIRECTIONS:

You will now read four different passages. Each passage is followed by comprehension and vocabulary questions. From the four choices for each item, choose the best answer. Then blacken in the correct circle on your answer sheet.

Read the following example passage and example question.

Example :

Bill Johnson lives in New York. He is 25 years old. He has four brothers and two sisters.

How many brothers does Bill Johnson have?

(a) one
(b) two
(c) three
(d) four

The correct answer is (d), so the circle with the letter (d) has been blackened.

ⓐ ⓑ ⓒ ●

NOW TURN THE PAGE AND BEGIN

TEST 3

PART 1. *Read the following biography article and answer the questions. The underlined words in the article are for vocabulary questions.*

CHRISTOPHER NOLAN

Christopher Nolan is an award-winning British-American director and screenwriter. Best known for their intricate plots and unusual narrative structures, several of Nolan's releases were huge box office hits, particularly *Inception* and *The Dark Knight* trilogy.

Nolan was born in London, England, on July 30, 1970. His father was a British copywriter, and his mother was an American flight attendant. He <u>developed</u> an interest in filmmaking at the age of seven when he shot a home movie using his father's Super 8 film camera. In 1989, he entered University College London to study English literature. His interest in filmmaking continued, however, and he joined the school's film society, serving as its president for two years.

After graduating in 1993, Nolan worked by producing training videos for companies while making short films in his spare time. His first full-length movie, *Following*, was released in 1998. Made with the help of friends from his college film society, this low-budget, black-and-white thriller tells the story of a writer who becomes obsessed with stalking strangers. The film was well-received in several film festivals across the world, and served as Nolan's "calling card" as a writer-director.

The success of *Following* attracted the attention of Newmarket Films, which acquired and produced Nolan's screenplay and next movie, *Memento*. This development launched his mainstream career. The independent film is based on a short story by Nolan's younger brother, Jonathan, and featured select sequences in a non-chronological order, essentially telling the story backwards. *Memento* was praised by critics, and nominated for Best Screenplay by both the Golden Globes and the Academy Awards.

Christopher Nolan's biggest break came when he directed *The Dark Knight* trilogy, a big-budget Hollywood adaptation of the Batman comic books. *Batman Begins*, the first of the series, pleased fans and critics alike when it was released in 2005. Its sequel, *The Dark Knight*, opened in 2008 and became the first movie to earn over $500 million in two days. Before completing the trilogy with *The Dark Knight Rises*, Nolan wrote and directed the critically <u>acclaimed</u> blockbuster *Inception*, which won four Academy Awards in 2011.

Christopher Nolan's complex storytelling and vivid visual style have made him a major figure in both independent and mainstream cinema. He has continued to be an important Hollywood figure, exploring genres such as science fiction and spy thrillers in his films.

53. What are Christopher Nolan's films best known for?

(a) their complex story lines
(b) their low production costs
(c) their simple narratives
(d) their basis as adaptations of comics

54. When did Christopher Nolan first get involved in filmmaking?

(a) when he joined a film organization
(b) when he made a home movie as a child
(c) when he took up moviemaking as a hobby
(d) when he graduated from college

55. According to the article, what did Nolan do immediately after finishing college?

(a) He released several short films.
(b) He made corporate training videos.
(c) He began his first full-length movie.
(d) He supervised his college's film society.

56. Which of the following makes the movie *Memento* distinctive?

(a) It was done on a limited budget.
(b) It was shot entirely in black-and-white.
(c) It was a collaboration with his college friends.
(d) It does not follow a normal sequence of events.

57. Based on the article, what can be said about *The Dark Knight* movie released in 2008?

(a) It is the last of the Batman series.
(b) It is Nolan's first comic book adaptation.
(c) It broke box office records.
(d) It earned Nolan many awards.

58. In the context of the passage, developed means _______.

(a) built
(b) rejected
(c) enhanced
(d) acquired

59. In the context of the passage, acclaimed means _______.

(a) praised
(b) censured
(c) disliked
(d) owned

PART 2. *Read the following magazine article and answer the questions. The underlined words in the article are for vocabulary questions.*

GLOBAL WARMING MAY SHRINK FISH

The size and body weight of much of the world's fish population could decrease by as much as 24% in the next 40 years. This finding from a study conducted by scientists at the University of British Columbia was published in the journal *Natural Climate Change*. The study demonstrates that the rising temperature of ocean water due to global climate change is causing a decrease in its oxygen levels. One result of this oxygen depletion is the inability of fish to develop into full-sized adults, threatening one of the world's major food sources.

The researchers designed a computer model to learn how global warming would affect more than 600 species of fish in different parts of the world. The study suggests that the average size of an adult fish in over 75% of the world's fish species can be expected to shrink by the year 2050. Those that would be most affected are the ones from the Indian Ocean, showing a potential decrease in average size by 24%. Because oxygen levels also decrease with depth in oceans, deep-sea fish will be the most vulnerable, including popularly harvested food sources like cod, haddock, and halibut.

The newly warmed water would also stimulate an increase in many species' metabolism. Any increase in a fish's basal metabolic rate, the rate an animal uses energy while awake and at rest, will consequently force it to consume more oxygen just to maintain normal bodily functions. This will contribute further to the depletion of the life-giving gas in the ocean and prevent other fish from growing properly.

The study further predicts that species will eventually relocate to colder waters where oxygen is more abundant. Like any organism, fish have adapted over time to thrive in their specific environments. As the oxygen levels change in their current habitats, fish will move toward areas where the gas levels are closer to those of their ideal environments. The larger the fish is, the colder the water it will relocate to. Populations of the biggest fish will most likely move closest to the North and South Poles where oxygen is most plentiful.

60. What is the direct cause of ocean fish shrinking in size?

(a) the decreasing supply of oxygen in the water
(b) the increasing number of fish species in the ocean
(c) the warming up of Earth's atmosphere
(d) the rising temperature of the oceans' water

61. Why will fish like cod and halibut be affected the worst by global warming?

(a) They are usually eaten by humans.
(b) They are the slowest to reproduce.
(c) They live deep within the oceans.
(d) They have very slow metabolic rates.

62. How does the increase in a fish's metabolic rate affect its behavior?

(a) It forces the fish to save available oxygen.
(b) It requires the fish to use up more oxygen.
(c) It induces the fish to become more restless.
(d) It encourages the fish to relocate.

63. Based on the article, where are smaller fish most likely to move to in cold waters?

(a) to the cold depths of the Indian Ocean
(b) to the cold waters that fishermen cannot reach
(c) closer to the Poles like bigger fish
(d) farther from the Poles than bigger fish

64. What is most likely the main concern addressed in the article?

(a) the destruction of the sea's ecosystems
(b) the harmful effects of climate change
(c) the looming shortage of a major source of food
(d) the movement of fish to remote seas

65. In the context of the passage, vulnerable means ________.

(a) tolerant
(b) sensitive
(c) immune
(d) risky

66. In the context of the passage, adapted means ________.

(a) moved
(b) rejected
(c) copied
(d) adjusted

PART 3. *Read the following encyclopedia article and answer the questions. The underlined words in the article are for vocabulary questions.*

TRUFFLES

Truffles are a type of mushroom that grows underground. They are typically found around certain types of trees on whose roots they rely upon for nourishment. They vary in size and come in two colors: black and white. Because of their irregularly round shape, truffles usually resemble the chocolate confection that bears the same name. Sought after for their earthy and pungent taste, truffles have been valued since ancient times, especially by the early Greeks and Romans. Today, truffles are highly prized in international *haute cuisine,* or high cuisine.

Truffles are so rare that they have been dubbed the "Diamonds of the Kitchen." They can only be harvested during certain times of the year, usually between September and May. They are also not easy to harvest; truffles can grow at depths of one meter underground, and it is usually difficult to determine which trees harbor them. Specially trained dogs and "truffle pigs" are normally used to sniff out mature truffles. All of these factors make truffles so expensive—one pound costs as much as $1,000—that the delicacy is normally served only in posh restaurants.

The two most well-known types of truffles are the black Perigord truffle, found in Perigord, France, and the white Alba Madonna truffle that is native to Piedmont, Italy. The black truffle is less costly than its white counterpart. It has a more refined flavor which has been described as "syrupy sweet." On the other hand, the white truffle has a flavor that hints of garlic and a musky aroma. Black truffles are best for cooking into sauces, creams, and stews. White truffles, however, are best served raw to retain their intense flavor and aroma.

Truffles go well with simple dishes like omelets, pastas, and salads. They are either shaved over or mixed into these dishes. Recently, truffle oil, which is basically olive oil infused with a small amount of either black or white truffles, has been introduced to the market as a more affordable substitute for truffles. It is also used to reproduce the essence of truffles in cooking.

67. Which of the following is NOT true about truffles?

(a) They grow on the roots of trees.
(b) They are prepared as an expensive candy.
(c) They come in different sizes and shapes.
(d) They have a strong, spicy taste.

68. According to the passage, why are truffles expensive?

(a) because they are difficult to find
(b) because they cannot be cultivated
(c) because the trees they live on are rare
(d) because they do not have a predictable harvest season

69. What is most likely a reason why dogs and pigs are used to locate truffles?

(a) They can dig deep into the ground.
(b) They know which trees to search.
(c) They have a strong sense of smell.
(d) They are easy to train.

70. Aside from their color, how else do white truffles differ from black truffles?

(a) They have a milder flavor.
(b) They can only be found in France.
(c) They are less expensive.
(d) They taste better uncooked.

71. Based on the article, what is most likely true about the way truffles are served?

(a) They are now served in ordinary restaurants.
(b) They can be served without using spices.
(c) They are not served as a main dish.
(d) They are generally served raw.

72. In the context of the passage, posh means ________.

(a) snobbish
(b) luxurious
(c) modern
(d) ordinary

73. In the context of the passage, substitute means ________.

(a) addition
(b) supplement
(c) alternative
(d) preference

PART 4. *Read the following business letter and answer the questions. The underlined words in the article are for vocabulary questions.*

Walter Jackson
8750 Roosevelt St.
San Diego, CA

Dear Mr. Jackson:

I am pleased to inform you that Collins University's School of Law has admitted you to its Juris Doctor degree program for next semester. You are among the select students whose academic achievements, diverse talents, and strong character qualify them for the program. We believe that you will contribute significantly to the academic rigor that <u>characterizes</u> our school.

To reserve your place at Collins University, please submit an initial deposit of 10% of your tuition fee along with a completed copy of the confirmation form enclosed with this letter. The deadline for confirming your participation in next semester's program is May 1, but we would appreciate hearing from you sooner. Please note that the initial deposit is non-refundable.

Your enrollment is subject to the condition that you present an official transcript of records verifying the completion of your bachelor's degree. Please prepare two notarized copies of your transcript(s), including the final grades for all courses taken, for our evaluation. Once we have reviewed your grades, we will send updates within the next few weeks about your scholarship and student loan options.

Along with this letter are admissions materials and brochures for you to <u>peruse</u>. Please go over the enclosed information sheet which highlights the deposit process and other important information. If you have any questions or concerns after reading this letter, you may contact our office at 555-0199, or send us an email.

We are looking forward to your attendance at Collins University.

Sincerely,

Samantha Goodman

Samantha Goodman
Dean of Admissions
Collins University

74. What is the main purpose of Samantha Goodman's letter to Walter Jackson?

(a) to ask him to pay his tuition fee
(b) to inform him of application requirements
(c) to invite him to enroll at a university
(d) to notify him of his acceptance at a college

75. According to the letter, why should Jackson make an initial deposit?

(a) to receive his bachelor's degree
(b) to acquire his transcript of records
(c) to confirm his intent to enroll at the university
(d) to be eligible for financial assistance

76. What could happen if Jackson does not submit his transcript of records?

(a) He will not qualify for a scholarship.
(b) He will be unable to apply to other schools.
(c) His slot in the college will be canceled.
(d) His initial deposit will be returned.

77. What most likely does Goodman need Jackson's transcript for?

(a) to determine if he qualifies for the Juris Doctor program
(b) to prevent him from backing out of the university
(c) to prove that he has completed his high school coursework
(d) to determine what kind of aid he is eligible for

78. Which of the following is Jackson not required to do after reading the letter?

(a) call the admissions office
(b) read the enclosed materials
(c) prepare his school records
(d) send his tuition fee deposit

79. In the context of the passage, characterizes means _______.

(a) designates
(b) defines
(c) distinguishes
(d) portrays

80. In the context of the passage, peruse means _______.

(a) review
(b) omit
(c) focus
(d) consider

THIS IS THE END OF THE TEST

G-TELP

퀵 지텔프 공식 문제집

필수 어휘 800

A

번호	단어 및 숙어	품사	뜻	Self-check		
				1	2	3
1	a variety of	phr.	다양한			
2	a wide array of	phr.	다수의			
3	abandoned	adj.	버려진			
4	abolish	v.	폐지하다, 없애다			
5	absence	n.	부재			
6	absorption	n.	흡수			
7	abundant	adj.	풍부한			
8	accept	v.	받아들이다			
9	accessibility	n.	접근 용이성			
10	accessory	n.	액세서리, 장신구			
11	accidentally	ad.	우연히, 잘못하면			
12	accommodating	v.	잘 협조하는			
13	accompany	v.	동행하다			
14	account executive	n.	(광고회사의) 거래처 담당 사원, 광고기획자			
15	account for	v.	책임지다. 차지하다			
16	account	n.	설명, 이야기			
17	accrue	v.	누적되다, 축적하다			
18	accurate	adj.	정확한			
19	accuse	v.	고발하다, 기소하다			
20	achieve	v.	달성하다			
21	achievement	n.	성취			
22	acquire	v.	얻다, 인수하다			
23	adapt (to)	v.	(상황에) 적응하다			
24	adapt	v.	각색하다, 맞추다			
25	adaptable	adj.	적응할 수 있는			
26	adaptation	n.	각색, 적응			
27	additional	adj.	추가적인			
28	additive	n.	첨가물			
29	address	v.	다루다, 해결하려 하다			
30	adjust to	phr v.	~에 적응하다			
31	admit	v.	입학을 허가하다			
32	advance	n.	발전			

A

번호	단어 및 숙어	품사	뜻	Self-check		
				1	2	3
33	advanced	adj.	고급의, 고도의, 선진의, 진보한			
34	advanced payment	n.	선불, 선지급			
35	advantage	n.	장점, 혜택			
36	advocate	v.	지지하다, 옹호하다			
37	afford	v.	~할 여유가 되다			
38	affordable	adj.	적당한, 알맞은 가격의			
39	aggressive	adj.	공격적인			
40	agreement	n.	계약			
41	allowance	n.	수당, 용돈			
42	ancient	adj.	고대의			
43	annual	adj.	연례의			
44	apparently	ad.	듣자 하니, 보아 하니			
45	appeal	n.	매력, 호소력			
46	appealing	adj.	매력적인			
47	applicable	adj.	해당되는			
48	application	n.	응용, 적용			
49	apply	v.	적용하다			
50	appreciate	v.	고마워하다, (어떤 상황 등을) 환영하다, 기뻐하다			
51	approachable	adj.	다가가기 쉬운			
52	appropriate	adj.	적합한			
53	appropriately	ad.	적당하게, 알맞게			
54	approximately	ad.	대략적으로			
55	aptitude	n.	소질, 적성			
56	aquatic	adj.	수생의, 수중의			
57	arouse	v.	불러일으키다, 각성시키다			
58	arrangement	n.	배치, 정돈			
59	artificial	adj.	인공적인			
60	ashamed	adj.	수치스러워하는			
61	aspiring	adj.	장차 ~가 되려고 하는			
62	assign	v.	(업무, 책임 등을) 배정하다, 맡기다			
63	assignment	n.	과제			
64	assist	v.	돕다			

A - B

번호	단어 및 숙어	품사	뜻	Self-check		
				1	2	3
65	associated	adj.	연관된			
66	assume	v.	(책임 등을) 맡다, 추정하다			
67	at short notice	phr.	촉박하게			
68	atmosphere	n.	대기			
69	attain	v.	달성하다			
70	attend to sth	phr v.	을 처리하다			
71	attend	v.	(학교 등에) 다니다, 출석하다			
72	attention	n.	보살핌, 주의			
73	audience	n.	관객			
74	augment	v.	늘리다, 증강하다			
75	autographed	adj.	사인된, 서명이 있는			
76	availability	n.	(이용, 구매) 가능성			
77	available	adj.	구할 수 있는, 이용 가능한			
78	average	adj.	평균의, 보통의			
79	avoid	v.	피하다			
80	award-winning	adj.	상을 받은			
81	awesome	adj.	멋진			
82	back out	phr v.	(하기로 했던 것을) 그만두다, 철회하다			
83	balance	n.	지불잔액, 잔금			
84	bandwidth	n.	대역폭			
85	barely	ad.	거의 ~아니게, 간신히			
86	barn	n.	헛간, 큰 건물			
87	be composed of	phr v.	~로 구성되어 있다			
88	be eager to	phr v.	~를 간절히 바라다			
89	be familiar with	phr v.	~에 대해 익히 알다			
90	be hard on	phr v.	~에 안 좋은 영향을 미치다			
91	be subject to	phr v.	~에 달려있다			
92	behave	v.	행동하다			
93	benefit concert	n.	자선 음악회			
94	benefit	n.	이점			
95	biodiversity	n.	생물의 다양성			
96	blowhole	n.	분수공			

B - C

번호	단어 및 숙어	품사	뜻	Self-check		
				1	2	3
97	bodily function	n.	생체 기능			
98	boost	v.	신장시키다, 증가시키다			
99	box office record	n.	박스 오피스 기록, 영화 흥행 기록			
100	branch out	phr v.	진출하다			
101	break down	phr v.	고장 나다			
102	breeze	n.	정말 쉬운 것			
103	budget	n.	예산, 지출 예상 비용			
104	buildup	n.	축적, 증가			
105	bump into	phr v.	~와 마주치다			
106	can't wait to	phr v.	싶어 하다			
107	candidate	n.	지원자			
108	capability	n.	능력			
109	capture	v.	포착하다			
110	carcass	n.	(큰 동물의) 시체			
111	career	n.	직업, 경력			
112	cash flow	n.	현금 유동성			
113	catastrophic	adj.	비극적인, 파멸의			
114	celebrate	v.	기념하다, 축하하다			
115	channel	n.	방법, 경로			
116	charge	v. n.	v. (요금 등을) 청구하다 n. 요금, 비용, 충전 기소, 고발, 보살핌(보호) 받는 아이			
117	charity	n.	자선, 자선단체			
118	classify	v.	분류하다			
119	client	n.	고객			
120	climate cycle	n.	기후주기			
121	climate	n.	기후			
122	collaboration	n.	공동작업			
123	collection	n.	모음집, 수집품			
124	collectively	ad.	집합적으로			
125	commentary	n.	논평, 논의			
126	commission	n.	(예술 관련) 의뢰			
127	commitment	n.	책무			
128	compatible	adj.	호환이 되는			

C

번호	단어 및 숙어	품사	뜻	Self-check		
				1	2	3
129	competent	adj.	능력 있는			
130	competition	n.	대회, 경쟁			
131	competitive	adj.	경쟁이 심한			
132	compilation	n.	모음집			
133	complain of	phr v.	(~로 아프다고) 호소하다			
134	complete	v.	완료하다, 끝마치다			
135	completion	n.	완료			
136	complex	adj.	복잡한			
137	complication	n.	(상황을 더 복잡하게 만드는) 문제, (의학) 합병증			
138	compose	v.	(사진, 그림 등의) 구도를 잡다, 작곡하다			
139	composition	n.	구도			
140	concentration	n.	밀집, 집중			
141	conduct	v.	(수행)하다			
142	confection	n.	당과 제품			
143	conference	n.	회의, 학회			
144	confine	v.	(질병 등으로) 얽매이게 하다			
145	confirm	v.	확인시켜주다			
146	confirmation form	n.	확인서			
147	conflict	n.	겹침, 갈등			
148	connectivity	n.	연결(성), 접속(성)			
149	consequently	ad.	결과적으로			
150	considerable	adj.	많은, 상당한			
151	consist of	phr v.	~로 구성되다			
152	constantly	ad.	지속적으로			
153	consult	v.	상의하다			
154	consume	v.	소모하다			
155	consumption	n.	섭취, 소비			
156	contain	v.	포함하다			
157	contentedly	ad.	행복하게			
158	contest	n.	대회			
159	continent	n.	대륙			
160	contribute to	phr v.	~에 기여하다, ~의 원인이 되다			

C - D

번호	단어 및 숙어	품사	뜻	Self-check		
				1	2	3
161	contributing	adj.	기여하는, 보조하는			
162	contribution	n.	공헌, 기여			
163	convenience	n.	편리함			
164	convent	n.	수녀원			
165	convention	n.	(대규모) 회의			
166	converge	v.	집중되다			
167	convert	v.	전환시키다			
168	cooperation	n.	협조			
169	coral	n.	산호			
170	counterpart	n.	상대, 대응관계에 있는 것			
171	coupling	n.	연결 부위(커플링)			
172	courteous	adj.	공손한			
173	crawl	v.	기어가다			
174	cross	v.	잡종을 만들다			
175	crowded	adj.	붐비는, 혼잡한			
176	damage	n.	피해, 손실			
177	damaged	adj.	손상된, 손해를 입은			
178	debt	n.	빚, 부채			
179	decade	n.	십 년			
180	decision-making	n.	의사결정			
181	declare	v.	공표하다			
182	decline	v.	감소하다			
183	declining	adj.	감소하는			
184	default on	phr v.	~를 불이행하다			
185	defeat	n.	패배			
186	degree	n.	학위			
187	delay	n.	지연			
188	deliberation	n.	숙고			
189	delicacy	n.	진미, 별미			
190	delicate	adj.	까다로운, 미묘한			
191	demand	v.	필요로 하다			
192	demanding	adj.	부담이 큰, 힘든			

D

번호	단어 및 숙어	품사	뜻	Self-check		
				1	2	3
193	demonstrate	v.	보여주다, 입증하다			
194	department	n.	(학)과			
195	depict	v.	묘사하다, 그리다			
196	depletion	n.	고갈			
197	deposit	n.	예치금, 보증금			
198	describe	v.	묘사하다, 표현하다			
199	desperate	adj.	간절한, 절망적인			
200	destruction	n.	파괴			
201	detention	n.	방과 후 남기, 구금			
202	determine	v.	알아내다, 결정하다			
203	detrimental	adj.	유해한			
204	development	n.	정세, 동향, 국면, 전개			
205	device	n.	기기, 장치			
206	diabetes	n.	당뇨			
207	dictator	n.	독재자			
208	disadvantage	n.	단점			
209	disappointed	adj.	실망한			
210	discipline	n.	절제력, 규율, 훈육			
211	discontent	n.	불만			
212	discuss	v.	논의하다			
213	discussion thread	n.	토론 게시판에 올라온 일련의 의견			
214	disfigured	adj.	흠이 있는, 흉한 외모를 가진			
215	distinct	adj.	구별되는			
216	distinctive	adj.	독특한, 눈에 띄는			
217	distracted	adj.	산만한			
218	diverse	adj.	다양한			
219	divide	v.	가르다, 나누다			
220	dormant	adj.	성장하지 않는, 활동을 하지 않는			
221	downside	n.	불리한 점			
222	dramatically	ad.	대폭으로, 극적으로			
223	draw	v.	(이목, 반응, 사람 등을) 끌다			
224	drawback	n.	문제점			

D - E

번호	단어 및 숙어	품사	뜻	Self-check		
				1	2	3
225	drift	n.	(서서히 일어나는) 이동			
226	dub	v.	별명을 붙이다			
227	durability	n.	내구성			
228	dwell	v.	서식하다, 살다			
229	dynamics	n.	소통하는/영향을 미치는 방식, 동역학			
230	earthy	adj.	흙 같은			
231	ease	n.	용이함			
232	effective	adj.	효과적인			
233	element	n.	요소			
234	elevated	adj.	높은			
235	eligible	adj.	~을 할 수 있는			
236	emphasize	v.	강조하다			
237	encouraging	adj.	희망을 주는			
238	endangered	adj.	위험에 처한			
239	engage	v.	하다, 참여하다			
240	enrich	v.	풍요롭게 하다, 질을 높이다			
241	enroll	v.	등록하다			
242	ensure	v.	반드시 ~하게 하다, 보장하다			
243	entail	v.	수반하다			
244	enterprising	adj.	진취적인			
245	enthusiasm	n.	열정, 열의			
246	enthusiast	n.	~에 열광하는 사람, -광			
247	enthusiastic	adj.	열정적인			
248	entice	v.	유인하다			
249	environment	n.	환경			
250	equip	v.	(장비 등을) 갖추다, 갖추게 하다			
251	equipment	n.	장비			
252	essential	adj.	기본적인, 필수적인			
253	establish	v.	확고히 하다			
254	establishment	n.	기관			
255	evaluation	n.	평가, 감정			
256	event	n.	사건			

E - F

번호	단어 및 숙어	품사	뜻	Self-check		
				1	2	3
257	evidence against	phr.	~에게 불리한 증거			
258	evolve	v.	진화하다, 진화시키다			
259	exceed	v.	넘어서다, 초과하다			
260	exceptionally	ad.	유난히			
261	exchange student	n.	교환학생			
262	excited	adj.	들뜬, 신이 난			
263	exclusive	adj.	고급의, 전용의			
264	exclusively	ad.	독점적으로			
265	exemption	n.	면제			
266	exhausted	adj.	기진맥진한			
267	expand	v.	확장하다			
268	expect	v.	예상하다			
269	expectation	n.	기대			
270	expense	n.	지출, 비용			
271	experiment	n.	실험			
272	expertise	n.	전문지식			
273	exploration	n.	탐구			
274	explore	v.	찾다, 탐험하다			
275	exposure	n.	출연, 노출			
276	extend	v.	연장하다			
277	external	adj.	외부의			
278	extinction	n.	멸종			
279	extravagant	adj.	화려한, 사치스러운			
280	face	v.	직면하다			
281	faculty	n.	교수진			
282	fairy tale	n.	동화, 우화			
283	falter	v.	흔들리다, 불안정해지다			
284	fatigue	n.	피로			
285	favorable	adj.	좋은, 적합한			
286	favorite	n.	(가장) 좋아하는 것			
287	feature	v. n.	v. 포함하다, 특징으로 삼다 n. 기능, 특성			
288	fiction	n.	소설, 허구			

F- G

번호	단어 및 숙어	품사	뜻	Self-check 1	2	3
289	fierce	adj.	사나운			
290	figure	n.	인물			
291	figure out	phr v.	~를 알아내다, 계산하다			
292	filling	adj.	포만감을 주는			
293	finance	v.	재원을 조달하다			
294	financial	adj.	재정적인			
295	firm	adj.	단호한			
296	flee	v.	도망치다			
297	flexibility	n.	유연성			
298	flexible	adj.	유연한, 융통성 있는			
299	flipper	n.	(물개 등의) 지느러미 발			
300	flooding	n.	홍수, 범람			
301	flourish	v.	잘 자라다, 번창하다			
302	fondness	n.	기호			
303	forecast	n.	예측, 예보			
304	forgo	v.	포기하다			
305	formation	n.	형성, 형성물			
306	fossil	n.	화석			
307	foul	adj.	더러운, 악취 나는			
308	fraction	n.	부분, 일부			
309	freshwater	adj.	담수의, 민물의			
310	frustrated	adj.	좌절한, 성공하지 못한			
311	fulfill	v.	이행하다			
312	function	v.	기능하다			
313	gadget	n.	장치, 기기			
314	gain acclaim for	phr v.	찬사를 받다			
315	gain	v.	얻다			
316	gait	n.	걸음걸이			
317	game-changing	adj.	결과(판도)를 바꾸는			
318	garage	n.	차고			
319	gear	v.	준비하다			
320	generate	v.	창출하다, 발생시키다			

G - I

번호	단어 및 숙어	품사	뜻	Self-check 1	2	3
321	gill	n.	아가미			
322	go at sth	phr v.	~을 열심히 하다			
323	good	adj.	(표 등이) 유효한			
324	grammar school	n.	(과거 영국의) 중등학교			
325	grant	v. n.	v. 주다 n. 보조금			
326	growing	adj.	증가하는			
327	halfway	ad.	중간쯤에			
328	handy	adj.	편리한			
329	harbor	v.	(동물 등의) 서식지가 되다			
330	harmful	adj.	해로운			
331	hectic	adj.	바쁜, 빡빡한			
332	hesitation	n.	망설임, 주저			
333	highlight	v.	강조하다, 표시하다			
334	highs and lows	n.	좋은 때와 힘든 때, 즐거움과 어려움			
335	hit the shelf	phr v.	(가게 등에) 나오다			
336	homeschool	v.	가정에서 교육하다, 홈스쿨링하다			
337	honor	v.	(약속 등을) 이행하다			
338	hood	n.	덮개			
339	housing	n.	덮개, 외관			
340	humanoid	adj.	인간형의			
341	ideal	n.	이상, 이상적인 것			
342	identification	n.	증명, 식별			
343	identify	v.	알아보다, 식별하다			
344	illegal	adj.	불법의			
345	imaginary	adj.	가상적인			
346	imitate	v.	모방하다			
347	immediate	adj.	즉각적인			
348	impact	n.	영향, 효과			
349	implement	v.	시행하다			
350	impress	v.	깊은 인상을 주다			
351	in addition	phr.	게다가			
352	in advance	phr.	미리, 사전에			

I

번호	단어 및 숙어	품사	뜻	Self-check		
				1	2	3
353	in contrast to	phr.	~와는 대조적으로			
354	in demand	phr.	수요가 많은			
355	in spurts	phr.	빠른 속도로 많이			
356	increase	v.	증가시키다, 증가하다			
357	incur	v.	(안 좋은 상황을) 초래하다, (비용 등을) 발생시키다			
358	indicate	v.	나타내다, 보여주다			
359	indistinguishable	adj.	구분할 수 없는			
360	individual	n.	개인			
361	indulge	v.	마음껏 하다			
362	industry	n.	산업, 업계			
363	infuse	v.	우리다, 주입하다			
364	ingredient	n.	재료			
365	inhabit	v.	서식하다			
366	injury	n.	부상			
367	inland	ad.	육지로			
368	innovative	adj.	획기적인			
369	inspire	v.	고무하다			
370	inspired	adj.	탁월한, 영감을 받은			
371	installment	n.	할부, 할부금			
372	instruction	n.	지도, 가르침, 기관			
373	instruction	n.	설명문, 안내문, 지시문			
374	intense	adj.	강렬한			
375	intensive	adj.	집중적인			
376	interactive	adj.	상호적인			
377	interest	n.	이자			
378	interfere	v.	방해하다			
379	intersection	n.	교차 지점			
380	intricate	adj.	복잡한			
381	intrigued	adj.	아주 흥미로워 하는			
382	invisible	adj.	보이지 않는			
383	involve	v. n.	v. 참여시키다, 수반하다, n. 송장			
384	involved	adj.	관련된			

I - L

번호	단어 및 숙어	품사	뜻	Self-check		
				1	2	3
385	irregularly	ad.	불규칙적으로			
386	job	n.	직무, 일, 직업, 일자리, 수술			
387	joint	adj. n.	adj. 공통의, 합동의 n. 이음매, 접합 부분, 접합(법)			
388	jolly	adj.	유쾌한, 즐거운			
389	jolt	v.	충격을 주다, 흔들다			
390	journal	n.	정기 간행물, 저널			
391	journey	n.	여행, 여정			
392	judge	v. n.	v. 판단하다, 심사하다 n. 판사			
393	jury	n.	배심원, 심사위원			
394	juvenile	adj.	청소년의, 아이다운			
395	keen	adj.	예민한, 정교한			
396	keep	v.	유지하다, 계속하다, 기르다			
397	knock	v.	두드리다, 때리다			
398	knowledge	n.	지식, 아는 것			
399	knowledgeable	adj.	지성이 있는, 박식한			
400	laboratory	n.	실험실			
401	lack	n.	부족			
402	landmark	n.	랜드마크, 주요 지형지물, 명소			
403	landscaping	n.	조경			
404	latest	adj.	(가장) 최근의, 최신의			
405	launch	v.	시작하다, 출시하다			
406	leading	adj.	가장 중요한, 주요한			
407	lean toward	phr v.	~쪽으로 마음이 기울다			
408	levelheaded	adj.	분별 있는			
409	liability	n.	채무			
410	limited	adj.	제한된			
411	line sth (with sth)	v.	~를 ~로 덧대다			
412	literary	adj.	문학의, 문학과 관련된			
413	livelihood	n.	생계			
414	local	adj.	지역의, 현지의			
415	location	n.	위치			
416	longingly	ad.	갈망하여			

L - M

번호	단어 및 숙어	품사	뜻	Self-check 1	2	3
417	looming	adj.	(안 좋은 일이) 서서히 다가오는			
418	looting	n.	약탈			
419	lower	v.	~을 내리다, 낮추다			
420	lug around	phr v.	끌고 다니다			
421	lyric	n.	노래 가사			
422	mainstay	n.	중심			
423	make ends meet	phr v.	먹고 살만큼만 벌다			
424	malfunction	n.	기능 불량			
425	manipulate	v.	조작하다			
426	marine	adj.	해양의			
427	mark	v.	표시하다			
428	market	v.	광고하다			
429	marsupial	n.	유대목 동물, 유대류			
430	massive	adj.	거대한			
431	master	n.	(구) 남자 선생			
432	masterpiece	n.	걸작, 명작			
433	material	n.	자료			
434	meet	v.	(요구, 기대 등을) 충족시키다			
435	memoir	n.	회고록, 전기			
436	metabolism	n.	신진대사			
437	migrant	n.	이민자			
438	mildly	ad.	약간			
439	missing	adj.	없어진, 행방불명의			
440	misunderstanding	n.	오해			
441	modern-day	adj.	현대의, 현재의			
442	monastery	n.	수도원			
443	monitor	v.	관찰하다, 감시하다			
444	monogamous	adj.	일부일처의			
445	motivate	v.	이유, 동기 부여를 하다			
446	multiple	adj.	많은, 다수의			
447	musical	n.	뮤지컬			
448	mysterious	adj.	기이한, 신비에 싸인			

N-O

번호	단어 및 숙어	품사	뜻	Self-check		
				1	2	3
449	narrative structure	n.	서사 구조			
450	navigate	v.	탐색하다			
451	need	n.	욕구, 수요			
452	negotiate	v.	협상하다			
453	non-fiction	n.	비소설, 실화			
454	non-stop	adj.	쉬지 않는, 직통의			
455	notarized	adj.	공증된			
456	notify	v.	고지하다, 알리다			
457	nourishment	n.	자양분			
458	novel	n.	소설			
459	nutrient	n.	영양소			
460	nutrition	n.	영양			
461	nutritious	adj.	영양가 높은			
462	obese	adj.	비만인			
463	obesity	n.	비만			
464	obligation	n.	의무			
465	occasional	adj.	가끔의			
466	occasionally	ad.	가끔			
467	occupy	v.	차지하다			
468	odor	n.	냄새, 악취			
469	offspring	n.	새끼, 자식			
470	operating system	n.	운영 체제			
471	operation	n.	사업, 운영			
472	option	n.	옵션, 선택(권)			
473	ordinary	adj.	보통의, 평범한			
474	organ	n.	장기			
475	organism	n.	생명체, 유기체			
476	outstanding	adj.	미지급된, 미해결된			
477	outweigh	v.	~보다 더 크다, 중요하다			
478	oversee	v.	감독하다, 관리하다			
479	overwhelm	v.	(너무 많은 것들이) 어쩔 줄 모르게 하다, 압도하다			
480	overworked	adj.	혹사당하는			

O - P

번호	단어 및 숙어	품사	뜻	Self-check		
				1	2	3
481	ownership	n.	소유권			
482	packed with	phr.	~로 꽉 찬			
483	paleontologist	n.	고생물학자			
484	pass away	phr v.	사망하다			
485	pass up	phr v.	(기회, 제안 등을) 거절하다, 놓치다			
486	patriotic	adj.	애국심이 많은			
487	patriotism	n.	애국심			
488	perfect	adj.	~에 꼭 알맞은, 완벽한			
489	perform	v.	공연하다, 연주하다			
490	performance	n.	공연, 성과, 실적			
491	periodically	ad.	주기적으로			
492	perk	n.	특전			
493	photography	n.	사진 촬영			
494	plain	adj.	평범한			
495	playhouse	n.	극장			
496	plead	v.	(법정에서) 답변하다			
497	pleasant	adj.	쾌적한			
498	pledge	v.	약속하다			
499	plentiful	adj.	풍부한			
500	plenty	n.	풍부한 양			
501	pool	v.	(자금, 기술 등을) 합치다			
502	population	n.	개체군, 인구			
503	position	v.	위치하다, ~에 자리를 잡다			
504	postural	adj.	자세의			
505	potential	adj.	잠재적인			
506	power outage	n.	정전			
507	practical	adj.	실용적인			
508	practically	ad.	사실상, 거의			
509	practice	n.	관행, 방식			
510	praise	v.	칭찬하다			
511	precede	v.	~에 앞서다			
512	precious	adj.	귀중한			

P

번호	단어 및 숙어	품사	뜻	Self-check		
				1	2	3
513	predator	n.	천적, 포식자			
514	predict	v.	예측하다			
515	prediction	n.	예측, 예견			
516	preference	n.	선호			
517	premise	n.	부지			
518	preparation	n.	준비, 준비과정			
519	prepare	v.	준비하다, 대비하다			
520	prerecorded	adj.	미리 녹음된			
521	presence	n.	진출			
522	present	v.	상연하다, 보여주다			
523	preservative	n.	방부제			
524	pressure	n.	압박, 압력			
525	prestigious	adj.	일류의			
526	presumably	ad.	아마도			
527	priceless	adj.	귀중한, 값을 매길 수 없는			
528	primary	adj.	주요한			
529	principle	n.	원리, 원칙			
530	prior to	phr.	~전에			
531	priority	n.	우선 사항			
532	prize	v.	귀하게 여기다			
533	proceed	v.	진행하다			
534	processor	n.	처리기			
535	productive	adj.	생산적인			
536	proficient	adj.	능숙한			
537	profitable	adj.	수익성이 있는			
538	program	v.	설정하다, 프로그램을 짜다			
539	promote	v.	홍보하다, 촉진하다, (분위기, 생각 등을) 조장하다			
540	promotional	adj.	홍보의			
541	prophecy	n.	예언			
542	protect	v.	보호하다			
543	prove	v.	~임이 드러나다			
544	provided (that)	conj.	~하는 조건 하에, 만약 ~라면			

P - R

번호	단어 및 숙어	품사	뜻	Self-check		
				1	2	3
545	publish	n.	게재하다, 출판하다			
546	pull into	phr v.	~에 도착하다			
547	pungent	adj.	톡 쏘는			
548	purchase	v.	구매하다			
549	pursue	v.	추구하다			
550	puzzling	adj.	혼란스러운			
551	quack	n.	돌팔이(가짜) 의사, (오리가)꽥꽥 우는 소리			
552	quadruped	adj.	네 발이 있는			
553	quail	v.	질리다, 움츠리다			
554	quaint	adj.	독특한, 예스러운			
555	qualified	adj.	자격이 있는, 적임의			
556	qualify	v.	자격을 주다, 적합하게 하다			
557	quantity	n.	양, 수량			
558	quash	v.	진압하다, 취소하다			
559	queasy	adj.	불안한, 불쾌한			
560	queer	adj.	괴상한, 수상한			
561	quench	v.	(불, 불꽃을) 끄다, 갈증을 풀다			
562	query	v.	질문하다			
563	question	v. n.	v. 질문하다, 심문하다 n. 질문, 의문, 문제			
564	queue	v.	줄을 서다			
565	quibble	n.	궤변, 애매한 말			
566	quintessence	n.	정수, 본질			
567	raffle	n.	복권식 판매, 추첨(행사)			
568	raise	v.	(자금 등을) 모으다			
569	range from A to B	phr v.	(범위가) A에서 B까지 다양하다			
570	rare	adj.	희귀한, 드문			
571	reach	v.	닿다, 도달하다			
572	read up on	phr v.	~에 대해 공부하다			
573	readily	ad.	쉽게			
574	reasonable	adj.	합리적인, 적당한			
575	recharge	v.	(재)충전하다			
576	recognition	n.	인식			

R

번호	단어 및 숙어	품사	뜻	Self-check		
				1	2	3
577	recognize	v.	인정하다			
578	record	adj.	기록적인 (가장 ~한)			
579	reef	n.	암초			
580	reenactment	n.	재현, 재연			
581	reference	n.	참고 문헌, 추천서			
582	refined	adj.	정제된			
583	refuse	v.	거부하다			
584	regarding	prep.	~에 대하여			
585	regardless (of sth)	adv.	개의치 않고, ~와 상관없이			
586	regrettable	adj.	유감스러운, 후회스러운			
587	regularly	ad.	정기적으로, 자주			
588	regulate	v.	조절하다			
589	related	adj.	(동물 등이) 같은 과에 속한, 동족인			
590	relatively	ad.	상대적으로			
591	release	v.	발표하다			
592	reliable	adj.	믿을 수 있는			
593	relief	n.	안도, 안심			
594	relocate	v.	이동하다			
595	remain	v. n.	v. 계속 ~하다 n. 잔해, 유해			
596	remind	v.	(~해야 할 것을) 상기시키다, 알려주다			
597	removable	adj.	떼어낼 수 있는, 이동식의			
598	renowned	adj.	유명한			
599	replace	v.	대체하다			
600	representative	adj.	대표하는			
601	reproduce	v.	번식하다			
602	reptile	n.	파충류			
603	reputation	n.	명성, 평판			
604	require	v.	필요하다, 요구하다			
605	requirement	n.	필요(요건)			
606	research	v.	연구하다			
607	resemble	v.	유사하다			
608	resident assistant	n.	기숙사 사감			

R - S

번호	단어 및 숙어	품사	뜻	Self-check 1	2	3
609	resign	v.	사임하다			
610	resist	v.	거부하다			
611	resistant	adj.	~에 잘 견디는			
612	rest assured	phr.	~를 믿어도 된다, 안심해도 된다			
613	retain	v.	유지하다, ~한 상태로 계속 고용하다			
614	reward	n.	보상			
615	rewarding	adj.	보람 있는			
616	rigid	adj.	엄격한			
617	rise	n.	발흥, 증가			
618	risk	n.	위험, 위험요소			
619	route	n.	노선			
620	run	v.	계속되다, 상연되다, 운영하다			
621	Sales Associate	n.	영업 사원			
622	sales quota	n.	판매 할당			
623	sales representative	n.	영업 사원			
624	salutatory	adj. n.	adj. 인사의 n. (졸업식에서 보통 차석 졸업생이 하는) 인사말			
625	sanitary	adj.	위생의, 청결한			
626	screech	v.	꽥 하는 소리를 내다			
627	sedentary	adj.	주로 앉아서 하는			
628	see through	phr v.	끝까지 해내다			
629	seek	n.	구하다, 찾다			
630	select	adj.	엄선된			
631	sense of smell	n.	후각			
632	sensitive	adj.	민감한			
633	separate	v.	가르다, 분리하다			
634	separated	adj.	분리된, 헤어진			
635	sequence	n.	(영화 장면 등의) 연속			
636	serve	v.	~ 역할을 하다			
637	set aside	phr v.	(돈, 시간 등을) 따로 떼어 두다			
638	set up	phr v.	~를 시작하다			
639	setback	n.	문제, 어려움			
640	settle	v.	지불하다, 정산하다			

S

번호	단어 및 숙어	품사	뜻	Self-check		
				1	2	3
641	setup	n.	구조			
642	shelter	n.	피신, 피난처			
643	shrink	v.	줄어들게 하다			
644	significantly	ad.	크게			
645	skip	v.	거르다, 건너뛰다			
646	slot	n.	자리			
647	smooth sailing	n.	순탄한 것, 조용한 항해			
648	sneeze	v.	재채기하다			
649	sole/single ownership	n.	개인 기업			
650	solicit	v.	요청하다, 간청하다			
651	species	n.	종(족), 종(족)들			
652	specific	adj.	특정한			
653	specimen	n.	표본			
654	spicy	adj.	강렬한			
655	split	v.	나누다			
656	sport	v.	자랑스럽게 선보이다			
657	stand out	phr v.	눈에 띄다			
658	stimulate	v.	자극하다, 촉진하다			
659	storage	n.	저장 공간			
660	strain	n.	(근육) 좌상			
661	strategy	n.	전략			
662	stretch	v.	펼쳐지다			
663	struggle	v.	허덕이다, 애쓰다			
664	subject	n.	피사체			
665	subordinate	n.	부하			
666	subsequently	ad.	나중에, 그 뒤에			
667	subtitle	v.	부제를 달다			
668	succeeding	adj.	계속되는, 다음의			
669	suffer	v.	(안 좋은 일을) 겪다, (질병 등에) 시달리다			
670	suggest	v.	제안하다, 시사하다			
671	suggestion	n.	제안			
672	sum	n.	돈, 합계			

S - T

번호	단어 및 숙어	품사	뜻	Self-check 1	2	3
673	superb	adj.	최상의			
674	supervise	v.	지휘하다, 지도하다			
675	supervisor	n.	상관, 관리자			
676	supplier	n.	공급자, 공급 업체			
677	supply	n.	저장품, 비축량			
678	support	v.	지원하다			
679	surrender	v.	포기하다, 항복하다			
680	surround	v.	둘러싸다			
681	surroundings	n.	주변, (주위) 환경			
682	swap	v.	맞바꾸다			
683	tactile	adj.	촉각의			
684	take sth on the road	phr v.	(연극 등을) 순회공연 하다			
685	take to sth	phr v.	~하는 습관이 생기다, ~를 좋아하기 시작하다			
686	technically	ad.	엄밀히 말하면			
687	temper	n.	성질, 기질			
688	temperamental	adj.	괴팍한			
689	temperature	n.	온도			
690	tend to	phr v.	~를 보살피다			
691	tendency	n.	경향			
692	terms	n.	(계약, 지불 등의) 조건			
693	texture	n.	촉감, 질감			
694	theatrical	adj.	연극(공연)의			
695	thorough	adj.	철저한			
696	threat	n.	위협			
697	threaten	v.	위협하다			
698	time-consuming	adj.	(많은) 시간이 걸리는			
699	tiny	adj.	매우 작은			
700	title	n.	서적, 제목			
701	tolerate	v.	용인하다			
702	tourist destination	n.	관광지			
703	tourist spot	n.	관광지, 명소			
704	trait	n.	특성			

T - U

번호	단어 및 숙어	품사	뜻	Self-check		
				1	2	3
705	transcript	n.	성적표			
706	transition	n.	전이			
707	trigger	v.	촉발시키다			
708	trilogy	n.	3부작			
709	tuition fee	n.	등록금			
710	turn off	phr v.	싫증나게 하다			
711	turn to	phr v.	(새로운 것을) 사용하기 시작하다			
712	typically	ad.	일반적으로, 보통			
713	ubiquitous	adj.	편재하는, 어디에나 존재하는			
714	ulcer	n.	궤양, 부패 상태			
715	ultimate	adj.	최고의, 궁극적인			
716	ultimatum	n.	최후통첩			
717	unaccountable	adj.	설명할 수 없는, 책임이 없는			
718	unanimity	n.	만장일치, 전원 합의			
719	unassuming	adj.	주제넘지 않는, 잘난 체하지 않는			
720	uncanny	adj.	불가사의한, 무시무시한			
721	uncomfortable	adj.	불편한			
722	unconscionable	adj.	비양심적인, 불합리한			
723	uncontaminated	adj.	오염되지 않은			
724	uncover	v.	발견하다, 알아내다			
725	under the hood	phr.	덮개 속에 (내부에)			
726	undercut	v.	(경쟁자보다) 싸게 팔다			
727	underdeveloped	adj.	미숙한			
728	undergo	v.	받다, 겪다			
729	underhand	adj.	일손이 모자라는, 비밀의			
730	underlying	adj.	기초를 이루는, 근원적인			
731	undermine	v.	몰래 손상시키다, 서서히 쇠퇴시키다			
732	underscore	v.	강조하다, 역설하다			
733	understate	v.	(수·양·정도 등을) 적게 말하다, 삼가서 말하다			
734	understatement	n.	삼가는 말, 줄잡아 말하기			
735	undertaker	n.	청부인, 기업가, 장의사			
736	undervalue	v.	실제 가격보다 낮게 평가하다			

U

번호	단어 및 숙어	품사	뜻	Self-check		
				1	2	3
737	unearth	v.	을 파내다, 발굴하다			
738	unearthly	adj.	이 세상의 것 같지 않은, 초자연적인			
739	unequivocal	adj.	모호하지 않은, 헷갈리지 않는			
740	unexceptionable	adj.	나무랄 데 없는, 더할 나위 없는			
741	unexpected	adj.	예상 밖의, 예기치 않은			
742	unexpectedly	ad.	갑자기, 예상치 못하게			
743	unfaltering	adj.	단호한			
744	unfeigned	adj.	거짓 없는, 진실한			
745	unfetter	v.	자유롭게 하다, 해방하다			
746	unfortunate	adj.	불행한			
747	ungainly	adj.	(사람·동작·자태 등이) 우아하지 않은, 보기 흉한			
748	uniformity	n.	획일, 일치			
749	unimpeachable	adj.	과실이 없는, 뚜렷한			
750	unique	adj.	특별한, 독특한			
751	unison	n.	일치, 조화			
752	universal	adj.	보편적인, 전 세계의			
753	unkempt	adj.	흐트러진, 어질러진			
754	unprecedented	adj.	전례없는			
755	unravel	v.	풀다, 해명하다			
756	unrealistic	adj.	비현실적인			
757	unruly	adj.	제멋대로 구는			
758	unsavory	adj.	맛 없는, 불미스러운			
759	unscathed	adj.	상처가 없는			
760	unseemly	adj. ad.	adj. 부적당한 ad. 꼴사납게			
761	unsullied	adj.	더럽혀지지 않은, 결백한			
762	untoward	adj.	뜻밖의			
763	unwarranted	adj.	부당한			
764	upcoming	adj.	다가오는, 앞으로 할			
765	upright	adj.	똑바로, 직립한			
766	urge (to)	v	촉구하다, 요구하다			
767	urgent	adj.	긴급한, 집요한			
768	usage	n.	사용, 관습			

U - Z

번호	단어 및 숙어	품사	뜻	Self-check		
				1	2	3
769	usurp	v.	빼앗다, 침해하다			
770	utopia	n.	유토피아, 이상향			
771	valedictorian	n.	수석			
772	vary	v.	다양하다			
773	venture	n.	벤처 (사업), 모험			
774	view	n.	견해, 관점			
775	vigor	n.	활력, 활기			
776	virtually	ad.	가상으로			
777	visionary	adj.	예지력이 있는			
778	vivid	adj.	선명한			
779	volume	n.	양, 책, 권			
780	waive	v.	(특정한 경우에 규칙 등을) 적용하지 않다, 포기하다			
781	war effort	n.	물자			
782	warranty	n.	품질보증서			
783	wary	adj.	경계하는, 조심하는			
784	waver	v.	흔들리다			
785	weigh	v.	저울질하다, 따져보다			
786	well known	adj.	잘 알려진, 유명한			
787	well-established	adj.	안정된, 잘 자리 잡은			
788	well-received	adj.	좋은 평을 받은			
789	wholesome	adj.	건강한			
790	wonder	n.	경이로운 것, 불가사의			
791	work	n.	작품			
792	xenophobia	n.	외국 혐오			
793	x-rated	adj.	미성년자 관람 금지로 지정된			
794	yearn	v.	갈망하다, 그리워하다			
795	yield	v.	산출하다, 포기하다			
796	yoke	v.	(사람·생각 등을) 한데 묶다, 결합시키다			
797	zany	adj.	익살스러운, 우스운			
798	zeal	n.	열의, 열중			
799	zest	n.	기분 좋은 자극, 산뜻한 풍미			
800	zone	v. n.	v. (주택·상업·학교 지구 등으로) 구획하여 규제하다 n. 지역, 대			

G-TELP |공|식|주|관|사|

G-TELP 영어연구소 저

퀵 지텔프

공식 모의고사 정답 및 해설

Level 2

G-TELP KOREA 출판사업본부

G-TELP

퀵 지텔프 공식 모의고사

정답 및 해설

- **Chapter 1.** Grammar
- **Chapter 2.** Listening
- **Chapter 3.** Reading

한 눈에 보는 정답

Chapter 1 Grammar

• 문법 모의고사 1회

1	(b)	2	(d)	3	(a)	4	(c)	5	(a)
6	(b)	7	(d)	8	(c)	9	(a)	10	(b)
11	(a)	12	(c)	13	(b)	14	(d)	15	(a)
16	(b)	17	(d)	18	(c)	19	(b)	20	(a)
21	(c)	22	(d)	23	(b)	24	(c)	25	(a)
26	(d)								

• 문법 모의고사 2회

1	(b)	2	(a)	3	(d)	4	(d)	5	(b)
6	(a)	7	(d)	8	(b)	9	(d)	10	(a)
11	(c)	12	(b)	13	(a)	14	(b)	15	(c)
16	(b)	17	(d)	18	(a)	19	(d)	20	(b)
21	(c)	22	(a)	23	(d)	24	(a)	25	(c)
26	(c)								

• 문법 모의고사 3회

1	(b)	2	(a)	3	(c)	4	(d)	5	(c)
6	(a)	7	(d)	8	(b)	9	(a)	10	(c)
11	(a)	12	(c)	13	(d)	14	(b)	15	(d)
16	(c)	17	(b)	18	(a)	19	(c)	20	(d)
21	(a)	22	(b)	23	(a)	24	(c)	25	(d)
26	(c)								

Chapter 2 Listening

• 청취 모의고사 1회

27	(b)	28	(a)	29	(c)	30	(d)	31	(a)
32	(b)	33	(d)	34	(d)	35	(c)	36	(a)
37	(d)	38	(b)	39	(a)	40	(a)	41	(d)
42	(c)	43	(d)	44	(b)	45	(a)	46	(b)
47	(c)	48	(d)	49	(c)	50	(c)	51	(b)
52	(a)								

• 청취 모의고사 2회

27	(b)	28	(a)	29	(c)	30	(d)	31	(a)
32	(c)	33	(c)	34	(d)	35	(d)	36	(a)
37	(b)	38	(a)	39	(b)	40	(b)	41	(d)
42	(a)	43	(c)	44	(a)	45	(c)	46	(a)
47	(b)	48	(d)	49	(a)	50	(c)	51	(d)
52	(c)								

• 청취 모의고사 3회

27	(a)	28	(b)	29	(a)	30	(c)	31	(b)
32	(d)	33	(c)	34	(b)	35	(c)	36	(c)
37	(d)	38	(b)	39	(a)	40	(c)	41	(d)
42	(a)	43	(b)	44	(a)	45	(b)	46	(c)
47	(d)	48	(a)	49	(b)	50	(d)	51	(c)
52	(a)								

Chapter 3 Reading & Vocabulary

• 독해 모의고사 1회

53	(b)	54	(a)	55	(c)	56	(d)	57	(a)
58	(c)	59	(d)	60	(a)	61	(b)	62	(d)
63	(c)	64	(a)	65	(c)	66	(b)	67	(c)
68	(a)	69	(b)	70	(d)	71	(a)	72	(b)
73	(d)	74	(c)	75	(d)	76	(a)	77	(b)
78	(c)	79	(a)	80	(b)				

• 독해 모의고사 2회

53	(d)	54	(b)	55	(c)	56	(a)	57	(b)
58	(a)	59	(a)	60	(a)	61	(c)	62	(b)
63	(d)	64	(a)	65	(d)	66	(b)	67	(d)
68	(b)	69	(a)	70	(c)	71	(d)	72	(a)
73	(c)	74	(c)	75	(b)	76	(b)	77	(d)
78	(a)	79	(a)	80	(b)				

• 독해 모의고사 3회

53	(a)	54	(b)	55	(b)	56	(d)	57	(c)
58	(d)	59	(a)	60	(a)	61	(c)	62	(b)
63	(d)	64	(c)	65	(b)	66	(d)	67	(b)
68	(a)	69	(c)	70	(d)	71	(c)	72	(b)
73	(c)	74	(d)	75	(c)	76	(c)	77	(d)
78	(a)	79	(b)	80	(a)				

Chapter 1

Grammar

01 문법 모의고사 1회

1	(b)	2	(d)	3	(a)	4	(c)	5	(a)
6	(b)	7	(d)	8	(c)	9	(a)	10	(b)
11	(a)	12	(c)	13	(b)	14	(d)	15	(a)
16	(b)	17	(d)	18	(c)	19	(b)	20	(a)
21	(c)	22	(d)	23	(b)	24	(c)	25	(a)
26	(d)								

1. 시제 (미래완료진행형)

해석 건축가들은 New Sears Tower의 설계를 완성하는 데만 2년이 걸릴 것으로 추정한다. 그들이 완성할 즈음에는, 오직 빌딩에 대한 설계, 전략, 허가 작업만 하고 있게 될 것이다.

해설 첫 번째 문장에서 조동사 'will'을 사용하여 미래의 일에 대해 예측(it will take two years)하고, 해당 문장에서는 이 일이 완성될 때쯤(by the time they are finished)의 상황을 예측하고 있으므로, 미래의 특정 시점까지 계속해서 진행되는 일에 대해 이야기할 때 쓰이는 미래완료진행형이 빈칸에 가장 적절하다. 따라서 정답은 (b)이다.

정답 (b)

어휘
architect **n.** 건축가
estimate **v.** 추정하다
complete **v.** 끝내다, 완성하다
by the time **conj.** ~할 때 쯤이면
permit **n.** 허가
strategy **n.** 전략

2. 동명사 (동명사를 목적어로 취하는 동사)

해석 David은 그의 상사가 사임하기 전까지 오랜 기간 동안 ABC 은행의 부팀장이었다. 그는 최근에 팀장으로 승진했고, 그의 책임은 이제 회사의 정책을 실행하는 것을 포함한다.

해설 'include'는 to 부정사가 아닌 동명사를 목적어로 취하므로 정답은 (d)이다. 참고로 동명사의 완료형(having + p.p.)은 해당 절의 시제보다 한 시제 앞설 때 사용한다.

정답 (d)

어휘
resign **v.** 사임하다
be promoted to **v.** ~로 승진하다
responsibility **n.** 책임
implement **v.** 시행하다
policy **n.** 정책

3. 시제 (현재진행형)

해석 사업 분석가로서, Dorothy는 일주일에 평균 60시간을 근무한다. 그 스트레스가 그녀에겐 너무 과한 것으로 드러났고, 그녀는 사직을 고려하고 있다. 지금 그녀는 인터넷에서 덜 힘든 직업을 검색하고 있다.

해설 두 번째 문장에 현재진행형(she is thinking of resigning)이 나오고, 해당 문장이 현재의 의미를 나타내는 부사구(right now)로 시작되며, 그녀가 덜 힘든 직업을 인터넷에서 검색하고 있는 중이라는 의미가 되어야 하므로, 현재진행형이 빈칸에 가장 적절하다. 따라서 정답은 (a)이다.

정답 (a)

어휘
average **adj.** 평균의
prove **v.** ~임이 드러나다
demanding **adj.** 부담이 큰, 힘든

4. 가정법 (미래)

해석 Alan은 그의 여자 친구를 자주 방문하지 않는다. 그녀는 시내 반대편에 살고, 그녀의 집으로 가는 버스는 매우 불편하다. 만약 그가 차를 산다면, 그는 더 자주 그녀를 방문할 것이다.

해설 실현 가능성이 낮은 상황을 가정(만약 그가 차를 산다면)할 때 "If 주어 + were to, 주어 + 조동사 과거형(would/could/should/might) + 동사원형" 형태를 주로 사용한다. if 절에 were to가 있으므로, 정답은 (c)이다.

정답 (c)

> **어휘**
> uncomfortable **adj.** 불편한
> often **ad.** 자주

5. 조동사 (문맥에 맞는 조동사)

해석 Sara의 자동차는 그녀가 중요한 회의를 가지기 한 시간 전에 고장이 났다. 원한다면 내 차를 사용해도 된다고 그녀에게 말했다. 나는 어쨌든 그날 갈 곳이 아무데도 없었다.

해설 첫 번째 문장에서 Sara의 자동차가 중요한 회의가 있기 한 시간 전에 고장이 났고, 해당 문장은 화자가 자신의 자동차를 사용해도 된다고 말했다는 의미가 되어야 하므로, 가능과 허가의 의미를 내포한 조동사 'could'가 가장 적절하다. 따라서 정답은 (a)이다.

정답 (a)

> **어휘**
> break down **phr v.** 고장이 나다
> important **adj.** 중요한

6. 시제 (과거진행형)

해석 Jerry는 그가 어제 슈퍼마켓에서 만났던 소녀에 대해 이야기하는 것을 멈출 수 없다. 그는 그 사랑스러운 여성을 우연히 마주쳤을 때 어떤 시리얼을 사야 할지 고르고 있던 중이었다고 말했다.

해설 단순과거시제와 과거진행형이 함께 쓰일 때, 긴 시간에 걸쳐 발생한 '배경'이 되는 행위나 상황은 과거진행형으로 나타내고, 그 와중에 발생한 상대적으로 짧은 시간의 행위나 상황은 단순과거시제로 나타낸다. 해당 문장의 종속절에 과거시제(bumped into)가 나오고, 주절은 Jerry가 어떤 시리얼을 사야할 지 고르던 중이었다고 말했다는 의미가 되어야 하므로, 과거진행형이 빈칸에 가장 적절하다. 따라서 정답은 (b)이다.

정답 (b)

> **어휘**
> accidentally **ad.** 우연히
> bump into **phr v.** ~와 마주치다

7. 가정법 (과거완료)

해석 Paul은 어제 교통체증에 갇혔을 때 중요한 출장을 가던 중이었다. 만약 그가 역으로 가는 다른 노선을 택했다면, 그는 기차를 놓치지 않았을 것이다.

해설 가정법 과거완료를 묻는 문제로, 과거의 사실에 반대되는 가정(만약 그가 역으로 가는 다른 노선을 택했다면)을 나타내고 있다. 가정법 과거완료 형식은 'if + 주어 + 과거완료동사(had p.p.), 주어 + 조동사 과거형(would/could/should/might) + 현재완료동사(have p.p.)'이므로, 정답은 (d)이다.

정답 (d)

> **어휘**
> get caught in **v.** ~에 갇히다, 휘말리다
> traffic jam **n.** 교통체증
> route **n.** 노선

8. 동명사 (동명사를 목적어로 취하는 동사)

해석 수영장 근처의 타일 부분은 물에 젖으면 매우 미끄러워져 위험한 조건을 만들 수 있습니다. 이것이 대부분의 수영 시설들이 특히 어린 아이들을 위해 달리기를 금지하는 규칙을 만드는 이유입니다.

해설 'forbid'는 to 부정사가 아닌 동명사를 목적어로 취하므로 정답은 (c)이다. 참고로 동명사의 완료형(having + p.p.)은 해당 절의 시제보다 한 시제 앞설 때 사용한다.

정답 (c)

어휘
extremely **ad.** 극도로, 극히
slippery **adj.** 미끄러운, 미끈거리는
hazardous **n.** 위험
facilities **n.** 설비, 시설

9. 관계사 (관계대명사)

해석 Martha는 그녀의 생일 파티에서 Lucy를 바래다주고 있던 남자에게 흥미를 느꼈다. Martha가 그가 누구냐고 묻자, Lucy가 "나와 함께 있던 사람은 내 사촌이야."라고 대답했다.

해설 빈칸의 절은 앞에 나온 명사구(the man)를 수식하며 '나와 함께 있던' 이라는 의미를 가진 관계사절이 되어야 한다. 선행사 'man'이 사람이며, 해당 절에서 관계대명사가 주어 역할을 하기 때문에 사람을 대체하는 주격 관계대명사(who 혹은 that)가 와야 한다. (d)의 that도 사람 선행사를 수식하지만, 주어(he)가 있어서 주격대명사로 쓰인 것이 아니므로 오답이다. 따라서 정답은 (a)이다.

정답 (a)

어휘
intrigued **adj.** 아주 흥미로워 하는
escort **v.** 호위하다, 바래다준다
reply **v.** 대답하다

10. 시제 (과거완료진행형)

해석 Janet은 감소하는 판매량과 치열해지는 온라인 책 판매자들과의 경쟁으로 인해 결국 그녀의 작은 서점을 폐업했다. 많은 사람들이 그녀의 결정으로 인해 슬퍼했다. 그녀는 우리 지역에서 15년 넘게 책을 판매해오고 있었다.

해설 첫 번째 문장과 두 번째 문장에 과거시제(Janet finally closed her small bookstore, A lot of people were saddened)가 과거 시점이 되고, Janet이 15년 이상 책을 판매해 왔던 것은 그 이전부터 폐업했던 과거 시점까지 계속되어 왔던 것이므로, 과거완료진행형이 빈칸에 가장 적절하다. 따라서 정답은 (b)이다.

정답 (b)

어휘
declining **adj.** 감소하는
growing **adj.** 증가하는
competition **n.** 경쟁

11. 연결어 (전치사)

해석 과학자들은 매일 긴 시간을 일하는 것이 결국 스트레스, 피로, 그리고 심장 문제를 일으킬 수 있다는 것을 확인했다. 이러한 발견에도 불구하고, 많은 사람들은 단지 먹고 살기 위해 직장에서 긴 시간을 보내고 있다.

해설 첫 번째 문장에서 과학자들이 매일 오랜 시간 근무하는 것이 여러 문제를 일으킬 수 있다는 것을 확인시켜 주었다고 하였으나, 두 번째 문장에서 사람들이 업무에 많은 시간을 들인다고 하였으므로, 빈칸 뒤 명사(this finding)와 함께 '이러한 발견에도 불구하고' 라는 양보의 의미를 완성할 수 있는 전치사가 빈칸에 가장 적절하다. 따라서 정답은 (a)이다.

정답 (a)

어휘
confirm **v.** 확인시켜주다
fatigue **n.** 피로
make ends meet **phr.** 먹고 살 만큼만 벌다

12. 조동사 (주장, 요구, 명령, 제안, 충고 등 의미의 동사 that절 동사원형)

해석 수업시간에 말썽을 부려 지난주에 방과 후에 남는 벌을 받은 이후, Tom은 똑같은 이유로 다시 교장실에 불려갔다. 그 소년을 걱정하며, 교장은 Tom이 진지한 상담을 받아야 한다고 요구했다.

해설 'demand' 뒤에 that절이 올 경우, 'that절의 주어가 ~해야 한다고 요구하다' 라는 의미가 된다. 이처럼 주절에 제안, 명령, 주장, 요구를 나타내는 동사가 올 경우, that절의 주어와 동사 사이에 있는 조동사 'should'가 종종 생략된다. 따라서 that절의 동사는 원형이 되어야 하므로, 정답은 (c)이다.

정답 (c)

어휘
receive **v.** 받다
detention **n.** 방과 후 남기, 구금
misbehaving **v.** 못된 짓을 하다, 비행을 저지르다
concerned **adj.** 걱정하는
counseling **n.** 상담

13. To 부정사 (To 부정사를 목적어로 취하는 동사)

해석 세계 인구가 너무 급격히 증가하고 있어 식량 공급에 어려움을 겪고 있다. 이에 대응하여, 과학자들은 질병에 강한 식물을 번식시켜 농작물의 수확량을 증대시키기를 바라면서 종자를 결합하고 조작하고 있다.

해설 동사 'hope' 뒤에는 that절, to 부정사, 전치사 for + 명사가 올 수 있는데, 빈칸에는 'hope'의 목적어(명사)가 되는 동시에 뒤따라오는 명사 'plants'를 목적어로 취하는 알맞은 형태의 동사가 와야 한다. 모든 조건을 만족시키는 형태는 to 부정사이므로, 정답은 (b)이다. 참고로 to 부정사의 완료형(to have + p.p.)은 해당 절의 시제보다 한 시제 앞설 때 사용한다.

정답 (b)

어휘
supplies **n.** 저장품, 비축량
splice **v.** 붙이다, 접합하다
manipulate **v.** 조작하다
resistant **adj.** ~에 잘 견디는

14. 시제 (미래진행형)

해석 시장 점유율을 높이기 위해, 어느 유명한 핸드폰 제조회사는 획기적인 스마트폰 시리즈를 출시할 계획이다. 그 회사는 이 핸드폰들을 7월 4일에 출시할 예정이다.

해설 첫 번째 문장에서 현재시제(plans to launch)를 사용하여 스마트폰들을 출시할 계획이라고 하고, 해당 문장은 미래의 특정한 시기(the fourth of July)에 그 핸드폰들을 출시할 예정이라는 의미가 되어야 하므로, 미래에 예정된 일에 대해 이야기할 때 쓰이는 미래진행형이 빈칸에 가장 적절하다. 따라서 정답은 (d)이다.

정답 (d)

어휘
market share **n.** 시장 점유율
launch **v.** 출시하다
innovative **adj.** 획기적인
introduce **v.** 소개하다, 출시하다

15. 가정법 (과거)

해석 Christina는 석사 학위를 위해 퇴근 후 야간 수업에 참석하고 있다. 이 일과가 그녀를 지치게 만들고 있다. 만약 그녀가 쉴 시간을 더 가진다면, 그녀는 그녀의 행복에 대해 훨씬 더 좋게 느낄 것이다.

해설 가정법 과거를 묻는 문제로, 현재의 사실에 반대되는 가정(만약 그녀가 쉴 시간을 더 가진다면)을 나타내고 있다. 가정법 과거는 'if + 주어 + 과거형 동사(had), 주어 + 조동사 과거형(would/could/should/might) + 동사원형'의 형태로 쓰이므로, 정답은 (a)이다.

정답 (a)

어휘
attend **v.** 참석하다
routine **n.** 일과
exhausted **adj.** 기진맥진한

16. 조동사 (문맥에 맞는 조동사)

해석 Henry는 그의 월말 보고서들을 작성하느라 너무 바빠서 다음 주 금요일 비즈니스 회의에 참석할 수 없다. 그의 상사는 Henry에게 그를 대신해서 회의에 참석하도록 부하 직원들 중 한 명을 배치해야 한다고 말했다.

해설 첫 번째 문장에서 Henry가 월말 보고서 때문에 너무 바빠서 회의에 참석할 수 없다고 하고, 해당 문장은 그의 상사가 그 대신 회의에 참석할 부하 한 명을 지정해야 한다고 말했다는 의미가 되어야 하므로, 의무와 충고의 의미를 내포한 조동사 'should'가 가장 적절하다. 따라서 정답은 (b)이다.

정답 (b)

어휘
be busy ~ing **v.** ~로 바쁘다
conference **n.** 회의, 학회
supervisor **n.** 상관, 관리자
subordinate **n.** 부하

17. 관계사 (관계대명사)

해석 내 친구는 내가 그의 결혼식에 갈 것인지 3번이나 물어봤고, 나는 계속해서 "응" 이라고 대답했다. 거의 1년 동안, 그는 이번 달 말에 열릴 그 큰 행사를 준비해왔다.

해설 빈칸의 절은 앞에 나온 명사구(the big event)를 수식하며 '이번 달 말에 열릴' 이라는 의미를 가진 관계사절이 되어야 한다. 선행사 'event'가 사물이며, 해당 절에서 관계대명사가 주어 역할을 하기 때문에 사물을 대체하는 주격 관계대명사(which 혹은 that)가 와야 한다. (c)의 which도 사물 선행사를 수식하지만, 주어(it)가 있어서 주격대명사로 쓰인 것이 아니므로 오답이다. 따라서 정답은 (d)이다.

정답 (d)

어휘
almost **ad.** 거의
prepare **v.** 준비하다
hold **v.** 열다, 개최하다

18. 연결어 (접속사)

해석 Mary는 어떤 것을 말을 하고 나서 정반대의 행동을 하는 경향이 있다. 비록 많은 사람들이 그녀의 행동에 싫증났지만, 그녀는 여전히 꽤 많은 친구들을 가지고 있다.

해설 빈칸 뒤를 보면 두 개의 절이 나오고 있으므로 빈칸에는 접속사가 들어가야 한다. 해당 문장은 Mary의 행동으로 사람들이 싫증이 났음에도 불구하고 친구가 많다는 의미가 되어야 하기 때문에 '~에도 불구하고' 라는 의미를 가진 접속사가 빈칸에 가장 적절하다. 따라서 정답은 (c)이다.

정답 (c)

어휘
tendency **n.** 경향
exact **adj.** 정확한
opposite **n.** 반대(의 사람, 일)
afterwards **ad.** 나중에
behavior **n.** 행동, 태도, 품행
therefore **ad.** 그러므로
although **conj.** ~에도 불구하고
unless **conj.** 만약 ~이 아니라면

19. 가정법 (과거완료)

해석 나는 사촌에게 100달러의 빚을 갚을 수 있도록 비용을 최소화하라고 말했다. 불행하게도, 그는 듣지 않았다. 만약 그가 내 충고를 받아들였다면, 그 빚이 지금의 2,000달러로 늘어나지는 않았을 것이다.

해설 가정법 과거완료를 묻는 문제로, 과거의 사실에 반대되는 가정(만약 그가 내 충고를 받아들였다면)을 나타내고 있다. 가정법 과거완료 형식은 'if + 주어 + 과거완료동사(had p.p.), 주어 + 조동사 과거형(would/could/should/might) + 현재완료동사(have p.p.)'이므로, 정답은 (b)이다.

정답 (b)

어휘
minimize **v.** 최소화하다
expense **n.** 지출, 비용

20. 조동사 (주장, 요구, 명령, 제안, 충고 등 의미의 동사 that절 동사원형)

해석 많은 프로 농구 선수들이 현재 스포츠맨답지 않은 행동을 하고 있다. 이 문제를 다루기 위하여, 연맹은 새로운 선수들이 선발되기 전과 후 모두 바른 행실에 대한 세미나에 참석해야 한다고 현재 주장한다.

해설 'insist' 뒤에 that절이 올 경우, 'that절의 주어가 ~해야 한다고 주장하다' 라는 의미가 된다. 이처럼 주절에 제안, 명령, 주장, 요구를 나타내는 동사가 올 경우, that절의 주어와 동사 사이에 있는 조동사 'should'가 종종 생략된다. 따라서 that절의 동사는 원형이 되어야 하므로, 정답은 (a)이다.

정답 (a)

어휘
engage **v.** 하다, 참여하다
unsportsmanlike **adj.** 스포츠맨답지 못한
conduct **n.** 행동
address **v.** 다루다, 해결하려 하다

21. To 부정사 (To 부정사 형용사적 용법)

해석 많은 사람들이 현재 영어를 세계 공용어라고 생각한다. 이것이 그 언어에 능숙하지 않은 사람들이 그들의 능력을 향상시키려고 노력하는 이유이다. 영어를 공부할 때 가장 먼저 배워야 할 것은 품사들이다.

해설 해당 문장에는 본동사 'are'이 있기 때문에, 빈칸에는 정형 동사(시제, 수를 나타내는 동사)가 올 수 없고, 앞에 오는 명사 'things'을 수식해주는 형용사구가 와야 한다. 모든 조건을 만족시키는 형태는 to 부정사(형용사적 용법)이므로, 정답은 (c)이다. 참고로 to 부정사의 완료형(to have + p.p.)은 해당 절의 시제보다 한 시제 앞설 때 사용한다.

정답 (c)

어휘
consider **v.** 고려하다; 여기다, 간주하다
universal **adj.** 보편적인
proficient **adj.** 능숙한
improve **v.** 향상시키다

22. 가정법 (과거완료)

해석 Tina는 학급 졸업생 대표가 되고 싶었지만, 그녀의 기말고사 결과는 그녀에게 단지 개회사 자격(차석 자격)만을 주었다. 만약 그녀가 시험을 더 잘 봤더라면, 그녀는 최고의 자리를 얻을 수 있었을 것이다.

해설 가정법 과거완료를 묻는 문제로, 과거의 사실에 반대되는 가정(만약 그녀가 시험을 더 잘 봤더라면)을 나타내고 있다. 가정법 과거완료 형식은 'if + 주어 + 과거완료동사(had p.p.), 주어 + 조동사 과거형(would/could/should/might) + 현재완료동사(have p.p.)'이므로, 정답은 (d)이다.

정답 (d)

어휘
valedictorian **n.** 수석
salutatory **adj.** 인사의 **n.** (졸업식에서 보통 차석 졸업생이 하는) 인사말

23. 동명사 (동명사를 목적어로 취하는 동사)

해석 Karl은 전국 과학 대회에서 졌을지도 모르지만, 그의 선생님들은 여전히 그를 매우 자랑스러워한다. Karl 또한 기분이 좋다. 1년 전만 해도, 그는 이런 권위 있는 대회에 나가는 것을 상상조차 할 수 없었을 것이다.

해설 imagine'은 to 부정사가 아닌 동명사를 목적어로 취하므로 정답은 (b)이다. 참고로 동명사의 완료형(having + p.p.)은 해당 절의 시제보다 한 시제 앞설 때 사용한다.

정답 (b)

어휘
competition **n.** 대회, 시합
be proud of **v.** ~을 자랑스러워 하다
prestigious **adj.** 일류의

24. 시제 (현재완료진행형)

해석 내가 읽고 있는 James Michener 소설인 <The Source>는 그의 가장 긴 소설임이 틀림없다. 나는 지금까지 그것을 두 달째 읽어 오고 있는데, 여전히 책의 중간쯤에도 미치지 못한다.

해설 첫 번째 문장에서 사용된 현재진행(I'm reading)시제, 그리고 해당 문장에서 그 책을 두 달 동안(for two months now) 계속 읽어 오고 있고 여전히 책의 중간쯤에도 미치지 못한다(I'm still not even halfway through the book)는 내용이 나오고 있으므로, 빈칸에는 현재 이전의 시점에 발생한 동작이나 상태가 현재 발화 시점에서 '진행' 되고 있는 중임을 나타낼 때 쓰이는 현재완료진행형이 가장 적절하다. 따라서 정답은 (c)이다. 현재완료형은 현재 이전에 시작된 동작이나 상태가 현재시점에서 '완료' 될 때 쓰이므로 (a)는 답이 될 수 없다.

정답 (c)

어휘
halfway **ad.** 중간쯤에

25. 가정법 (미래)

해석 Alice가 23번가를 지날 때마다, 그녀는 가게 창문에 진열되어 있는 명품 가방들을 오랫동안 쳐다본다. 그녀는 가방을 모으는 것을 좋아하며, 만약 전시된 가방이 세일 중이라면, 그녀는 가방을 구매할 것이다.

해설 실현 가능성이 낮은 상황을 가정(만약 전시된 가방이 세일 중이라면)할 때 "If 주어 + were to, 주어 + 조동사 과거형(would/could/should/might) + 동사원형" 형태를 주로 사용한다. if 절에 were to가 있으므로, 정답은 (a)이다.

정답 (a)

어휘
longingly **ad.** 갈망하여
on display **phr.** 전시 중인

26. 조동사 (중요성, 필요성, 의무 등 의미의 형용사 that절 동사원형)

해석 Dave Edwards는 범죄행위로 기소되었다. 그러나 그의 변호사는 그에 대한 직접적인 증거가 부족하다고 말한다. 따라서 변호사는 Dave가 혐의에 대해 "무죄"를 주장하는 것이 중요하다고 말한다.

해설 'important'와 같이 중요, 당연, 의무 등의 의미를 내포하고 있는 형용사가 주절에 있을 경우, that절의 주어와 동사 사이에 있는 조동사 'should'가 종종 생략된다. 따라서 that절의 동사는 원형이 되어야 하므로, 정답은 (d)이다.

정답 (d)

어휘
accuse **v.** 고발하다, 기소하다
evidence against **n.** ~에게 불리한 증거
plead **v.** (법정에서) 답변하다
charge **n.** 기소, 고발

Chapter 1

Grammar

02 문법 모의고사 2회

1	(b)	2	(a)	3	(d)	4	(d)	5	(b)
6	(a)	7	(d)	8	(b)	9	(d)	10	(a)
11	(c)	12	(b)	13	(a)	14	(b)	15	(c)
16	(b)	17	(d)	18	(a)	19	(d)	20	(b)
21	(c)	22	(a)	23	(d)	24	(a)	25	(c)
26	(c)								

1. 가정법 (과거완료)

해석 Frank는 사무실에서 고객을 위한 보고서를 작성하고 있었기 때문에, 지난 주말 친구들과 함께 골프를 칠 수 없었다. 만약 그가 보고서를 더 일찍 끝냈더라면, 골프장에서 친구들과 함께 할 수 있었을 것이다.

해설 가정법 과거완료를 묻는 문제로, 과거의 사실에 반대되는 가정(만약 그가 보고서를 더 일찍 끝냈더라면)을 나타내고 있다. 가정법 과거완료 형식은 'if + 주어 + 과거완료동사(had p.p.), 주어 + 조동사 과거형(would/could/should/might) + 현재완료동사(have p.p.)'이므로, 정답은 (b)이다.

정답 (b)

어휘
client **n.** 고객
finish **v.** 끝내다

2. 조동사 (문맥에 맞는 조동사)

해석 지난밤 교통 체증이 너무 심해서 집에 가는데 2시간이 아닌 4시간이 걸렸다. 마침내 집 진입로에 들어섰을 때는 10시였을 것이다.

해설 첫 번째 문장에서 지난밤에 집에 가는데 2시간이 아닌 4시간이 걸렸다고 하고, 해당 문장은 이러한 사실을 바탕으로 도착한 시간을 추측하고 있으므로, have + 과거분사형(been)과 함께 쓰일 때 추측의 의미를 내포하는 조동사 'must'가 가장 적절하다. 따라서 정답은 (a)이다.

정답 (a)

어휘
instead of **prep.** ~대신에
by the time **conj.** ~할 때쯤이면
finally **ad.** 마침내
pull into phr **v.** ~에 도착하다
driveway **n.** 진입로, 차도

3. 연결어 (접속부사)

해석 Jean은 사람들과 소통하는 데 있어서 자신의 스마트폰이 가장 중요한 장치라고 생각한다. 더욱이 그녀는 와이파이가 연결될 때마다 인터넷 서핑을 하는 데 중독된다.

해설 첫 번째 문장에서 Jean이 사람들과 소통하는 데 있어서 스마트폰이 가장 중요한 장치라고 생각한다고 하였고, 두 번째 문장에서 인터넷 서핑에 중독되어 있다고 하였으므로, '더욱이' 라는 첨가/부연의 의미를 가진 접속 부사가 빈칸에 가장 적절하다. 따라서 정답은 (d)이다.

정답 (d)

어휘
essential **adj.** 중요한, 필수적인
be addicted to **v.** ~에 중독되다, 빠지다

4. 시제 (현재진행형)

해석 Harold의 어머니는 자신이 다음 주에 시내에 있을 거라며 그의 아파트에서 지내고 싶다는 것을 그에게 알리기 위해 전화를 했다. 그 때문에, 그는 어머니의 방문에 대비하여 지금 집을 청소하고 있다.

해설 첫 번째 문장에 과거시제(called)가 나오지만, 해당 문장에 현재 시점을 나타내는 부사(now)가 있으며, 그가 미래에 어머니가 방문할 것을 대비하여 지금 집을 청소하고 있는 중이라는 의미가 되어야 하므로, 현재진행형이 빈칸에 가장 적절하다. 따라서 정답은 (d)이다.

정답 (d)

어휘
inform **v.** 알리다
hence **ad.** 그 때문에, 그러므로
prepare **v.** 준비하다, 대비하다

5. 가정법 (과거완료)

해석 Karl은 John Grisham의 <A Painted House>를 읽기 시작했으나, 단지 약간 흥미롭다고 느꼈다. 만약 이 베스트셀러 작가가 새로운 성인 소설 대신에 또 다른 법정 스릴러물을 집필했더라면, Karl은 그것을 더 즐겼을 것이다.

해설 가정법 과거완료를 묻는 문제로, 과거의 사실에 반대되는 가정(만약 이 베스트셀러 작가가 새로운 성인 소설 대신에 또 다른 법정 스릴러물을 집필했더라면)을 나타내고 있다. 가정법 과거완료 형식은 'if + 주어 + 과거완료동사(had p.p.), 주어 + 조동사 과거형(would/could/should/might) + 현재완료동사(have p.p.)'이므로, 정답은 (b)이다.

정답 (b)

어휘
mildly **ad.** 약간
interesting **adj.** 흥미로운
author **n.** 작가
coming-of-age **n.** 성인, 성년

6. 조동사 (주장, 요구, 명령, 제안, 충고 등 의미의 동사 that절 동사원형)

해석 한 소년이 쇼핑몰에서 부모님과 떨어져 있었다. 그 길 잃은 소년을 가엽게 여긴 한 여자는 소년의 부모님에게 알리기 위해 그 소년을 안내데스크로 데려다 주어야 한다고 안전 요원에게 주장했다.

해설 'insist' 뒤에 that절이 올 경우, 'that절의 주어가 ~ 해야 한다고 주장하다' 라는 의미가 된다. 이처럼 주절에 제안, 명령, 주장, 요구를 나타내는 동사가 올 경우, that절의 주어와 동사 사이에 있는 조동사 'should'가 종종 생략된다. 따라서 that절의 동사는 원형이 되어야 하므로, 정답은 (a)이다.

정답 (a)

어휘
separated **adj.** 분리된, 헤어진
take pity on **v.** ~을 불쌍히 여기다
notify **v.** 알리다

7. 동명사 (동명사를 목적어로 취하는 동사)

해석 Alex는 학교 농구팀에 합류한 후 형편없는 성적을 받기 시작했다. 그는 농구 하는 것을 너무 좋아해서 그가 해야 할 만큼 공부에 집중할 수 없었다.

해설 'enjoy'는 to 부정사가 아닌 동명사를 목적어로 취하므로 정답은 (d)이다. 참고로 동명사의 완료형(having + p.p.)은 해당 절의 시제보다 한 시제 앞설 때 사용한다.

정답 (d)

어휘
focus on **v.** ~에 집중하다

8. 시제 (과거진행형)

해석 지금쯤 새로운 화장실 세면대가 사용될 준비가 되었기를 바란다. 내가 마지막으로 배관공을 보았을 때, 그는 폐수 파이프의 연결 부위를 조이고 있었고, 이는 한 시간도 더 된 일이었다.

해설 단순과거시제와 과거진행형이 함께 쓰일 때, 긴 시간에 걸쳐 발생한 '배경'이 되는 행위나 상황은 과거진행형으로 나타내고, 그 와중에 발생한 상대적으로 짧은 시간의 행위나 상황은 단순과거시제로 나타낸다. 해당 문장의 종속절에 과거시제(saw)가 나오고, 주절은 배관공이 폐수 파이프의 연결 부위를 조이고 있던 중이었다는 의미가 되어야 하므로, 과거진행형이 빈칸에 가장 적절하다. 따라서 정답은 (b)이다.

정답 (b)

어휘
by now **ad.** 지금쯤
plumber **n.** 배관공
tighten **v.** 조이다
coupling **n.** 연결 부위

9. 조동사 (문맥에 맞는 조동사)

해석 8살인 내 조카딸은 방금 배운 최신 마술 묘기를 자랑하게 되어 매우 신이 났다. "날 봐요, 삼촌! 내가 이 평범한 손수건을 꽃으로 변하게 할 거에요." 라고 그녀는 선언했다.

해설 첫 번째 및 두 번째 문장에 과거시제(was, declared)가 나오지만, 해당 문장은 마술을 시작하려는 조카의 말을 직접 인용한 부분으로, 의지와 미래의 의미를 내포한 조동사 'will'이 빈칸에 가장 적절하다. 따라서 정답은 (d)이다.

정답 (d)

어휘
turn A into B **v.** A를 B로 바꾸다
ordinary **adj.** 평범한
declare **v.** 선언하다

10. 시제 (현재완료진행형)

해석 Claire는 Smith 교수의 역사 수업에서 더 높은 점수를 받길 원한다. 최근에 그녀가 수업시간에 잘 하지 못해왔기 때문에, 그녀는 곧 있을 토론 주제들에 대해 조사하면서 주말마다 도서관에서 시간을 보낼 계획이다.

해설 해당 문장의 주절을 보면 현재시제(plans)를 사용하여 Claire가 도서관에서 매 주말 시간을 보낼 계획이라고 하고, 빈칸이 포함된 절에는 '최근에(lately)'라는 의미를 가진 부사가 있으므로, 해당 절은 Claire가 과거부터 현재까지 수업시간에 잘 하지 못해오고 있다는 의미가 되어야 한다. 따라서 현재완료진행형이 빈칸에 가장 적절하므로, 정답은 (a)이다.

정답 (a)

어휘
lately **adj.** 최근에
upcoming **adj.** 다가오는, 앞으로 할
discussion **n.** 토론
topic **n.** 주제

11. 시제 (미래완료진행형)

해석 당신은 Jeremy의 예전 아파트에서는 그를 찾을 수 없을 것이다. 그는 샌프란시스코의 대학 중 한 곳의 교수직을 받아들이면서 샌프란시스코로 오래 전 이사를 갔다. 4월이 되면, 그는 그곳에서 5년간 사는 것이 될 것이다.

해설 두 번째 문장에 과거시제(moved, accepted)가 나오지만, 해당 문장에서는 4월이 될 때쯤(By April)의 상황을 이야기하고 있으므로, 미래의 특정 시점까지 계속해서 진행되는 일에 대해 이야기할 때 쓰이는 미래완료진행형이 빈칸에 가장 적절하다. 따라서 정답은 (c)이다.

정답 (c)

어휘
accept **v.** 받아들이다

12. 조동사 (주장, 요구, 명령, 제안, 충고 등 의미의 동사 that절 동사원형)

해석 Chris는 복권에 당첨되면 정말로 전 세계를 여행하고 싶어 한다. 나는 그가 당첨 확률을 높이기 위해서는 더 많은 복권을 사야 한다고 제안했다.

해설 'suggest' 뒤에 that절이 올 경우, 'that절의 주어가 ~해야 한다고 제안하다' 라는 의미가 된다. 이처럼 주절에 제안, 명령, 주장, 요구를 나타내는 동사가 올 경우, that절의 주어와 동사 사이에 있는 조동사 'should'가 종종 생략된다. 따라서 that절의 동사는 원형이 되어야 하므로, 정답은 (b)이다.

정답 (b)

어휘
would like to V v. ~하고 싶어 하다
increase v. 증가하다, 증가시키다

13. 연결어 (접속사)

해석 Bill은 자동차 경주가 수반하는 위험에도 불구하고 그것을 정말 좋아한다. 그는 심지어 결혼하기 전부터 그것을 해오고 있는 중이다. 사실, 그는 아내가 끊임없이 그에게 간청했음에도 불구하고 자동차 경주를 포기하기를 거부한다.

해설 해당 문장은 아내가 지속적으로 자동차 경주를 포기하라고 애원하는데도 Bill이 이를 거절한다는 의미가 되어야 하므로, 주절과 상반되는 상황을 소개하며 '~에도 불구하고' 라는 의미를 가진 접속사가 빈칸에 가장 적절하다. 따라서 정답은 (a)이다.

정답 (a)

어휘
despite prep. ~에도 불구하고
involve v. 수반하다
in fact ad. 사실은
refuse v. 거절하다, 거부하다
give up v. 포기하다
constantly ad. 끊임없이
beg v. 간청하다

14. 가정법 (과거)

해석 Cynthia는 너무 똑똑해서 반에서 1등을 할 수도 있었다. 하지만, 그녀는 과제에 손을 대지 않은 채, 비디오 게임을 하며 대부분의 밤을 보낸다. 만약 내가 그녀라면, 나는 주말에만 비디오 게임을 할 것이다.

해설 가정법 과거를 묻는 문제로, 현재의 사실에 반대되는 가정(만약 내가 그녀라면)을 나타내고 있다. 가정법 과거는 'if + 주어 + 과거형 동사(were), 주어 + 조동사 과거형(would/could/should/might) + 동사원형'의 형태로 쓰이므로, 정답은 (b)이다.

정답 (b)

어휘
assignment n. 과제
untouched adj. 손을 대지 않은

15. 시제 (미래진행형)

해석 Mary는 내일 차로 Todd를 태우러 갈 때 혼잡한 공항에서 그를 찾는데 어떤 어려움도 겪지 않을 것이다. 그는 주황색 하와이안 셔츠, 형광 초록색 반바지, 그리고 큰 밀짚모자를 쓰고 있을 거라고 말한다.

해설 Mary가 공항에 Todd를 데리러 가는 것은 미래(tomorrow)에 있을 일이고, 해당 절은 그가 미래에 어떤 복장을 하고 있을 것이라는 내용이 되어야 하므로, 앞으로 벌어질 미래의 한 시점에 진행되고 있을 동작이나 상태를 나타낼 때 쓰이는 미래진행형이 빈칸에 가장 적절하다. 따라서 정답은 (c)이다.

정답 (c)

어휘
have difficulty ~ing v. ~하는 데 어려움을 겪다
crowded adj. 붐비는, 혼잡한

16. 가정법 (미래)

해석 Jenny는 집에 피아노가 없어서 실망했다. 그녀는 만약 그녀 자신만의 피아노를 갖게 된다면, 그녀가 가장 좋아하는 모든 노래들을 연주할 수 있을 때까지 매일 연습할 것이라고 말한다.

해설 실현 가능성이 낮은 상황을 가정(만약 그녀 자신만의 피아노를 갖게 된다면)할 때 "If 주어 + were to, 주어 + 조동사 과거형(would/could/should/might) + 동사원형" 형태를 주로 사용한다. if 절에 were to가 있으므로, 정답은 (b)이다.

정답 (b)

어휘
disappointed adj. 실망한, 낙담한
favorite adj. 가장 좋아하는

17. 관계사 (관계대명사)

해석 Ernest Cline은 상을 받은 책인 <Ready Player One>으로 가장 잘 알려진 미국 소설가이다. 가상의 사회를 중심으로 한 이 책은 박스오피스에서 꽤 성공한 영화로 각색되었다.

해설 선행사는 'The book'이고 동사는 'was adapted'이므로, 콤마(,) 사이에 들어갈 내용은 앞에 나온 명사구(The book)에 대한 부연 설명이 되어야 한다. 사물인 책을 부연 설명하며, 콤마(,) 뒤에 와서 계속적 용법으로 쓰일 수 있는 관계대명사 which로 해당 절을 시작해야 한다. (a)의 that도 사물 선행사를 수식하지만, 콤마 뒤에 올 수 없으므로 오답이다. 따라서 정답은 (d)이다.

정답 (d)

어휘
adapt **v.** 각색하다
successful **adj.** 성공적인

18. 가정법 (과거완료)

해석 태양이 지구와 관련하여 그렇게 이상적으로 위치하는 것은 행운이다. 과학자들은 만약 태양이 지구에 조금만 더 가까웠거나 멀었더라면, 지구상의 생명체는 수십억 년 전에 시작될 수 없었을 것이라고 말한다.

해설 가정법 과거완료를 묻는 문제로, 과거의 사실에 반대되는 가정(만약 태양이 지구에 조금만 더 가까웠거나 멀었더라면)을 나타내고 있다. 가정법 과거완료 형식은 'if + 주어 + 과거완료동사(had p.p.), 주어 + 조동사 과거형(would/could/should/might) + 현재완료동사(have p.p.)'이므로, 정답은 (a)이다.

정답 (a)

어휘
position **v.** 위치하다, ~에 자리를 잡다
ideally **ad.** 이상적으로
in relation to **prep.** ~와 관련하여

19. To 부정사 (To 부정사를 목적어로 취하는 동사)

해석 Sarah는 물리 숙제를 하기 위해 Harper Lee의 <To Kill a Mockingbird>를 읽는 것을 포기해야 한다. 그녀는 그 소설을 다시 읽을 수 있도록 숙제를 빨리 끝내기를 바란다.

해설 동사 'hope' 뒤에는 that절, to 부정사, 전치사 for + 명사가 올 수 있는데, 빈칸에는 'hope'의 목적어(명사)가 되는 동시에 뒤따라오는 명사 'assignment'를 목적어로 취하는 알맞은 형태의 동사가 와야 한다. 모든 조건을 만족시키는 형태는 to 부정사이므로, 정답은 (d)이다. 참고로 to 부정사의 완료형(to have + p.p.)은 해당 절의 시제보다 한 시제 앞설 때 사용한다.

정답 (d)

어휘
forgo **v.** 포기하다

20. 시제 (과거완료진행형)

해석 수학 시험의 결과를 받은 후, Betty는 낮은 점수를 보고도 전혀 놀라지 않았다. 그 시험을 보기 전에, 그녀는 해야 했던 만큼의 공부를 하지 않았었다.

해설 첫 번째 문장에서 과거시제(was)가 나오고, 그녀가 시험을 봤던 것 역시 과거 시점이다. 그녀가 충분히 공부를 해오지 않았던 것은 시험을 봤던 시점 직전까지 계속되어 왔던 것이므로, 과거완료진행형이 빈칸에 가장 적절하다. 따라서 정답은 (b)이다.

정답 (b)

어휘
prior to **prep.** ~전에

21. 동명사 (동명사를 목적어로 취하는 동사)

해석 Finley씨가 그녀의 수업시간에는 단지 몇 개의 규칙만 있음을 알렸다. 그러나 그녀는 어떤 형태로든 부정행위를 용인하지 않을 것임을 분명히 했다.

해설 'tolerate'는 to 부정사가 아닌 동명사를 목적어로 취하므로 정답은 (c)이다. 참고로 동명사의 완료형(having + p.p.)은 해당 절의 시제보다 한 시제 앞설 때 사용한다.

정답 (c)

어휘
tolerate **v.** 용인하다

22. 조동사 (주장, 요구, 명령, 제안, 충고 등 의미의 동사 that절 동사원형)

해석 Samantha는 Glamour 출판사가 그녀에게 제안하는 자리를 수락하는 것을 진지하게 고려하고 있다. 하지만, 나는 그녀가 그 일을 수락하기 전에 급여를 협상하기를 제안했다. 적어도 그녀의 현재 월급보다 많아야 한다.

해설 'suggest' 뒤에 that절이 올 경우, 'that절의 주어가 ~해야 한다고 제안하다' 라는 의미가 된다. 이처럼 주절에 제안, 명령, 주장, 요구를 나타내는 동사가 올 경우, that절의 주어와 동사 사이에 있는 조동사 'should'가 종종 생략된다. 따라서 that절의 동사는 원형이 되어야 하므로, 정답은 (a)이다.

정답 (a)

어휘
consider **v.** 고려하다; 여기다, 간주하다
accept **v.** 수락하다
offer **v.** 제안하다
negotiate **v.** 협상하다

23. 가정법 (과거완료)

해석 Bernard는 그의 선생님이 자신을 에세이 쓰기 대회에 참가하게 한 것이 실수였다고 생각하는데, 그는 결국 실패하였다. 그는 만약 자신이 수학 대회에 대신 나갔더라면, 훨씬 더 좋은 성적을 냈을 것이라고 믿는다.

해설 가정법 과거완료를 묻는 문제로, 과거의 사실에 반대되는 가정(만약 자신이 수학 대회에 대신 나갔더라면)을 나타내고 있다. 가정법 과거완료 형식은 'if + 주어 + 과거완료동사(had p.p.), 주어 + 조동사 과거형(would/could/should/might) + 현재완료동사(have p.p.)'이므로, 정답은 (d)이다.

정답 (d)

어휘
subsequently **ad.** 나중에, 그 뒤에
instead **ad.** 대신에

24. 관계사 (관계대명사)

해석 당신은 패널 인터뷰에서 인사부 부장을 조심하는 것이 낫다. 그녀는 날카로운 질문을 한다. 당신은 그녀가 묶어 올린 머리를 한 패널리스트라는 것을 알 수 있다.

해설 빈칸에는 앞에 나온 명사구(the panelist)를 수식하며 '묶어올린 머리를 한'이라는 의미를 가진 관계사절이 되어야 한다. 해당 절에서 관계대명사가 주어 역할을 하기 때문에 사람을 대체하는 주격 관계대명사가 와야 한다. (d)의 that도 사람 선행사를 수식하지만, 주어(she)가 있어서 주격대명사로 쓰인 것이 아니므로 오답이다. 따라서 정답은 (a)이다.

정답 (a)

어휘
wary **adj.** 경계하는, 조심하는
pointed **adj.** (말이) 날카로운
recognize **v.** 알아보다

25. 동명사 (동명사를 목적어로 취하는 동사)

해석 Hill씨는 자신이 이끄는 합창단이 단체 보컬 대회에서 금메달을 딸 것이라고 매우 자신한다. 준비하기 위해, 그녀의 그룹은 현재 몇 주 동안 그들의 곡을 부르는 연습을 하고 있다.

해설 'practice'는 to 부정사가 아닌 동명사를 목적어로 취하므로 정답은 (c)이다. 참고로 동명사의 완료형(having + p.p.)은 해당 절의 시제보다 한 시제 앞설 때 사용한다.

정답 (c)

어휘
competition **n.** 대회, 경쟁
be confident that **v.** ~에 대해 확신하다

26. To 부정사 (To 부정사를 목적어로 취하는 동사)

해석 제약 회사의 영업 사원들은 이번 분기에 자신들이 할당량을 달성하고, 심지어 넘어서는 데 성공했다. 그들의 좋은 실적에 보답하기 위해서, 회사의 대표는 모든 사원에게 두둑한 보너스를 지급하기로 결정했다.

해설 동사 'decide'는 to 부정사를 목적어로 취하므로, 정답은 (c)이다. 참고로, to + have + 과거분사형(given)은 문장의 본동사보다 먼저 일어난 일에 대해 말할 때 쓰이므로 (b)는 정답이 될 수 없다.

정답 (c)

어휘
sales representative **n.** 영업 사원
exceed **v.** 넘어서다, 초과하다
hefty **adj.** 많은, 두둑한

Chapter 1

Grammar

03 문법 모의고사 3회

1	(b)	2	(a)	3	(c)	4	(d)	5	(c)
6	(a)	7	(d)	8	(b)	9	(a)	10	(c)
11	(a)	12	(c)	13	(d)	14	(b)	15	(d)
16	(c)	17	(b)	18	(a)	19	(c)	20	(d)
21	(a)	22	(b)	23	(a)	24	(c)	25	(d)
26	(c)								

1. 시제 (현재진행형)

해석 오늘 일찍 나는 Alicia를 축구 경기에 초대하기 위해 그녀의 집에 잠깐 들렀다. 그러나 내가 그녀를 봤을 때 그녀는 거의 서 있지 못했다. 보아하니 그녀는 지난주에 입었던 다리 부상에서 여전히 회복 중이다.

해설 모든 문장에 과거시제(dropped, could stand, got)가 나오지만, Alicia를 방문했던 건 오늘(today)이고, 해당 문장은 그녀가 지난주에 입었던 다리 부상에서 여전히 회복 중이라는 의미가 되어야 하므로, 현재진행형이 빈칸에 가장 적절하다. 따라서 정답은 (b)이다.

정답 (b)

어휘
drop by **v.** ~에 들르다
barely **ad.** 거의 ~아니게, 간신히
apparently **ad.** 보아하니, 보기에
recover from **v.** ~로부터 회복하다

2. 가정법 (과거완료)

해석 Ryan은 친구의 결혼식에 티셔츠와 청바지를 입고 갈 뻔했다. 만약 그가 떠나기 전에 내가 검정색 넥타이 드레스 코드를 그에게 상기시키지 않았다면, 그는 공식적인 행사에 적절한 복장을 갖추지 못했을 것이다.

해설 가정법 과거완료를 묻는 문제로, 과거의 사실에 반대되는 가정(만약 그가 떠나기 전에 내가 검정색 넥타이 드레스 코드를 그에게 상기시키지 않았다면)을 나타내고 있다. 가정법 과거완료 형식은 'if + 주어 + 과거완료동사(had p.p.), 주어 + 조동사 과거형(would/could/should/might) + 현재완료동사(have p.p.)'이므로, 정답은 (a)이다.

정답 (a)

어휘
nearly **ad.** 거의
remind **v.** 상기시키다
appropriately **ad.** 적당하게, 알맞게
formal **adj.** 공식의

3. 조동사 (주장, 요구, 명령, 제안, 충고 등 의미의 동사 that절 동사원형)

해석 많은 아이들이 신체 활동 부족으로 인해 비만이 되고 있다. 이 문제를 방지하기 위해서 전문가들은 아이들이 컴퓨터 게임을 하는 데 시간을 보내는 대신 활동적인 운동에 참여하기를 권장한다.

해설 'recommend' 뒤에 that절이 올 경우, 'that절의 주어가 ~해야 한다고 권고하다' 라는 의미가 된다. 이처럼 주절에 제안, 명령, 주장, 요구를 나타내는 동사가 올 경우, that절의 주어와 동사 사이에 있는 조동사 'should'가 종종 생략된다. 따라서 that절의 동사는 원형이 되어야 하므로, 정답은 (c)이다.

정답 (c)

어휘
obese **adj.** 비만인
inactivity **n.** 활동하지 않음
avoid **v.** 피하다
recommend **v.** ~을 권하다
active **adj.** 활동적인

TEST 3

4. 시제 (미래완료진행형)

해석 Peggy는 저녁 파티를 열 거라서, 정오부터 계속 요리를 하는 중이다. 손님들이 도착할 때 즈음이면 그녀는 다섯 시간 연속으로 음식을 준비하고 있는 것이 될 것이다. 그들이 오기 전에 그녀가 옷을 갈아입을 시간이 있길 바란다.

해설 첫 번째 문장에서 현재완료진행형(has been cooking)을 사용하여 Peggy가 요리를 해오고 있다고 하고, 해당 문장에서는 손님들이 도착할 때 즈음(by the time her guests arrive) 그녀가 요리를 다섯 시간 동안 쭉 하고 있을 거라고 추측하고 있으므로, 미래의 특정 시점까지 계속해서 진행되는 일에 대해 이야기할 때 쓰이는 미래완료진행형이 빈칸에 가장 적절하다. 따라서 정답은 (d)이다.

정답 (d)

어휘
host **v.** (행사를) 주최하다, 열다
by the time **conj.** ~할 때쯤이면
arrive **v.** 도착하다
prepare **v.** 준비하다

5. 문맥에 맞는 조동사

해석 며칠 전에 Emilia의 아파트가 불에 탔고, 심각하게 손상되었다. 그녀는 현재 머물 곳을 찾는 중이다. 나는 그녀의 오랜 친구로서, 그 동안에 나와 같이 살아도 된다고 말했다.

해설 첫 번째 문장에서 Emilia의 아파트가 불에 타 심각하게 손상되었다고 하고, 해당 문장은 화자가 자신과 함께 살아도 된다고 말했다는 의미가 되어야 하므로, 빈칸에는 가능과 허가의 의미를 내포한 조동사 'could'가 가장 적절하다. 따라서 정답은 (c)이다.

정답 (c)

어휘
damaged **adj.** 손상된, 손해를 입은
in the meantime **ad.** 그 동안에

6. 동명사 (동명사를 목적어로 취하는 동사)

해석 Kate Winslet은 세계에서 가장 훌륭한 배우 중 한 명이다. 연기자 집안에서 자란 것이 이점이 된 것으로 증명되었다. 그녀는 어린 나이에 연극과 TV 쇼에 노출되었던 것을 회상한다.

해설 해당 문장에서 동사는 recalls이고 to 부정사와 동명사 모두 목적어가 가능하다. 이때 to 부정사는 앞으로 할 행동(미래)를 나타내고, 동명사는 과거에 이미 했던 행동들을 언급하는데 쓰인다. 주어진 문장에서는 그녀의 어린 시절(at an early age), 즉 과거에 무대에 무대 연극에 노출되었던 것을 회상하는 것이므로, 정답은 동명사인 (a)이다. 참고로 동명사의 완료형(having + p.p.)은 해당 절의 시제보다 한 시제 앞설 때 사용한다.

정답 (a)

어휘
raise **v.** 기르다, 키우다
prove to V **v.** ~라고 입증되다
gain **v.** 얻다
exposure **n.** 출연, 노출

7. 시제 (현재완료진행형)

해석 캐나다의 많은 부모들이 인상되는 대학교 등록금에 대해 화가 나 있다. 한 보도에 따르면 캐나다에서는 1980년 이래로 사무직 종사자 월급 인상률의 거의 2배에 달하는 비율로 등록금이 인상되어오고 있다고 한다.

해설 첫 번째 문장에서 현재시제(are)를 사용하여 부모들이 화가 나 있다고 하고, 해당 문장은 과거 시점인 1980년 이래로(since 1980) 등록금이 인상되어오고 있다는 의미가 되어야 하므로, 빈칸에는 현재완료진행형이 가장 적절하다. 따라서 정답은 (d)이다.

정답 (d)

어휘
upset **adj.** 화가 난
tuition fee **n.** 등록금
nearly **ad.** 거의

8. 가정법 (과거완료)

해석 뉴욕의 한 잡지사가 나를 그래픽 아티스트로 채용하고 싶어 했지만, 나는 그 제안을 거절했다. 만약 그들이 내가 바라는 연봉에 합의했다면, 나는 망설임 없이 그 일자리를 받아들였을 것이다.

해설 가정법 과거완료를 묻는 문제로, 과거의 사실에 반대되는 가정(만약 그들이 내가 바라는 연봉에 합의했다면)을 나타내고 있다. 가정법 과거완료 형식은 'if + 주어 + 과거완료동사(had p.p.), 주어 + 조동사 과거형(would/could/should/might) + 현재완료동사(have p.p.)'이므로, 정답은 (b)이다.

정답 (b)

어휘
decline **v.** 거절하다
agree **v.** 동의하다
without hesitation **phr.** 망설임 없이, 주저하지 않고

9. 동명사 (동명사를 목적어로 취하는 동사)

해석 어떤 종류의 운동 전에 준비운동을 하는 것은 부상 가능성을 줄이는 데 도움이 되기 때문에 중요하다. 전문가들은 스트레칭을 준비운동으로 권장한다. 그것은 근육의 유연성을 향상시킴으로써 근육의 긴장을 방지한다.

해설 'advise'는 to 부정사가 아닌 동명사를 목적어로 취하므로 정답은 (a)이다. 참고로 동명사의 완료형(having + p.p.)은 해당 절의 시제보다 한 시제 앞설 때 사용한다.

정답 (a)

어휘
reduce **v.** 줄이다
advise **v.** 권하다
prevent **v.** 막다, 예방하다
strain **n.** (근육) 좌상
flexibility **n.** 유연성

10. 관계사 (관계대명사)

해석 미국의 세 번째 대통령인 Thomas Jefferson은 14세까지 홈스쿨링을 받았다. 그의 선생님은 William Douglas라고 불리는 성직자였는데, 이 사람에게서 그는 그리스어, 이탈리아어, 그리고 프랑스어를 배웠다.

해설 빈칸 앞의 절이 주어(His tutor)와 동사(was)를 갖춘 완전한 절이므로, 빈칸이 포함된 부분은 앞에 나온 명사구(a clergyman named William Douglas)에 대한 부연 설명이 되어야 한다. 앞서 언급한 성직자에 대해 부연 설명하며, 동시에 전치사(from)의 목적어가 될 수 있는 것은 관계대명사 whom이다. 일반적으로 전치사 뒤에 that절은 올 수 없으므로 (a)는 오답이다. 따라서 정답은 (c)이다.

정답 (c)

어휘
homeschool **v.** 홈스쿨링을 받다, 가정에서 교육하다
clergyman **n.** 성직자

11. 시제 (미래진행형)

해석 최근 Luke는 멜버른 대학교에서 대학원 전액 장학금을 받았다. 그는 앞으로 2년을 호주에서 경영학 석사 과정을 마치는데 보내게 될 것이다.

해설 빈칸을 포함한 문장에서는 다음 2년(next two years) 동안 이루어질 행위를 이야기하고 있으므로, 앞으로 벌어질 미래의 한 시점에 진행되고 있을 동작이나 상태를 나타낼 때 쓰이는 미래진행형이 빈칸에 가장 적절하다. 따라서 정답은 (a)이다.

정답 (a)

어휘
recently **ad.** 최근에
grant **v.** 주다
complete **v.** 완료하다, 끝마치다
master's degree **n.** 석사 과정

12. 가정법 (과거)

해석 Katherine은 고모의 고양이들을 좋아하지만, 그녀가 그들 주변에 있을 때 재채기를 많이 하는 경향이 있다. 만약 고양이 털 알레르기가 없다면, 그녀는 다음 주 이모의 집에 방문하는 것에 대해 더 신이 날 것이다.

해설 가정법 과거를 묻는 문제로, 현재의 사실에 반대되는 가정(만약 고양이 털 알레르기가 없다면)을 나타내고 있다. 가정법 과거는 'if + 주어 + 과거형 동사(were), 주어 + 조동사 과거형(would/could/should/might) + 동사원형'의 형태로 쓰이므로, 정답은 (c)이다.

정답 (c)

어휘
be fond of **v.** ~을 좋아하다
tend to V **v.** ~하는 경향이 있다
sneeze **v.** 재채기하다
be allergic to **v.** ~에 알레르기가 있다
excited **adj.** 신이 난, 즐거워 하는

13. 연결어 (접속부사)

해석 Anthony가 그의 Ford Focus를 1만 달러에 판매하려고 내놓았을 때, 그는 구매자를 찾는 데 어려움을 겪었다. 결국, 그는 가격을 8천 달러로 낮추었고, 곧 그 자동차는 판매되었다.

해설 첫 번째 문장에서 Anthony가 자동차를 1만 달러에 판매하려고 내놓았다가 구매자를 찾는 데 어려움을 겪었다고 하고, 빈칸 뒤 문장에서는 8천 달러로 가격을 낮추어 자동차가 금방 판매되었다는 내용이므로, '결국' 이라는 의미를 가진 접속 부사가 빈칸에 가장 적절하다. 따라서 정답은 (d)이다.

정답 (d)

어휘
have a hard time ~ing **v.** ~하는 데 어려움을 겪다
lower **v.** ~을 내리다, 낮추다
nevertheless **ad.** 그럼에도 불구하고
despite **prep.** ~에도 불구하고
meanwhile **ad.** 그 동안에, 한편
eventually **ad.** 결국

14. To 부정사 (To 부정사를 목적어로 취하는 동사)

해석 물리학은 Jeremy가 가장 싫어하는 과목이다. 그는 수업 중 대부분 진도를 따라가는 데 어려움을 겪는다. 교수님이 풀어야 할 문제를 내줄 때마다, Jeremy는 그 문제를 풀려고 노력하는데 너무 많은 시간을 쓴다.

해설 동사 'try' 뒤에는 to 부정사와 동명사가 올 수 있는데, to부정사와 쓰이면 '~하려고 노력하다' 라는 의미가 되고 동명사와 쓰이면 '시험 삼아 ~를 해보다' 라는 의미가 된다. 해당 문장은 문제를 풀려고 노력하는데 너무 많은 시간을 쓴다는 의미가 되어야 하므로, 정답은 (b)이다. 참고로 to 부정사의 완료형(to have + p.p.)은 해당 절의 시제보다 한 시제 앞설 때 사용한다.

정답 (b)

어휘
least **adj.** 가장 적은, 최소의
have a hard time ~ing **v.** ~하는 데 어려움을 겪다
solve **v.** 해결하다
figure out **phr v.** ~를 알아내다, 계산하다

15. 시제 (과거완료진행형)

해석 Brian과 그의 아내는 Cedar Creek 호수 근처로 낚시를 갔다. 그들은 여행을 가려고 지난 몇 주 동안 계획하고 있었는데, 비 오는 날씨 때문에 계속 미뤄오고 있었다.

해설 첫 문장에서 과거시제(went)를 사용하여 Brian과 그의 아내가 낚시를 갔다고 하고, 몇 주 동안 여행 계획을 세웠으나 계속 미뤄온 것은 낚시를 갔다고 하는 과거 시점보다 전에 발생해왔던 일이므로, 빈칸에는 과거 이전부터 과거까지 계속됐던 일에 대해 이야기할 때 쓰이는 과거완료진행형이 가장 적절하다. 따라서 정답은 (d)이다.

정답 (d)

어휘
finally **ad.** 마침내
nearby **adj.** 근처의
postpone **v.** 미루다, 연기하다
due to **prep.** ~때문에

16. 동명사 (동명사를 목적어로 취하는 동사)

해석 Emma는 결혼식 설계사라는 그녀의 새 직업에 대해 굉장히 열정적이다. 지금 그녀는 미팅 중이다. 첫 번째 고객과 대화를 마친 후, 그녀는 한 공급 업체와 이야기하기 위해 시내로 향할 것이다.

해설 'finish'는 to 부정사가 아닌 동명사를 목적어로 취하므로 정답은 (c)이다. 참고로 동명사의 완료형(having + p.p.)은 해당 절의 시제보다 한 시제 앞설 때 사용한다.

정답 (c)

어휘
enthusiastic **adj.** 열정적인
supplier **n.** 공급자, 공급업체

17. 가정법 (미래)

해석 비록 광고기획자(AE)로 종사하고 있지만, Lisa는 매주 토요일 아이들을 위한 발레 선생님으로 봉사 활동을 한다. 그녀는 만약 시간과 돈이 있다면, 자신만의 발레 학교를 열 것이라고 말한다.

해설 실현 가능성이 낮은 상황을 가정(만약 시간과 돈이 있다면)할 때 "If 주어 + were to, 주어 + 조동사 과거형(would/could/should/might) + 동사원형" 형태를 주로 사용한다. if 절에 were to가 있으므로, 정답은 (b)이다.

정답 (b)

어휘
account executive **n.** (광고회사의) 거래처 담당 사원, 광고기획자
volunteer **v.** 자원하다, 자원 봉사로 하다

18. 관계사 (관계대명사)

해석 보도에 따르면 매년 1억 마리 이상의 동물들이 미국 실험실에서 연구와 실험으로 인해 죽임을 당한다고 한다. 이에 대응하여 동물 권리 보호 운동가들은 제품을 위해 동물 실험을 하는 회사를 반대하는 캠페인을 벌이고 있다.

해설 빈칸이 포함된 절은 앞에 나온 명사(companies)를 수식하며 '동물 실험을 하는'의 의미를 가진 관계사절이 되어야 한다. 해당 절에서 관계대명사가 주어 역할을 하기 때문에 사물을 대체하는 주격 관계대명사(which 혹은 that)가 와야 한다. (d) which도 사물 선행사를 수식하지만, 주어(they)가 있어서 주격 대명사로 쓰인 것이 아니므로 오답이다. 따라서 정답은 (a)이다.

정답 (a)

어휘
laboratory **n.** 실험실
experiment **n.** 실험
activist **n.** 운동가
campaign **v.** 캠페인(운동)을 벌이다

19. 조동사 (주장, 요구, 명령, 제안, 충고 등 의미의 동사 that절 동사원형)

해석 역사 수업에서 우리의 기말 과제는 프랑스 혁명에 관한 창의적인 발표를 하는 것이다. 우리 그룹의 한 조원은 우리가 역사적 재현으로 발표를 시작해야 한다고 제안했다.

해설 'propose' 뒤에 that절이 올 경우, 'that절의 주어가 ~해야 한다고 제안하다' 라는 의미가 된다. 이처럼 주절에 제안, 명령, 주장, 요구를 나타내는 동사가 올 경우, that절의 주어와 동사 사이에 있는 조동사 'should'가 종종 생략된다. 따라서 that절의 동사는 원형이 되어야 하므로, 정답은 (c)이다.

정답 (c)

어휘
creative **adj.** 창의적인
presentation **n.** 발표
historical **adj.** 역사의
reenactment **n.** 재현, 재연

20. 시제 (현재완료진행형)

해석 사장님이 Leonard에게 조퇴하라고 말했다. Leonard는 사무실에 도착한 이래로 두통을 호소해오고 있다. 두통이 곧 사라지지 않는다면, 그는 병원에 가야 할 것이다.

해설 해당 문장의 부사절에서 과거시제(arrived)를 사용하고 있고, 해당 문장은 Leonard가 사무실에 도착했던 과거 시점부터 현재까지 두통을 호소해오고 있다는 의미가 되어야 하므로, 빈칸에는 현재완료진행형이 가장 적절하다. 따라서 정답은 (d)이다.

정답 (d)

어휘
complain of **phr v.** (~로 아프다고) 호소하다

21. To 부정사 (To 부정사를 목적격 보어로 취하는 동사)

해석 Wendy의 목표 중 하나는 미국의 모든 유명 랜드마크 앞에서 그녀의 사진을 찍는 것이다. 지난주에 그녀는 10번째 사진을 위해 워싱턴에 있는 링컨 기념관에 동행해달라고 나에게 부탁했다.

해설 동사 'ask'는 to 부정사를 목적격 보어로 취하므로, 정답은 (a)이다. 참고로 to 부정사의 완료형(to have + p.p.)은 해당 절의 시제보다 한 시제 앞설 때 사용한다.

정답 (a)

어휘
goal **n.** 목표
landmark **n.** 명소
accompany **v.** 동행하다

22. 가정법 (과거완료)

해석 전기 회사가 오늘 밤 6시부터 8시간의 정전이 있을 것이라고 공지했다. 만약 내가 아버지에게 이를 상기시키지 않았다면, 그는 오늘 일찍 비상 손전등을 충전하는 것을 잊었을 것이다.

해설 가정법 과거완료를 묻는 문제로, 과거의 사실에 반대되는 가정(만약 내가 아버지에게 이를 상기시키지 않았다면)을 나타내고 있다. 가정법 과거완료 형식은 'if + 주어 + 과거완료동사(had p.p.), 주어 + 조동사 과거형(would/could/should/might) + 현재완료동사(have p.p.)'이므로, 정답은 (b)이다.

정답 (b)

어휘
announce **v.** 발표하다
power outage **n.** 정전
remind **v.** 상기시키다
recharge **v.** (재)충전하다
forget **v.** 잊다

23. 연결어 (접속부사)

해석 많은 사람들이 믿는 것과는 반대로, 고래는 물고기가 아닌 포유류이다. 그들은 물고기와 여러 면에서 다르다. 예를 들면, 고래는 물고기처럼 아가미를 가지고 있지 않다. 대신 그들은 공기를 들이마시기 위해 분수공을 사용한다.

해설 빈칸 앞에서 고래가 물고기와 많은 면에서 다르다(differ from fish in many ways)고 하고, 빈칸 뒤에서는 아가미가 없다는 것을 하나의 예로 들고 있으므로, 빈칸에는 '예를 들면' 이라는 의미를 가진 접속부사가 가장 적절하다. 따라서 정답은 (a)이다.

정답 (a)

어휘
contrary to **prep.** ~와 달리
mammal **n.** 포유류
differ from **v.** ~와 다르다
gill **n.** 아가미
blowhole **n.** 분수공
for example **ad.** 예를 들면
in conclusion **ad.** 결론적으로
furthermore **ad.** 게다가

24. 조동사 (문맥에 맞는 조동사)

해석 Samantha는 오늘 밤 친구들과 콘서트에 갈 예정이다. 일기예보에 따르면, 오늘 폭풍이 올 것 같다. 나는 그녀가 떠날 때 우산을 챙겨가는 것을 잊지 않길 바란다.

해설 빈칸이 포함된 문장의 주어와 동사가 'it seems'로 '~인 것 같다' 라는 의미이므로, 빈칸에는 약한 추측과 가능성을 나타내는 조동사 'might'가 가장 적절하다. 따라서 정답은 (c)이다.

정답 (c)

어휘
forecast **n.** 예측, 예보

25. 조동사 (주장, 요구, 명령, 제안, 충고 등 의미의 동사 that절 동사원형)

해석 Benedict는 지시문을 충분히 주의 깊게 읽지 않기 때문에 종종 시험에 떨어진다. 나는 그가 각 문제에 답하기 전에 적어도 두 번씩 읽어야 한다고 제안했다. 그렇지 않으면 그는 계속 시험에 떨어질 것이다.

해설 'suggest' 뒤에 that절이 올 경우, 'that절의 주어가 ~해야 한다고 제안하다' 라는 의미가 된다. 이처럼 주절에 제안, 명령, 주장, 요구를 나타내는 동사가 올 경우, that절의 주어와 동사 사이에 있는 조동사 'should'가 종종 생략된다. 따라서 that절의 동사는 원형이 되어야 하므로, 정답은 (d)이다.

정답 (d)

어휘
fail to V **v.** ~하는 데 실패하다
instructions **n.** 설명문, 안내문, 지시문
otherwise **ad.** 그렇지 않으면

26. 가정법 (과거완료)

해석 Tiffany는 Warren의 파티에 참석하는 데 동의했다. 그러나 만약 그녀가 채식주의자라는 것을 그에게 말하지 않았더라면, Warren은 모두 고기 메뉴로 진행했을 것이다. 결국에는 모든 사람이 추가 요리인 아티초크 버섯 라자냐를 맛있게 먹었다.

해설 가정법 과거완료를 묻는 문제로, 과거의 사실에 반대되는 가정(만약 그녀가 채식주의자라는 것을 그에게 말하지 않았더라면)을 나타내고 있다. 가정법 과거완료 형식은 'if + 주어 + 과거완료동사(had p.p.), 주어 + 조동사 과거형(would/could/should/might) + 현재완료동사(have p.p.)'이므로, 정답은 (c)이다.

정답 (c)

어휘
agree **v.** 동의하다
attend **v.** 참석하다
additional **adj.** 추가적인

TEST 3

Chapter 2
Listening

01 청취 모의고사 1회

27	(b)	28	(a)	29	(c)	30	(d)	31	(a)
32	(b)	33	(d)	34	(d)	35	(c)	36	(a)
37	(d)	38	(b)	39	(a)	40	(a)	41	(d)
42	(c)	43	(d)	44	(b)	45	(a)	46	(b)
47	(c)	48	(d)	49	(c)	50	(c)	51	(b)
52	(a)								

Part 1 Q. 27-33

27: Why did Edmund go to see Rose?
28: How did Rose become familiar with *The Phantom of the Opera*?
29: According to Edmund, what is most likely a sign that the musical is popular outside the theater world?
30: What is the reason Edmund was so surprised when he got his tickets?
31: According to Edmund, why doesn't Rose need to win a raffle?
32: What is most likely the producers' reason for wanting to reach a bigger audience?
33: Why does Edmund want to see the musical on the first night?

M: Good morning, Rose. [27] I have two tickets for a Broadway musical. Would you like to go with me?
M: 좋은 아침이야, Rose. 나한테 브로드웨이 뮤지컬 티켓이 두 장 있어. 같이 보러 갈래?

F: Really, Edmund? Which musical are the tickets for?
F: 정말, Edmund? 어떤 뮤지컬 티켓이야?

M: The Phantom of the Opera.
M: <오페라의 유령>이야.

F: Wow, I know The Phantom of the Opera. It's one of the most successful musicals of all time, and the longest running show on Broadway, too.
F: 와, 나 <오페라의 유령> 알아. 그거 역대 가장 성공적인 뮤지컬들 중 하나잖아. 브로드웨이에서 가장 오래 상연되고 있는 작품이기도 하고.
M: Correct. Have you seen it?
M: 맞아. 본적 있어?

F: [28] Not onstage. I've only seen one of the film versions. I'm sure watching a live performance would be an awesome experience! By the way, isn't *The Phantom of the Opera*'s music composed by Andrew Lloyd Webber?
F: 무대 공연을 본 적은 없어. 영화화된 걸로만 딱 한 번 봤거든. 라이브 공연을 보는건 분명 멋진 경험이 될 거야! 그건 그렇고, Andrew Lloyd Webber가 <오페라의 유령> 음악 작곡하지 않았니?

M: That's right. Many of Webber's musicals have run or are still running in the West End in London and on Broadway in New York.
M: 맞아. Webber의 뮤지컬들 중 많은 작품들이 런던의 웨스트엔드와 뉴욕의 브로드웨이에서 상연된 적 있거나 여전히 상연 중이야.

F: I also understand the play is based on a novel by the French writer Gaston Leroux.
F: 나 또한 그 연극이 프랑스 작가 Gaston Leroux의 소설에 기반을 두고 있다고 알고 있어.

M: That's correct. The story is about a mysterious and disfigured musical genius who falls madly in love with a beautiful soprano.
M: 맞아. 아름다운 소프라노와 열렬히 사랑에 빠진 기이하고 흉측한 외모를 가진 음악 천재에 관한 이야기지.

F: Yes, I remember the plot from the movies. It's a powerful love story, and I adore the songs in it. The melodies and lyrics are so haunting.
F: 응, 나 그 영화에 나온 줄거리 기억나. 강렬한 사랑 이야기고, 난 거기에 나온 노래들을 좋아해. 멜로디와 가사가 너무 기억에 남아.

M: I agree. [29] Many of the songs in the musical have become popular outside the theater. "All I Ask of You" was even recorded as a pop single.
M: 나도 동의해. 그 뮤지컬의 노래들 중 많은 곡들이 극장 밖에서도 유명해졌잖아. "All I Ask of You"는 심지어 싱글 팝송으로 기록을 세웠지.

F: I'm sure it will be totally different to hear that music performed live. Hey, how much did the tickets cost you? I bet they are expensive.
F: 그 노래가 라이브로 공연되는 걸 듣는 건 분명 다를거

야. 야, 그 티켓 구하는데 얼마나 들었어? 틀림없이 비쌀텐데.

M: Well, they are expensive, but they didn't cost me a penny. I won the tickets in a raffle held by Century Department Store. 30) I was quite surprised when I found out I won. I'd practically forgotten about joining the raffle.

M: 음, 비싸긴 한데, 한 푼도 안 들었어. Century 백화점이 주최한 추첨행사에서 그 티켓에 당첨됐거든. 당첨된 걸 알았을 때 상당히 놀랐어. 그 추첨 행사에 참가한 걸 거의 잊어버리고 있었다니까.

F: Wow! I wish I were as lucky as you, Edmund. 31) I'd surely appreciate winning those tickets.

F: 와! 나도 너만큼 운이 좋았으면 좋겠어, Edmund. 내가 그 티켓에 당첨되면 분명 기뻤을 텐데.

M: 31) But you don't have to, Rose. I'm already asking you to go to the theater with me! So, will you come with me tomorrow?

M: 그럴 필요 없어, Rose. 이미 너한테 극장에 같이 가자고 하고 있잖아! 자, 내일 나랑 같이 갈래?

F: Of course! I've never been to a musical before. How can I pass up this chance? But how do we get to New York on such short notice?

F: 물론이지! 뮤지컬을 보러 간 적이 한 번도 없었거든. 내가 어떻게 이 기회를 놓칠 수 있겠어? 그런데 우리가 어떻게 그렇게 갑자기 뉴욕에 가지?

M: Oh, we won't have to go Broadway to see it. They're bringing it here! They're performing *The Phantom of the Opera* at the Maryland Center Stage Theater.

M: 아, 우리는 그걸 보러 브로드웨이에 갈 필요는 없어. 그들이 여기서 공연을 할 예정이거든. Maryland Center Stage 극장에서 <오페라의 유령>을 공연을 하게 될 거야.

F: Fantastic! That's just a stone's throw away from where we live. But why are they bringing the show here?

F: 멋진데! 거긴 우리가 사는 곳에서 아주 가깝잖아. 그런데 왜 그들이 여기에서 공연을 하려는 거야?

M: 32) Well, the production company wants to branch out into a broader market. And, since not everyone can get to Broadway, the producers decided to take the musical on the road.

M: 음, 제작사가 더 넓은 시장으로 진출하기를 원해. 그리고, 모두가 브로드웨이에 갈 수는 없으니까, 제작자들이 그 뮤지컬로 순회공연 하기로 했어.

F: I see··· How long will the musical be running here?

F: 그렇구나. 그 뮤지컬이 여기서 얼마나 상연되려나?

M: It will only run for two days, but 33) our tickets are good for either day. However, I can't wait to see it, so I suggest we watch the show during its first performance tomorrow night.

M: 이틀밖에 상연 안 하긴 하지만, 우리 티켓은 어느 날이든 유효해. 그런데, 나는 그 공연을 빨리 보고 싶으니까, 내일 밤에 하는 첫 번째 공연을 보자.

F: That will be perfect, Edmund. Thank you for inviting me.

F: 그거 좋은데, Edmund. 초대해줘서 고마워.

M: You're welcome, Rose. I'll pick you up at seven.

M: 천만에, Rose. 7시에 데리러 갈게.

어휘

musical **n.** 뮤지컬
run **v.** (영화)상영되다, (공연)상연되다, 계속되다
perform **v.** 공연하다, 연주하다
performance **n.** 공연
awesome **adj.** 멋진
compose **v.** 작곡하다
novel **n.** 소설
mysterious **adj.** 기이한, 신비에 싸인
disfigured **adj.** 흠이 있는, 흉한 외모를 가진
lyrics **n.** 노래 가사
raffle **n.** 추첨(행사), 복권식 판매
practically **ad.** 거의, 사실상
appreciate **v.** 기뻐하다, 고마워하다, (어떤 상황 등을) 환영하다
pass up **phr v.** (기회, 제안 등을) 놓치다, 거절하다
branch out **phr v.** 진출하다
take sth on the road **phr v.** (연극 등을) 순회공연 하다
suggest **v.** 제안하다
good **adj.** (표 등이) 유효한
can't wait to **phr v.** 빨리 ~하고 싶어 하다

27. 세부사항

왜 Edmund는 Rose를 보러 갔는가?

(a) 그녀에게 대회에서 우승한 것에 대해 말하기 위해
(b) 그녀에게 무료 티켓을 주기 위해
(c) 공연 행사에 그녀를 초대하기 위해
(d) 그가 본 연극에 대해 그녀에게 말하기 위해

해설 Edmund의 첫 번째 대사를 보면, 그가 브로드웨이 공연 티켓을 두 장 가지고 있다며 Rose에게 같이 가자고 제안하고(I have two tickets for a Broadway musical. Would you like to go with me?) 있으므로, 정답은 (b)이다.

정답 (b)

어휘
contest **n.** 대회
theatrical **adj.** 공연의, 연극의

28. 세부사항

Rose는 어떻게 <오페라의 유령>에 대해 잘 알게 되었는가?

(a) 영화 버전을 봄으로써
(b) 작곡가의 팬이 됨으로써
(c) 비평가들의 비평을 읽음으로써
(d) 라이브 공연을 봄으로써

해설 Rose의 세 번째 대사를 보면, 무대 공연을 본 적은 없고 영화로 만들어진 작품으로 딱 한 번 봤다고(Not onstage. I've only seen one of the film versions.) 말하고 있으므로, 정답은 (a)이다.

정답 (a)

어휘
be familiar with **phr v.** ~에 대해 익숙하다[잘 알다]

29. 추론

Edmund에 따르면, 이 뮤지컬이 연극계 밖에서 인기 있다는 가장 좋은 신호는 무엇인가?

(a) 브로드웨이에서 오랫동안 상연되었다.
(b) 로맨틱한 줄거리가 잘 알려져 있다.
(c) 싱글로 발매된 곡이 있었다.
(d) 베스트셀러 소설로 각색되었다.

해설 Edmund의 여섯 번째 대사를 보면 그 뮤지컬의 노래들 중 많은 곡들 이 극장 밖에서도 유명했으며 싱글 팝송으로 기록도 세웠다는 것을(Many of the songs in the musical have become popular outside the theater. "All I Ask of You" was even recorded as a pop single.) 알 수 있으므로, 정답은 (c)이다.

정답 (c)

어휘
storyline **n.** 줄거리
release **v.** 발매하다, 발표하다

30. 특정정보

Edmund가 표를 받았을 때 그렇게 놀란 이유는 무엇인가?

(a) 그는 추첨에 참여하는 것을 잊어버렸다.
(b) 그는 그것들이 너무 비싸다고 생각했다.
(c) 그는 표가 다 팔렸다고 생각했다.
(d) 그는 추첨에 참가한 것을 기억하지 못했다.

해설 Edmund의 일곱 번째 대사를 보면, 추첨에 참가했다는 사실을 까맣게 잊고 있어서 당첨되었다는 사실에 놀랐다는(I was quite surprised when I found out I won. I'd practically forgotten about joining the raffle.)내용이므로, 정답은 (d)이다.

정답 (d)

어휘
expensive **adj.** 비싼, 돈이 많이 드는
raffle **n.** 추첨, 제비뽑기

31. **특정정보**
Edmund에 따르면, 왜 Rose는 복권에 당첨될 필요가 없는가?

(a) 그가 그녀와 함께 뮤지컬을 보길 원하기 때문에
(b) 구할 수 있는 티켓이 많기 때문에
(c) 그 뮤지컬이 단 이틀 동안만 공연하기 때문에
(d) 그가 그녀에게 그의 티켓 중 한 장을 팔 것이기 때문에

해설 Rose의 일곱 번째 대사를 보면, 본인도 뮤지컬 티켓에 당첨되었으면 정말 기뻐했을 것이라고(I'd surely appreciate winning those tickets.) 하자, Edmund가 여덟 번째 대사에서 본인이 같이 가자고 하고 있으니 그럴 필요가 없다고(But you don't have to, Rose. I'm already asking you to go to the theater with me!) 말하고 있으므로, 정답은 (a)이다.

정답 (a)

어휘
plenty of **adj.** 많은, 풍부한
available **adj.** 구할 수 있는, 이용 가능한

32. **추론**
제작자들이 더 많은 관객에게 다가가고 싶어하는 이유는 무엇인 것 같은가?

(a) 브로드웨이의 재정적 손실을 극복하기 위해
(b) 제작사의 티켓 판매량을 증가시키기 위해
(c) 제휴 백화점들을 지원하기 위해
(d) 지역 극장 회사들을 지원하기 위해

해설 Edmund의 열 번째 대사를 보면, 왜 메릴랜드에서 뮤지컬 공연을 하냐는 Rose의 질문에 제작사가 조금 더 넓은 시장으로 진출하고 싶어하고 (the production company wants to branch out into a broader market), 브로드웨이에서 공연을 볼 수 없는 사람들을 위해 순회공연을 한다고(And, since not everyone can get to Broadway, the producers decided to take the musical on the road.) 말하고 있으므로, 판매량을 늘리기 위함이라고 추론할 수 있다. 따라서 정답은 (b)이다.

정답 (b)

어휘
audience **n.** 관객
increase **v.** 증가시키다, 증가하다
support **v.** 지원하다

33. **세부사항**
왜 Edmund는 첫째 날 밤에 뮤지컬을 보길 원하는가?

(a) 그는 첫 공연들이 항상 더 낫다고 생각한다.
(b) 그는 첫 공연 티켓만 가지고 있다.
(c) 그는 Rose에게 밤이 더 낫다는 것을 알고 있다.
(d) 그는 가능한 빨리 그것을 보고 싶어한다.

해설 Edmund의 열한 번째 대사를 보면, 티켓이 이틀 중 어느 때나 유효하지만(our tickets are good for either day.) 본인이 공연을 빨리 보고 싶으니 첫 번째 공연을 보자고 제안하고(I can't wait to see it, so I suggest we watch the show during its first performance tomorrow night.) 있으므로, 정답은 (d)이다.

정답 (d)

어휘
performance **n.** 공연, 성과
as soon as possible **phr.** 가능한 빨리, 빠른 시일 내에

Part 2 **Q. 34-39**

34: What is the speaker promoting for the company?
35: Why most likely is Cosmic Technologies now concentrating on the tablet market?
36: What part of the Cosmic T1 makes using it feel immersive?
37: According to the speaker, how most likely did Cosmic Technologies make the tablet better than a laptop?
38: How can the Cosmic T1's development be described best?
39: Based on the talk, what is the advantage of reserving the Cosmic T1 in advance?

Good morning, ladies and gentlemen. I'm a product manager with Cosmic Technologies, and 34) I'm here today to introduce to you our latest product, the Cosmic T1. The Cosmic T1 is a 13-inch tablet featuring the convenience of a smart phone and the power of a desktop computer. Ready or not, when this game-changing device hits the shelves this coming spring, the computing world will never be the same.
좋은 아침입니다, 신사 숙녀 여러분. 저는 Cosmic Technologies의 제품 관리자입니다. 저는 여기서 오늘 여러분께 우리의 최신 제품인 Cosmic T1을 소개하고자 합니다. Cosmic T1은 스마트폰의 편리함과 데스크탑 컴퓨터의 힘을 특징으로 하는 13인치 태블릿입니다. 준비가 됐든 안 됐

든, 이 획기적인 장치가 다가오는 봄에 출시되면, 컴퓨팅 세계는 결코 예전 같지 않을 것입니다.

Many of you may be wondering why we are expanding our focus to tablets when our company is best known for our cutting-edge smart phones. It may seem like a risky proposition, especially since the tablet market has grown extremely competitive over the years. Well, we want to be known as more than just a maker of advanced but affordable phones. 35) Through research we have also learned that a large part of our customer base is constantly on the move. Whether they're working from home, taking international business trips, or finishing projects during vacation, people's technology needs are shifting.
많은 분들이 저희 회사가 최첨단 스마트폰으로 가장 잘 알려져 있는데 왜 태블릿에 초점을 맞추고 있는지 궁금해하실 겁니다. 특히 태블릿 시장이 수년간 매우 경쟁적으로 성장했기 때문에 이것은 위험한 일처럼 보일 수 있습니다. 음, 우리는 단지 성능은 우수하지만 가격은 합리적인 전화기 제조사 이상으로 알려지기를 원합니다. 또한 연구를 통해 고객층의 상당 부분이 끊임없이 바뀌고 있다는 사실을 알게 되었습니다. 그들이 집에서 일하든, 해외 출장을 가든, 휴가 동안 프로젝트를 끝내든, 사람들의 기술 요구는 변하고 있습니다.

At Cosmic Technologies, we have set our sights on a lofty goal. We aim to market a tablet so durable, so powerful, and so dynamic that consumers will never need a desktop or laptop ever again. We hope that the Cosmic T1 tablet will be considered the ultimate universal device.
저희 Cosmic Technologies는 높은 목표를 세웠습니다. 저희 회사는 내구성이 뛰어나고, 강력하며, 역동적이어서 소비자들이 다시는 데스크톱이나 노트북을 찾을 필요가 없는 태블릿을 출시하는 것을 목표로 합니다. 우리는 Cosmic T1 태블릿이 궁극적인 범용 장치로 여겨지기를 바랍니다.

Running on the latest operating system, the Cosmic T1 can compete with all of the top models of the established brands. 36) It sports a whopping 13-inch display that rivals any laptop's screen to make watching movies and playing online games a truly immersive experience. It has a triple camera that will give your photos and videos more depth. If you are a gaming enthusiast, the T1's superfast processor and vivid graphics won't disappoint. It also has an incredible storage capacity of one terabyte that keeps our tablet in pace with most desktop computers.
최신 운영 체제에서 실행되는 Cosmic T1은 기성 브랜드들의 모든 상위 모델과 경쟁할 수 있습니다. 그것은 다른 노트북 화면에 필적하는 거대한 13인치 디스플레이를 자랑하며 영화 시청과 온라인 게임 플레이를 진정 몰입도 높은 경험으로 만들어줍니다. 그것은 당신의 사진과 비디오를 더 깊이 있게 해줄 3중 카메라를 가지고 있습니다. 만약 당신이 게임 매니아라면, T1의 초고속 프로세서와 생생한 그래픽은 실망시키지 않을 것입니다. 또한 대부분의 데스크탑 컴퓨터 수준에 버금가는 1테라바이트의 놀라운 저장 용량을 갖추고 있습니다.

The Cosmic T1 has the advantage over laptops when it comes to convenience. Even the sleekest laptops can be bulky, heavy, and easy to break, requiring a special bag for transport. Our tablet, however, can go practically anywhere! 37) With its polycarbonate housing, you can throw it into any large bag without worrying about bumping or scratching your device.
편의성 면에서 Cosmic T1은 노트북보다 우월합니다. 심지어 가장 날렵한 노트북도 부피가 크고, 무겁고, 부서지기 쉬우며, 운송을 위해 특별한 가방이 필요합니다. 그러나 당사의 태블릿은 사실상 어디든 갈 수 있습니다! 폴리카보네이트 하우징으로, 장치를 부딪치거나 긁힐 염려 없이 어떤 큰 가방에도 태블릿을 넣을 수 있습니다.

Under the hood, the tablet has a battery that can last for 20 hours on one charge. This exceptionally long life is made possible by equipping the tablet with the latest, most powerful lithium-ion battery on the market. It also comes with a USB cable, earphones, and a charger. The Cosmic T1 is backed up by a one-year warranty on parts and services.
내부를 보면, 한 번 충전하면 20시간 동안 지속될 수 있는 배터리가 있습니다. 이 유난히 긴 수명은 시중에서 가장 강력한 최신 리튬 이온 배터리를 태블릿에 탑재함으로써 가능해집니다. 또한, USB 케이블, 이어폰, 충전기도 함께 제공됩니다. Cosmic T1은 부품과 서비스에 대해 1년 보증이 지원됩니다.

38) Cosmic Technologies' entry into the tablet market is preceded by years of research and de-

velopment. After careful market deliberation, we have come up with the ultimate tablet in terms of versatility and strength. Our products also have a very reasonable pricing structure considering the top-notch quality. With the Cosmic T1, you pay for nothing more than superb performance and great styling. Be the envy of your friends. 39) If you make a reservation for the Cosmic T1 now, you can get a wireless keyboard and smart pencil at a highly discounted price.

Cosmic Technologies의 태블릿 시장 진출에는 수년간의 연구와 개발이 선행되었습니다. 신중한 시장에 대한 심사숙고 끝에, 저희 회사는 다양한 기능과 내구성 측면에서 최고의 태블릿을 고안해냈습니다. 최고급 품질을 고려할 때 저희 제품은 또한 매우 합리적인 가격 구조를 가지고 있습니다. Cosmic T1과 함께, 당신이 지불한 것은 최고의 성능, 그리고 멋진 스타일에 불과합니다. 친구들에게 부러움의 대상이 되세요. 지금 Cosmic T1을 예약하시면 무선 키보드와 스마트 펜슬을 매우 할인된 가격에 받으실 수 있습니다.

어휘
latest **adj.** (가장) 최신의, 최근의
advanced **adj.** 고급의, 선진의
feature **v.** 특징으로 삼다, 포함하다 **n.** 기능, 특성
connectivity **n.** 연결(성), 접속(성)
game-changing **adj.** 판도를 바꾸는
device **n.** 장치, 기기
hit the shelves **phr v.** (새롭게) 출시되다
competitive **adj.** 경쟁적인
need **n.** 요구, 수요
sport **v.** 자랑스럽게 선보이다
enthusiast **n.** ~에 열광하는 사람, -광
storage **n.** 용량, 저장 공간
housing **n.** 외관
under the hood **phr.** 내부에
charge **n.** 충전
exceptionally **ad.** 예외적으로
equip **v.** (장비 등을) 갖추다, 갖추게 하다
deliberation **n.** 고려, 숙고
ultimate **adj.** 궁극적인, 최고의
superb **adj.** 최고의

34. 특정정보
화자는 회사를 위해 무엇을 홍보하고 있는가?

(a) 최신 스마트폰
(b) 고급 디지털 카메라
(c) 향상된 운영 체제
(d) 새 전자 기기

해설 첫 번째 문단을 보면, 회사의 최신 제품인 Cosmic T1을 소개하러 왔다고(I'm here today to introduce to you our latest product, the Cosmic T1.) 하고, 스마트폰의 편리함과 데스크탑 컴퓨터의 힘을 특징으로 하는 13인치 태블릿(The Cosmic T1 is a 13-inch tablet featuring the convenience of a smart phone and the power of a desktop computer.)이라고 설명하고 있으므로, 정답은 (d)이다.

정답 (d)

어휘
promote **v.** 홍보하다
operating system **n.** 운영 체제
gadget **n.** 기기, 장치

35. 추론
왜 Cosmic Technologies가 현재 태블릿 시장에 집중하고 있는 것 같은가?

(a) 시장에 저렴한 태블릿이 부족하기 때문에
(b) 그들이 전화선을 중단했기 때문에
(c) 사람들이 기술을 사용하는 방식이 변화하고 있기 때문에
(d) 소비자가 데스크톱에 싫증을 느끼고 있기 때문에

해설 두 번째 문단을 보면, 연구를 통해 고객층의 상당 부분이 끊임없이 바뀌고 있다는 사실을 알게 되었다고(Through research we have also learned that a large part of our customer base is constantly on the move.) 말하고 있으며, 사람들의 기술 요구가 변화하고 있다고(people's technology needs are shifting.) 말하고 있기 때문에, 태블릿에 집중하고 있다는 것을 추론할 수 있다. 따라서 정답은 (c)이다.

정답 (c)

어휘
affordable **adj.** 알맞은, 줄 수 있는
consumer **n.** 소비자

TEST 1

36. 특정정보

Cosmic T1의 어떤 부분이 그것을 사용하는 데 몰입감을 느끼게 하는가?

(a) 화면의 상당한 크기
(b) 심층 카메라 기술
(c) 신속한 처리 능력
(d) 뛰어난 저장 용량

해설 네 번째 문단을 보면, 영화 시청과 온라인 게임 플레이를 몰입도 높은 경험으로 만들기 위해 다른 노트북 화면에 필적하는 13인치의 거대한 디스플레이를 자랑스럽게 선보이고 있다고(It sports a whopping 13-inch display that rivals any laptop's screen to make watching movies and playing online games a truly immersive experience) 나와있으므로, 정답은 (a)이다.

정답 (a)

어휘
considerable **adj.** 상당한, 많은
capacity **n.** 용량, 수용력

37. 추론

화자에 따르면, Cosmic Technologies는 노트북보다 태블릿을 어떻게 더 뛰어나게 만들었는가?

(a) 특수 운반 케이스와 함께 판매함으로써
(b) 연장된 배터리 수명을 제공함으로써
(c) 내장된 이어폰으로 제작함으로써
(d) 손상을 더 어렵게 함으로써

해설 다섯 번째 문단을 보면, 폴리카보네이트 하우징으로 장치를 부딪치거나 긁을 염려 없이 어떠한 큰 가방에도 태블릿을 넣을 수 있다는(With its polycarbonate housing, you can throw it into any large bag without worrying about bumping or scratching your device.)내용이 나와 있으므로, 손상을 더 어렵게 함으로써 뛰어나게 제작했다는 것을 추론할 수 있다. 따라서 정답은 (d)이다.

정답 (d)

어휘
damage **n.** 손상, 피해

38. 추론

Cosmic T1의 발전이 어떻게 가장 잘 설명될 수 있는가?

(a) 1년 안에 완성되었다.
(b) 많은 준비과정을 수반했다.
(c) 회사에 많은 위험을 제기한다.
(d) 다른 회사의 기술에 기반을 두었다.

해설 마지막 문단을 보면, 태블릿 시장에 진입하기 이전에 수년간의 연구와 개발이 선행되었다고 하고(Cosmic Technologies' entry into the tablet market is preceded by years of research and development.), 심사숙고 끝에 최고의 태블릿을 만들어냈다고(After careful market deliberation, we have come up with the ultimate tablet) 말하고 있으므로, 제품을 개발하는 데 많은 준비과정을 거쳤다는 것을 추론할 수 있다. 따라서 정답은 (b)이다.

정답 (b)

어휘
preparation **n.** 준비, 준비과정
involve **v.** 수반하다
risk **n.** 위험, 위험요소

39. 추론

강연 내용에 따르면, Cosmic T1을 미리 예약하는 것의 이점은 무엇인가?

(a) 일부 액세서리를 더 저렴한 비용으로 구입하는 것
(b) 모든 친구들이 질투하게 하는 것
(c) 태블릿 가격을 크게 할인 받는 것
(d) 한정 출시품에 대한 독점 구매 기회를 갖는 것

해설 마지막 문단을 보면, 지금 예약하면 무선 키보드와 스마트 펜슬을 할인된 가격에 받을 수 있다는(If you make a reservation for the Cosmic T1 now, you can get a wireless keyboard and smart pencil at a highly discounted price.) 내용이 나와있으므로, 정답은 (a)이다.

정답 (a)

어휘
jealous **adj.** 질투하는, 시기하는
discount **n.** 할인

Part 3 Q. 40-45

40: What does Patty want to see Philip for?
41: According to Philip, what is an advantage of a business with sole ownership?
42: According to Philip, what is a benefit of a partnership?
43: According to Patty, why are business matters hard for partners to handle?
44: Which aspect of a partnership most likely appeals to Patty the least?
45: Based on the exchange, what has Patty probably decided after the conversation?

F: Hello, Philip. I'm glad to see you here at the park.
F: 안녕, Philip. 여기 공원에서 널 보니 기뻐.

M: Hi, Patty. It's nice to see you here, too. What's up?
M: 안녕, Patty. 나도 여기서 널 보니 좋다. 무슨 일이야?

F: Well, I've been thinking about something for days now. You see, 40) I want to start a business, but I don't know whether to start a business on my own or with a partner.
F: 음, 나는 지금 며칠째 무언가에 대해서 생각해 오고 있어. 있잖아, 내가 사업을 시작하고 싶은데 나 혼자 사업을 시작해야 할지 아니면 동업자와 함께 시작해야 할지 모르겠어.

M: I see… 40) And you want my opinion on which business setup is better? I'd be happy to help. How about we discuss the advantages and disadvantages of both? That way, you can decide for yourself.
M: 그렇구나. 그래서 어떤 사업 구조가 더 좋을지에 대한 내 의견을 원하는 거니? 내가 도움이 된다면 기쁠 거야. 우리가 그 모두의 장점과 단점에 대해 의논해보는 건 어떨까? 그렇게 하면, 네가 스스로 결정할 수 있을 거야.

F: Sounds good to me. Where should we start?
F: 좋은 생각이야. 어디서부터 시작할까?

M: Let's begin with running a business on your own. The first advantage of sole or single ownership is that the business is easier to set up because there is less paperwork and fewer legal requirements involved. 41) Also, you have complete control of the business once you set it up.
M: 너 혼자 사업을 운영하는 걸로 시작해보자. 개인 혹은 단독 기업의 첫 번째 장점은 수반되는 서류 작업과 법적 요구 사항이 더 적기 때문에 사업을 시작하는 게 더 쉽다는 거야. 또한, 네가 그걸 시작하면 그 사업에 대한 완전한 주도권을 가질 수 있지.

F: That sounds great. You mean I get to make all the business rules and have direct control over the decision-making process?
F: 그거 정말 좋은 것 같아. 네가 의미하는 게 내가 모든 사업 규정들을 만들고 의사 결정 과정에 있어서 직접적인 주도권을 갖게 된다는 거니?

M: Correct. There are also tax advantages for a solely-owned business. More importantly, all the profit the business makes is yours.
M: 맞아. 또 단독 소유 사업을 위한 세금 혜택들도 있어. 더 중요한 건, 그 사업이 창출하는 모든 수익이 네 것이라는 거지.

F: That sounds very encouraging, Philip. Now, what about the disadvantages?
F: 정말 용기를 북돋워주네, Philip. 자, 그럼 단점들은 어떻지?

M: The downside to a sole ownership is that working alone may overwhelm you and limit the company's growth. You will also have to take personal responsibility for any of the company's missteps and failures.
M: 개인 기업의 불리한 점은 혼자 일한다는 게 너를 압도해서 회사의 성장을 제한할 지도 모른다는 거야. 또한 회사의 어떠한 실수와 실패에 대해 개인적인 책임을 져야 해.

F: I see... And since I'm running the business alone, I could have a hard time raising funds for its growth. Isn't that right?
F: 그렇구나… 그리고 나 혼자서 기업을 운영하기 때문에, 회사의 성장을 위한 자금을 조달하는데 힘든 시간을 보낼 수 있겠구나. 그렇지 않니?

M: That's right. In addition, being the only manager, it will not be easy for you to take a vacation or be away from your business for a few days when needed.
M: 맞아. 게다가, 유일한 관리자이기 때문에, 필요할 때 휴가를 내거나 며칠 동안 업무로부터 떨어져 있기가 쉽지 않을 거야.

F: That would be really hard on both the business and my family. Now, what about a partnership?
F: 그건 그 사업과 내 가족들 모두에게 정말 안 좋은 영향을 미칠 거야. 자, 그럼 동업은 어때?

M: One of the advantages of a partnership is that you could have more money to start the business since you and your partner will combine your resources. You would also 42) have the added benefit of splitting the tasks, responsibilities, and risks of the business with your partner.
M: 동업의 장점들 중 하나는 너와 네 동업자가 자산을 합칠 것이기 때문에 사업을 시작하기 위해 더 많은 자본을 가질 수 있다는 거야. 너는 또한 그 사업의 업무, 책무, 그리고 위험요소들을 동업자와 분담할 수 있다는 추가적인 이점도 가질 거야.

F: I see. That could make it easier for both of us to run the company. And, in contrast to sole ownership, I can have someone attend to the business in case I decide to take a vacation. Okay, so what are the drawbacks of a partnership?
F: 알았어. 그건 두 사람 모두 회사를 운영하기가 수월하게 만들 수 있겠다. 그리고, 개인 기업과는 다르게, 내가 휴가를 가기로 결심하는 경우 그 업무를 처리해줄 누군가를 가질 수도 있는 거네. 알았어, 그럼 동업의 문제점들은 뭘까?

M: One of the biggest risks of a partnership is the possibility of conflicts between partners.
M: 동업의 가장 큰 위험요소 중 하나는 동업자 간 갈등의 가능성이야.

F: I agree, Philip. 43) Business matters can be sensitive issues that even the most reasonable partners may find difficult to deal with.
F: 동의해, Philip. 사업상의 문제는 가장 합리적인 동업자들조차 다루기 힘들어 할 지도 모르는 민감한 사안이 될 수 있지.

M: That's true. Also, you will have to share the business's profits with your partner. And lastly, 44) if your partner fails to pay his or her debts or breaks a contract, you might have to share the legal consequences or suffer penalties, too.
M: 그건 사실이야. 또한, 사업의 수익을 너의 동업자와 나눠야 할 거야. 그리고 마지막으로, 만일 동업자가 빚을 갚지 못하거나 계약을 파기한다면, 너는 또한 법적 책임을 공유하거나 처벌을 받아야 할지도 몰라.

F: Really? Hmmm··· 44) That pretty much outweighs all the benefits of a partnership for me. I didn't know a partnership could involve that much risk!
F: 정말? 흠··· 나에겐 동업의 모든 혜택들보다 그게 꽤 더 큰 것 같은데. 나는 동업이 그렇게 많은 위험요소를 수반할 수 있는지 몰랐어!

M: 45) Not very encouraging when you're just starting out in business, huh?
M: 네가 막 사업을 시작하려고 할 때 그다지 희망을 주는 건 아니지, 응?

F: 45) Definitely not. Thank you very much, Philip. You've been a great help.
F: 절대로 아니지. 매우 고마워, Philip. 네가 큰 도움이 되었어.

M: You're welcome, Patty. I'm glad I could help you make a decision.
M: 천만에, Patty. 네가 결정을 할 수 있게 도와줄 수 있었다니 기뻐.

어휘
setup **n.** 구조
advantage **n.** 장점, 혜택
disadvantage **n.** 단점
run **v.** 운영하다
decision-making **n.** 의사결정
encouraging **adj.** 힘을 북돋아 주는, 희망을 주는
downside **n.** 불리한 점
overwhelm **v.** (너무 많은 것들이) 압도하다, 어쩔 줄 모르게 하다
raise **v.** (자금 등을) 조달하다, 모으다
in addition **ad.** 게다가
be hard on **phr.** ~에 안 좋은 영향을 미치다
split **v.** 분담하다, 나누다
operation **n.** 사업, 운영
in contrast to **ad.** ~와는 대조적으로
attend to sth **phr v.** ~을 처리하다
drawback **n.** 문제점
sensitive **adj.** 민감한
outweigh **v.** ~보다 더 크다, 중요하다

40. 세부사항
무엇을 위해 Patty는 Philip을 만나고 싶어하는가?

(a) 그녀가 두 종류의 사업 중에서 선택하도록 돕기 위해
(b) 그녀에게 어떤 서비스를 제공할지 결정하는 것을 돕기 위해
(c) 그에게 전문적인 요구 사항에 대해 물어보기 위해
(d) 그에게 그녀의 새로운 벤처 사업에 대해 이야기하기 위해

해설 Patty의 두 번째 대사를 보면, 그녀가 사업을 시작하고 싶은데 개인 기업으로 시작할지 동업자와 시작할지 모르겠다고(I want to start a business, but I don't know whether to start a business on my own or with a partner.) 하자, 그 다음 대사에서 Philip이 어느 사업 구조가 더 나은지 본인의 의견을 원하는 거냐며(And you want my opinion on which business setup is better?) 확인하고 있으므로, Patty는 Philip이 두 가지 사업 형태 중 하나를 선택할 수 있게 도와주기를 원하는 것임을 알 수 있다. 따라서 정답은 (a)이다.

정답 (a)

어휘
venture **n.** 벤처 (사업), 모험

41. 특정정보
Philip에 따르면, 개인 기업의 이점은 무엇인가?

(a) 더 높은 성공 가능성
(b) 더 적은 복잡한 법적 분쟁
(c) 근로자 고용의 용이성 증대
(d) 사업에 대한 완전한 주도권

해설 Philip의 세 번째 대사를 보면, 개인 기업의 경우 그 사업에 대한 완전한 주도권을 가질 수 있다고(Also, you have complete control of the business once you set it up.) 말하고 있으므로, 정답은 (d)이다.

정답 (d)

어휘
ease **n.** 용이함

42. 특정정보
Philip에 따르면, 동업의 이점은 무엇인가?

(a) 특별한 세금 면제를 받는다.
(b) 성공하는데 더 적은 일을 요구한다.
(c) 동업자들이 의무를 분담할 수 있다.
(d) 동업자들이 함께 여행을 갈 수 있다.

해설 Philip의 일곱 번째 대사를 보면, 업무, 책무, 위험요소 등을 분담할 수 있다는 추가적인 이점이 있다고(have the added benefit of splitting the tasks, responsibilities, and risks of the business with your partner) 말하고 있으므로, 정답은 (c)이다.

정답 (c)

어휘
exemption **n.** 면제
obligation **n.** (업무상) 의무

43. 세부사항
Patty에 따르면, 왜 사업상의 문제들은 동업자들이 다루기 어려운가?

(a) 항상 오해로 이어진다.
(b) 종종 사업을 불안정하게 만든다.
(c) 개인에 의해 더 잘 다루어 진다.
(d) 민감한 파트너에게도 긴장을 일으킬 수 있다.

해설 Patty의 아홉 번째 대사를 보면, 사업상의 문제들이 가장 합리적인 동업자들도 다루기 어려워하는 민감한 사안이 될 수 있다고(Business matters can be sensitive issues that even the most reasonable partners may find difficult to deal with) 말하고 있으므로, 정답은 (d)이다.

정답 (d)

어휘
misunderstanding **n.** 오해
falter **v.** 불안정해지다, 흔들리다
individual **n.** 개인
sensible **adj.** 민감한

44. 추론
어떤 파트너십의 특징이 Patty가 가장 마음에 들어 하지 않을 것 같은가?

(a) 사업의 완전한 주도권을 갖지 못하는 것
(b) 동업자의 빚을 책임져야 할 수도 있는 것
(c) 동업자가 자리를 비울 때 사업을 혼자 운영해야 하는 것
(d) 동업자와 수익을 나누는 것

해설 Philip의 아홉 번째 대사를 보면, 만약 동업자가 빚을 갚지 못하거나 계약을 파기한다면, 본인이 법적 책임을 공유하거나 처벌을 받아야 할 수도 있다는 (if your partner fails to pay his or her debts or breaks a contract, you might have to share the legal consequences or suffer penalties, too.) 내용이 나와있고, 이에 대해 Patty가 동업의 모든 혜택들보다 이 단점이 더 크다고(That pretty much outweighs all the benefits of a partnership for me) 말하며 그렇게 많은 위험요소를 수반할 줄 몰랐다고(I didn't know a partnership could involve that much risk!) 말하고 있으므로 동업자의 빚을 책임져야 하는 것이 가장 마음에 들지 않는다는 것을 추론할 수 있다. 따라서 정답은 (b)이다.

정답 (b)

어휘
debt **n.** 빚, 부채

45. 추론
이 대화에 근거하여, 대화 이후에 Patty는 무엇을 하기로 결정했을 것 같은가?

(a) 개인 사업자로 사업을 시작하기
(b) 동업을 신청하기
(c) 신뢰할 수 있는 비즈니스 파트너를 찾기
(d) 더 많은 자금을 벌 수 있는 방법을 생각하기

해설 Philip이 열 번째 대사를 보면, 그가 동업자의 채무나 계약을 대신 이행할 수도 있다는 점이 사업을 시작할 때 그다지 희망을 주는 건 아니지 않냐고(Not very encouraging when you're just starting out in business, huh?) 하자, Patty가 절대 아니라며 (Definitely not.) Philip의 말에 동의하고 있으므로, 동업을 하지 않고 개인 기업을 설립할 것이라고 추론할 수 있다. 따라서 정답은 (a)이다.

정답 (a)

어휘
seek **n.** 찾다, 구하다
reliable **adj.** 신뢰할 수 있는

Part 4 Q. 46-52

46: What is the talk all about?
47: Why most likely should one choose members who are highly enthusiastic?
48: How can one handle setbacks when organizing an event?
49: Based on the talk, what is one way of raising as much money as possible?
50: Based on the talk, what can one do to make the event known to as many people as possible?
51: How can taking some time off help in solving a problem?
52: Based on the talk, why does having fun most likely lead to success?

Hello, everyone. Welcome to Nashville's Annual Charity Workers Convention. I'm sure most of you would like to find a way to raise more money for your favorite charity. Now, there are many events that you can organize to raise funds, but the one that's most likely to draw the biggest crowd—and the most funds—is a benefit concert. 46) Let me tell you about the steps involved in organizing a benefit concert.
안녕하세요, 여러분. Nashville의 연례 자선 노동자 회의에 오신 것을 환영합니다. 여러분 대부분은 분명 여러분이 가장 좋아하는 자선단체를 위해 더 많은 돈을 모을 방법을 찾고 싶어할 것입니다. 자, 여러분이 기금을 모으기 위해 조직할 수 있는 많은 행사들이 있지만, 가장 많은 관중과 기금을 모을 가능성이 가장 높은 행사는 자선 콘서트입니다. 자선 콘서트를 조직하는 것과 관련된 단계에 대해 말씀드리겠습니다.

The first step is to form a team to assist you. 47) It must consist of individuals who share your enthusiasm, passion, and stamina. After all, as volunteers, they're not getting paid for the job. Surround yourself with people who are always positive and encouraging—even at the end of an unpleasant day. They should also be intelligent, trustworthy, and hardworking.
첫 번째 단계는 여러분을 도울 팀을 꾸리는 것입니다. 그것은 여러분의 열의, 열정, 그리고 체력을 공유하는 사람들로 구성되어야 합니다. 어쨌든, 자원봉사자로서, 그들은 그 일에 대한 보수를 받지 않을 것입니다. 심지어는 기분 나쁜 하루가 끝날 무렵이라도 언제나 긍정적이고 희망을 주는 사람들을 여러분 주변에 두십시오. 또한 그들은 똑똑하고, 신뢰할 수 있으며, 근면해야 합니다.

Next, 48) learn how to deal with the highs and lows of organizing a charity event. You'll probably be enthusiastic at the start, especially if many sponsors have pledged support and great bands have signed up. 48) However, there will be times when you'll be disappointed when a sponsor or a band backs out or a useful team member quits. These are the realities of organizing a benefit concert or any charitable event. 48) To see the project through, you must have flexibility and an open mind.
그 다음으로, 자선 행사를 준비하는 것의 즐거움과 어려움을 다룰 줄 아는 방법을 배우세요. 여러분은 아마 처음엔 열정적일 것입니다. 특히 많은 후원자들이 후원을 약속하고 대단한 음악밴드들이 계약했다면 말이죠. 그러나, 어떤 후원자나 음악밴드가 약속을 철회하거나 유능한 팀원이 그만 둘 때 여러분이 실망감을 느낄 때가 있을 거에요. 이들은 자선 콘서트 혹은 어떤 자선 행사를 준비하는 것의 현실입니다. 프로젝트를 끝까지 해내기 위해서, 여러분은 융통성이 있어야 하고 열린 마음을 가지고 있어야 합니다.

The third step is to handle your budget wisely. The goal of a benefit concert is to raise as much money as possible. This means spending as little of your money as you can in the process. 49) You may not succeed if you don't know how to manage your money. Unless you are certain an expense will pay off, try to cut back on your spending. And remember to look for deals where you can earn something for your services.
세 번째 단계는 예산을 현명하게 처리하는 것입니다. 자선 콘서트의 목표는 가능한 한 많은 돈을 모금하는 것입니다. 이는 당신이 그 과정에서 할 수 있는 한 적은 돈을 쓰는 것을 의미합니다. 돈을 관리하는 방법을 모르면 당신은 성공하지 못할 지도 모릅니다. 당신이 성공적인 지출을 확신할 수 없다면, 소비를 줄이도록 노력하세요. 그리고 여러분의 서비스를 위해 무언가를 얻을 수 있는 데서 거래를 찾는 것을 잊지 마십시오.

The fourth step is 50) to advertise aggressively. Make sure that your event is known to as many people as possible. Use all channels available to you, like social networking sites, newspapers and magazines, posters, and, especially, word of mouth. The more people that come to your benefit concert, the better it is for you and the charity.
네 번째 단계는 적극적으로 광고하는 것입니다. 반드시 여러분의 행사를 가능한 한 많은 사람들에게 알게 하십시오. 소셜 네트워크 사이트, 신문과 잡지, 포스터, 특히 입소문과 같은, 여러분이 이용 가능한 모든 수단을 사용하세요. 여러분의 자선 콘서트에 더 많은 사람들이 올수록, 여러분과 자선단체에 더 좋습니다.

51) To ensure the success of your event, take breaks on a regular schedule. As much as you want your event to succeed, going at it 24/7 is never your best option. Keep your mind fresh and your body healthy by taking some time off and doing something enjoyable. Go to the movies, or visit your favorite nature park. 51) Besides, doing something different for even an hour or so may help you find a solution to a problem you're facing.
행사의 성공을 보장하기 위해, 정기적인 일정에 따라 휴식을 취하십시오. 여러분은 행사가 성공하기를 원하시겠지만, 그 일에 하루종일 매진하는 것은 절대로 최선의 선택이 아닙니다. 휴식을 취하고 즐거운 일을 함으로써 여러분의 마음을 상쾌하게 하고 몸을 건강하게 유지하세요. 영화를 보러 가거나, 여러분이 가장 좋아하는 자연 공원을 방문하세요. 게다가, 한 시간 정도라도 다른 것을 하는 것은 여러분이 직면하고 있는 문제에 대한 해결책을 찾는데 도움이 될 수 있습니다.

52) I also advise that you smile and have fun. Being a great leader means inspiring those you lead. To do this, you must be inspired yourself. Enjoy the experience and appreciate every moment. Whether you are meeting a potential sponsor or assigning a team member to do a task, 52) your work will feel lighter and you're more likely to succeed if you have a smile on your face.
저는 또한 여러분이 미소를 짓고 즐겨야 한다고 조언하겠습니다. 좋은 리더는 여러분이 이끄는 사람들에게 열의를 심어주는 것을 의미합니다. 그러기 위해, 여러분 스스로 열의가 있어야 합니다. 그 경험을 즐기고 매 순간에 감사함을 느끼세요. 여러분이 잠재적인 후원자를 만나거나 팀원에게 해야 할 업무를 배정하든 간에, 여러분 얼굴에 미소를 짓는다면 여러분의 일은 더 쉽게 느껴질 것이고 그러면 여러분이 성공할 가능성이 더 높아질 것입니다.

Organizing a benefit concert may not be a walk in the park, but if you really devote yourself to it and work hard, then it will be one of the most rewarding experiences you'll have.
자선 콘서트를 조직하는 것은 아주 쉬운 일이 아닐지도 모르지만, 여러분이 정말 그것에 스스로 몰두하고 열심히 일한다면, 그건 여러분이 할 가장 보람 있는 경험들 중 하나가 될 것입니다.

어휘
annual **adj.** 연례의
charity **n.** 자선, 자선단체
convention **n.** (대규모) 회의
draw **v.** (이목, 반응, 사람 등을) 끌다
benefit concert **n.** 자선 콘서트
assist **v.** 돕다
onsist of **phr v.** ~로 구성되다
enthusiasm **n.** 열정, 열의
surround **v.** 두다, 둘러싸다
highs and lows **n.**즐거움과 어려움, 좋은 때와 힘든 때
pledge **v.** 계약하다, 약속하다
disappointed **adj.** 실망한
back out **phr v.** (하기로 했던 것을) 철회하다, 그만두다
see through **phr v.** 끝까지 해내다
flexibility **n.** 융통성, 유연성
budget **n.** 예산, 지출 예상 비용
channel **n.** 수단, 방법, 경로
ensure **v.**보장하다, 반드시 ~하게 하다
go at sth **phr v.** ~을 열심히 하다
24/7 **ad.** 하루 24시간, 1년 내내, 언제나
face **v.** 직면하다
inspire **v.** 영감을 주다, (열의를 갖도록) 고무하다
appreciate **v.** 감사하다, 고마워하다
potential **adj.** 잠재적인
assign **v.** (업무, 책임 등을) 배정하다, 맡기다

46. 주제

연설의 주제는 무엇인가?

(a) 자선단체를 지원하는 방법
(b) 콘서트를 계획하는 단계
(c) 좋은 리더가 되는 방법들
(d) 이벤트를 홍보하는 방법

해설 첫 번째 문단을 보면, 자선 콘서트를 조직하는 단계에 대해서 말해줄 것이라고(Let me tell you about the steps involved in organizing a benefit concert.) 말하고 있으므로, 정답은 (b)이다.

정답 (b)

어휘
support **v.** 지원하다

47. 추론

왜 매우 열정적인 구성원들을 선택해야 할 것 같은가?

(a) 다른 구성원들이 그들의 열정을 따라갈 수 있기 때문에
(b) 그들이 사람들을 더 잘 설득할 수 있기 때문에
(c) 그들은 급여에 의해 동기부여 되지 않을 것이기 때문에
(d) 그들은 더 오랜 시간 근무할 수 있기 때문에

해설 두 번째 문단을 보면, 팀 구성원들이 그 일에 대한 보수를 받지 않을 것이기(After all, as volunteers, they're not getting paid for the job.) 때문에, 함께 열의, 열정과 체력을 나눌 사람들로 팀이 구성되어야 한다고(It must consist of individuals who share your enthusiasm, passion, and stamina.) 말하고 있으므로, 정답은 (c)이다.

정답 (c)

어휘
motivate **v.** 동기를 부여하다

48. 세부사항

행사를 조직할 시 문제들을 어떻게 다룰 수 있는가?

(a) 적극적인 구성원들이 떠나지 않도록 설득함으로써
(b) 믿을 수 있는 사람들만을 대함으로써
(c) 많은 후원자들을 가입시킴으로써
(d) 실망스러운 상황에 적응함으로써

해설 세 번째 문단을 보면, 자선 행사를 준비하는 것의 즐거움과 어려움을 다루는 방법을 배우라고(learn how to deal with the highs and lows of organizing a charity event.) 하며, 어떤 후원자나 음악 밴드가 약속을 철회하거나, 유능한 팀원이 그만두면 여러분이 실망감을 느낄 때가 있을 것(However, there will be times when you'll be disappointed when a sponsor or a band backs out or a useful team member quits.)이라고 말하고 있다. 그 프로젝트를 끝까지 해내기 위해선 융통성이 있어야 하고 열린 마음을 가져야 한다고(To see the project through, you must have flexibility and an open mind.) 말하고 있으므로, 정답은 (d)이다.

정답 (d)

어휘
convince **v.** 설득하다, 납득시키다
disappointing **adj.** 실망스러운, 기대에 못 미치는

49. 특정정보

이 연설에 따르면, 가능한 많은 돈을 모금할 수 있는 하나의 방법은 무엇인가?

(a) 여가 시간을 생략함으로써
(b) 항상 일함으로써
(c) 가능한 한 적은 비용을 소비함으로써
(d) 예산 담당자를 고용함으로써

해설 네 번째 문단을 보면, 돈을 관리하는 방법을 모르면 성공하지 못할 수도 있다고(You may not succeed if you don't know how to manage your money.) 말하고 있으며, 당신이 성공적인 지출을 확신할 수 없다면, 소비를 줄이도록 노력하라고(Unless you are certain an expense will pay off, try to cut back on your spending.) 말하고 있으므로, 정답은 (c)이다.

정답 (c)

어휘
skip **v.** 생략하다, 거르다, 건너뛰다

50. 특정정보

이 대화에 따르면, 이 행사를 가능한 많은 사람들에게 알리기 위해 할 수 있는 일은 무엇인가?

(a) 가장 큰 수단에서만 광고하기
(b) 모든 친구에게 적극적으로 연락하기
(c) 다양한 홍보 방법을 사용하기
(d) 콘서트에는 유명 밴드만 고용하기

해설 다섯 번째 문단을 보면, 적극적으로 광고하기(to advertise aggressively)를 통해 행사를 가능한 한 많은 사람들에게 알려야 한다고(Make sure that your event is known to as many people as possible.) 하며, 소셜 네트워크 사이트, 신문과 잡지, 포스터, 특히 입소문과 같은, 이용 가능한 모든 수단을 사용하라고(Use all channels available to you, like social networking sites, newspapers and magazines, posters, and, especially, word of mouth.) 말하고 있으므로, 정답은 (c)이다.

정답 (c)

어휘
aggressively **ad.** 적극적으로
a variety of **phr.** 다양한, 여러 가지의

51. 세부사항

문제 해결에 시간을 갖는 것이 어떻게 도움이 될 수 있는가?

(a) 그것은 문제를 완전히 피할 수 있게 한다.
(b) 해결책에 대해 생각할 시간을 한 번 줄 수 있다.
(c) 문제가 해결될 것임을 보장한다.
(d) 스스로 문제를 해결할 수 있도록 한다.

해설 여섯 번째 문단을 보면, 행사의 성공을 보장하는데 도움이 되려면 정기적으로 휴식을 취하라고(To ensure the success of your event, take breaks on a regular schedule.) 하며, 한 시간 정도라도 다른 것을 하는 것은 여러분이 직면하고 있는 문제에 대한 해결책을 찾는데 도움이 될 수 있다고(Besides, doing something different for even an hour or so may help you find a solution to a problem you're facing.) 말하고 있으므로, 정답은 (b)이다.

정답 (b)

어휘
completely **ad.** 완전히, 전적으로
solution **n.** 해법, 해결책

52. 추론

이 연설에 따르면, 왜 즐기는 것이 성공으로 이어지는 것 같은가?

(a) 일을 더 쉬워 보이도록 한다.
(b) 후원자들로 하여금 더 많이 기부하도록 한다.
(c) 그 업무의 성공을 보장한다.
(d) 문제에 대한 새로운 해결책을 제시한다.

해설 마지막 문단을 보면, 항상 미소를 짓고 즐기라고(I also advise that you smile and have fun) 충고하며 얼굴에 미소를 띠고 있으면 일이 더 쉬워지고 성공할 가능성이 더 있다고(your work will be lighter and you're more likely to succeed if you have a smile on your face.) 말하고 있으므로, 즐기며 일을 하는 것이 일을 더 쉽게 만들어준다는 것을 추론할 수 있다. 따라서 정답은 (a)이다.

정답 (a)

어휘
donate **v.** 기부하다
completion **n.** 성공, 완료, 완성

TEST 1

Chapter 2
Listening

02 청취 모의고사 2회

27	(b)	28	(a)	29	(c)	30	(d)	31	(a)
32	(c)	33	(c)	34	(d)	35	(d)	36	(a)
37	(b)	38	(a)	39	(b)	40	(b)	41	(d)
42	(a)	43	(c)	44	(a)	45	(c)	46	(a)
47	(b)	48	(d)	49	(a)	50	(c)	51	(d)
52	(c)								

Part 1 Q. 27-33

27: Why was Carol in France?
28: What was one of the difficulties Carol first encountered in France?
29: According to Carol, what probably is one factor that makes France a nice country to visit?
30: Why was it necessary for Carol to learn French?
31: How did Carol define a fashion designer?
32: What was Jason's prediction about Carol's future as a fashion designer?
33: What will Jason most likely do after the conversation?

M: Hi, Carol! It's nice to see you again. When did you come back from France?
M: 안녕, Carol! 다시 보니 반갑구나. 언제 프랑스에서 돌아왔어?

F: Hello, Jason! I got back on Saturday.
F: 안녕, Jason! 나는 토요일에 돌아왔어.

M: Well, 27) how was it in France?
M: 그래, 프랑스는 어땠어?

F: 27) Pretty good, actually. Being an exchange student in a foreign country can be very rewarding.
F: 사실, 꽤 좋았어. 다른 나라에서 교환학생으로 지내는 건 매우 보람찰 수 있어.

M: I can imagine how exciting it must have been! You studied there for four years, right?
M: 얼마나 신났을지 상상이 가! 너 거기서 4년간 공부했지, 그렇지?

F: Yes, I did. But of course, I spent my school breaks back here at home.
F: 응, 맞아. 하지만 물론, 학교 방학 때는 여기 돌아와서 집에서 지냈어.

M: That's right, we never really had a chance to talk. So, what was it like being an exchange student?
M: 맞아, 우리가 정말 이야기할 기회가 전혀 없었지. 그래서, 교환학생으로 지내는 건 어땠어?

F: Well, 28) it was hard at first—you know, learning a new language and adjusting to a different culture. But once I got over that, it was smooth sailing all the way.
F: 음, 처음에는 힘들었어. 너도 알다시피, 새로운 언어를 배우고 다른 문화에 적응하는 것 말이야. 그런데 그걸 이겨내고 나니까, 그 뒤로는 계속 순탄하게 흘러갔어.

M: Did you stay with a host family?
M: 홈스테이 가족과 함께 지냈니?

F: Yes, I did. Living with a host family was part of the exchange program. I was lucky enough to stay with a very friendly and accommodating family. Everybody spoke English well, too.
F: 응, 그랬어. 홈스테이 가족이랑 사는 게 교환 프로그램의 일부였거든. 나는 운 좋게도 굉장히 친절하고 협조적인 가족과 지낼 수 있었지. 모두가 영어를 잘하기도 하고 말이야.

M: Good for you! But tell me more about France. How is it over there?
M: 잘 됐네! 그건 그렇고 프랑스에 대해서 더 말해줘. 거긴 어땠어?

F: 29) France is one of the nicest countries in Europe. It generally has cool winters and mild summers. And the city of Paris is really a very romantic place.
F: 프랑스는 유럽에서 가장 좋은 국가들 중 하나야. 보통 그곳은 일반적으로 시원한 겨울과 온화한 여름을 가지고 있어. 그리고 파리는 정말 낭만적인 곳이야.

M: I see. Which landmarks did you see in Paris?
M: 그렇구나. 파리에서 어떤 명소를 봤어?

F: Well, I visited the Eiffel Tower, the Louvre Museum, the Cathedral of Notre Dame, and the Latin Quarter.
F: 음, 지금까지 에펠 탑, 루브르 박물관, 노트르담 성당,

그리고 라틴 구를 방문했어.

M: Wow, I've only seen those landmarks in the movies! Say, 30) were you able to speak French fluently?
M: 와, 나는 그런 명소들은 영화에서만 봤는데! 야, 너 프랑스어는 유창하게 할 수 있었어?

F: Oh yes, 30) I had to. The French people are very patriotic, and they believe that tourists and migrants must learn their language and not the other way around.
F: 그럼, 그렇게 해야 했어. 프랑스 사람들은 굉장히 애국적이고, 관광객들과 이민자들이 자신들의 언어를 배워야 한다고 생각해. 그 반대가 아니라.

M: I understand. After all, you went there to study, and I'm assuming French must have been the main language of instruction. By the way, what program did you end up taking there?
M: 그렇구나. 어쨌든, 넌 공부하기 위해 그곳에 갔고, 프랑스어가 수업의 주 언어였을테고. 그건 그렇고, 거기서 결국 무슨 프로그램을 들었어?

F: Oh, I was studying fashion design at the Paris American Academy.
F: 아, 나는 Paris American Academy에서 패션 디자인을 공부하고 있었어.

M: Oh la la! Sounds like a very exclusive course. So, are you a fashion designer now?
M: 올랄라! 굉장히 전문 과정 같은데. 그래서, 지금 패션 디자이너가 된 거야?

F: I guess I am now, at least, by training.
F: 적어도, 교육받은 바로는 그런 것 같아.

M: Cool. So, what exactly did they train you to do?
M: 멋진데. 그래서, 그들이 정확히 뭘 하라고 훈련 시켰니?

F: Well, 31) as a fashion designer, I've been trained to design and create dresses, shoes, and clothing accessories. I have also been taught to research the latest trends in fashion, draw sketches of clothing designs, and select fabrics with the right colors and textures. I also learned how to oversee the creation of my own designs.
F: 음, 패션 디자이너로서, 드레스, 신발 그리고 의류용 장신구를 제작하고 디자인하는 교육을 받았어. 그리고 패션 분야의 최신 유행을 연구하고, 의류 디자인을 스케치하고, 딱 맞는 색깔과 감촉을 지닌 직물을 선택하는 것도 배웠지. 그리고 나만의 디자인을 만드는 걸 관리하는 법도 배웠어.

M: Impressive! 32) You might become a famous fashion designer someday. So, are you going to work first for a designer, or just start your own business?
M: 인상적인데! 넌 언젠가 유명한 패션 디자이너가 될 지도 몰라. 그래서 처음에 디자이너를 위해 일할 거니, 아니면 그냥 네 사업을 시작할 거니?

F: I believe I'd learn more working for a clothing company first.
F: 난 우선 의류 회사에서 일하면서 더 배워보고 싶어.

M: Sounds good, Carol. I wish I had joined an exchange program like you did. I know I can always visit France as a tourist anytime, but to have studied and lived there would have taught me a lot more about the country and its people.
M: 그거 좋은 생각이야, Carol. 나도 너처럼 교환학생 프로그램에 참가했다면 좋았을 텐데. 물론 언제든지 관광객으로 프랑스에 갈 수 있다는 건 알지만, 그곳에서 공부하면서 사는 건 그 나라와 사람들에 대해서 더 많은 걸 가르쳐 줄 테니까.

F: You could still do that, Jason. 33) Why not apply for one?
F: 지금도 할 수 있어, Jason. 지원해보는 게 어때?

M: I guess I will. 33) I hear the university's still accepting applicants. Maybe I'll give it a try. Thanks, Carol!
M: 그래야겠다. 아직 대학교에서 지원자들을 받는다고 들었어. 한 번 시도해보지 뭐. 고마워, Carol!

어휘
rewarding **adj.** 보람 있는
adjust to **phr v.** ~에 적응하다
smooth **adj.** 순탄한
accommodating **adj.** 협조적인
landmark **n.** 명소, 역사적인 건물
patriotic **adj.** 애국적인, 애국심이 많은
migrant **n.** 이민자
assume **v.** 생각하다, 가정하다, 추정하다
instruction **n.** 수업, 지도, 가르침
exclusive **adj.** 전용의, 고급의
texture **n.** 감촉, 질감
oversee **v.** 관리하다, 감독하다

TEST 2

27. 세부사항

왜 Carol은 프랑스에 있었는가?

(a) 그녀는 파리를 방문하고 싶었다.
(b) 그녀는 교환학생이었다.
(c) 그녀는 친구 Jason과 그곳에 방문했다.
(d) 그녀는 패션 디자이너로 근무하고 있었다.

해설 Carol의 두 번째 대사를 보면, 프랑스에서 어떻게 지냈냐는(How was it in France?) Jason의 질문에 굉장히 좋았다고(Pretty good) 하며 외국에서 교환학생으로 지내는 게 매우 보람찰 수 있다고(Being an exchange student in a foreign country can be very rewarding.) 말하고 있으므로, 정답은 (b)이다.

정답 (b)

어휘
exchange student **n.** 교환학생

28. 특정정보

Carol이 프랑스에서 처음에 겪었던 어려움 중 하나는 무엇인가?

(a) 프랑스어를 배우는 것
(b) 후원 가정에 적응하는 것
(c) 프랑스인의 애국심을 받아들이는 것
(d) 학교생활에 적응하는 것

해설 Carol의 네 번째 대사를 보면, 새로운 언어를 배우고 다른 문화에 적응하는 것이 처음에 힘들었다고(it was hard at first—you know, learning a new language and adjusting to a different culture.) 말하고 있으므로, 정답은 (a)이다.

정답 (a)

어휘
accept **v.** 받아들이다
patriotism **n.** 애국심

29. 사실확인

Carol에 따르면 프랑스를 방문하기 좋은 나라로 만드는 요인은 무엇인가?

(a) 유럽에서 가장 많은 명소 보유
(b) 가장 낭만적인 사람들이 있는 곳
(c) 대부분 좋은 날씨
(d) 매우 가족 지향적인 국가

해설 Carol의 여섯 번째 대사를 보면, 프랑스가 유럽에서 가장 좋은 국가들 중 하나라고(France is one of the nicest countries in Europe.) 하며 시원한 겨울과 온화한 여름을 가지고 있다고(It generally has cool winters and mild summers.) 말하고 있으므로, 정답은 (c)이다.

정답 (c)

어휘
landmark **n.** 명소, 역사적인 건물
decent **adj.** 좋은, 적당한, 적절한
family-oriented **phr.** 가족 지향의, 가정적인

30. 세부사항

Carol이 프랑스어를 배워야 했던 이유는 무엇인가?

(a) 패션 산업의 일자리를 찾기 위해
(b) 후원 가족과 의사소통하기 위해
(c) 패션 업계의 사람들에게 깊은 인상을 주기 위해
(d) 그 나라의 관습을 따르기 위해

해설 Carol의 여덟 번째 대사를 보면, 프랑스어를 유창하게 할 수 있었냐는(Were you able to speak French fluently?) Jason의 질문에 그렇게 해야 했다고(I had to) 하며 프랑스 사람들은 굉장히 애국적이라 관광객들과 이민자들이 프랑스어를 배워야 된다고 생각한다고(The French people are very patriotic, and they believe that tourists and migrants must learn their language) 말하고 있으므로, 정답은 (d)이다.

정답 (d)

어휘
industry **n.** 산업, 업계
impress **v.** 인상을 심어주다

31. 특정정보
Carol은 패션 디자이너를 어떻게 규정했는가?

(a) 패션 의류를 디자인하고 만드는 사람
(b) 의류와 장신구를 광고하는 사람
(c) 패션에 깊은 관심이 있는 사람
(d) 패션 산업에 많은 경험이 있는 사람

해설 Carol의 열한 번째 대사를 보면, 패션 디자이너로서 드레스, 신발 및 의류용 장신구를 디자인하고 만드는 교육을 받아왔다고(as a fashion designer, I've been trained to design and create dresses, shoes, and clothing accessories) 말하고 있으므로, 정답은 (a)이다.

정답 (a)

어휘
market **v.** 광고하다
considerable **adj.** 많은, 상당한

32. 세부사항
패션 디자이너로서 Carol의 미래에 대한 Jason의 예측은 무엇인가?

(a) 그녀는 곧 자신만의 사업을 시작할 것이다.
(b) 그녀는 성공적인 프랑스 패션 디자이너가 될 것이다.
(c) 그녀는 언젠가 패션계에서 유명해질지도 모른다.
(d) 그녀는 미래에 유명한 디자이너를 위해 일할 것이다.

해설 Jason의 열두 번째 대사를 보면, Carol에게 언젠가 유명한 패션 디자이너가 될지도 모른다고(You might become a famous fashion designer someday.) 말하고 있으므로, 정답은 (c)이다.

정답 (c)

어휘
well known **adj.** 유명한, 잘 알려진

33. 추론
대화 후에 Jason은 무엇을 할 것 같은가?

(a) 프랑스의 역사에 대해 조사하기
(b) 유명한 프랑스 디자이너들에 대해 공부하기
(c) 학교의 교환학생 프로그램 부서에 방문하기
(d) Carol과 상의하여 패션 관련 조언을 받기

해설 Carol과 Jason의 마지막 대화를 보면, 교환학생 프로그램에 지원하는 게 어떠냐고(Why not apply for one?) 제안하는 Carol에게 Jason이 학교가 아직 지원자를 받는다고 들었다며(I hear the university's still accepting applicants.) 시도해보겠다고(Maybe I'll give it a try.) 말하고 있으므로, 교환학생 프로그램 부서에 방문할 예정이라는 것을 추론할 수 있다. 따라서 정답은 (c)이다.

정답 (c)

어휘
research **v.** 조사하다, 연구하다
read up on **phr v.** ~에 대해 공부하다
consult **v.** 상의하다

Part 2 Q. 34-39

34: What is the purpose of this talk?
35: Why did Driscoll Robotics create the humanoid robot?
36: Where did the company have its office when it was starting out?
37: According to the speaker, what makes the humanoid robot the first of its kind?
38: What do the research teams hope to achieve with the next-generation of robots?
39: Based on the talk, why are the practical uses of humanoid robots almost limitless?

Good morning, everyone! My name is Lou Carter and I represent Driscoll Robotics. 34) I'm here today to introduce the Anthro One, a new humanoid robot by Driscoll Robotics and a result of decades of continuous research and development. Since the start of the company, Driscoll Robotics has never wavered in taking on new challenges in its efforts to create new products and advance new technologies. The company has been doing all of this with the aim of using technology to improve people's lives.
안녕하세요, 여러분! 제 이름은 Lou Carter이고 Driscoll Robotics를 대표하여 나왔습니다. 저는 Driscoll Robotics에서 만든 새 인간형 로봇이자 수십 년간 계속된 연구 개발의 산물인 Anthro One을 소개하러 오늘 이곳에 왔습니

TEST 2

다. 회사의 초창기부터, Driscoll Robotics는 신상품을 개발하고 신기술을 발전시키려는 노력으로 새로운 활동에 도전하는 데 있어서 결코 흔들린 적이 없었습니다. 당사는 사람들의 삶을 향상시키기 위해 기술을 사용하려는 목적으로 이 모든 것을 해오고 있습니다.

35) In order to realize our goal of bettering lives, we looked to the area of humanoid robotic research and we have developed the Anthro One humanoid robot. "But, what is a humanoid robot?" you may ask. It's a robot which takes on the form of the human body and is designed to perform human functions.
삶을 개선시키려는 당사의 목표를 실현하기 위해, 인간형 로봇 연구 분야를 살펴봤고 Anthro One 인간형 로봇을 개발했습니다. "그러나, 인간형 로봇이 뭐지?"라고 질문할 지도 모르겠습니다. 인간형 로봇은 인체의 형상을 띠며 인체 기능을 수행하기 위해 고안된 로봇입니다.

Before I proceed, let me first give you a brief background of our company. Driscoll Robotics was established in 1995 by an enterprising young engineer from Milan, Ohio, named George Driscoll. 36) Starting out in a small, abandoned, one-story building in Brooklyn, New York, the humble company premises have grown into a five-building industrial complex. Today, we maintain an international presence with offices in key locations including Japan, China, Australia, New Zealand, South Africa, Saudi Arabia, and Mexico.
진행하기 전에, 우선 여러분께 당사의 간략한 배경에 대해 설명 드리겠습니다. Driscoll Robotics는 오하이오주 밀란 출신인 George Driscoll이라는 진취적이고 젊은 기술자에 의해 1995년에 설립되었습니다. 뉴욕시 브루클린에 있는 작고 버려진 1층짜리 건물에서 시작하면서, 이 초라한 회사 부지는 건물 5개의 공업 단지로 성장하였습니다. 오늘날, 저희는 일본, 중국, 호주, 뉴질랜드, 남아프리카, 사우디아라비아, 그리고 멕시코를 포함한 주요 지역에 사무실을 운영하며 국제적으로 진출해 있습니다.

Our products are used around the world, and I'm eager to talk to you about our latest innovation, the Anthro One. 37) This humanoid robot is the first of its kind in that it can actually make decisions. When we at Driscoll began to develop Anthro One, we focused on three essential factors needed for a robot to do human tasks as effectively as possible. First, we designed it to have good postural balancing. This allows it to remain upright and maintain its posture. Second, we gave it external recognition. This ability lets the robot sense things in its surroundings and analyze those things in relation to its task. Lastly, we enabled it to engage in independent behavior. This means the robot can process the information it gathers and determine its next move regarding a task or a situation without being told to do so.
저희 제품은 전 세계에서 사용되고 있고, 여러분께 저희의 최신 기술 혁신 제품인 Anthro One에 대해 말씀드리고 싶습니다. 이 인간형 로봇은 실제로 결정을 내릴 수 있다는 점에서 유일무이한 최초의 로봇입니다. 저희 Driscoll 사에서 Anthro One을 개발하기 시작했을 때, 로봇이 인간의 과업을 가능한 효과적으로 수행하는데 필요한 세 가지 필수 조건에 초점을 맞추었습니다. 첫째, 저희는 이 로봇이 훌륭한 자세 균형을 갖도록 설계하였습니다. 이는 로봇이 똑바로 서있고 자세를 유지하게끔 해줍니다. 둘째, 외부 인식 기능을 탑재했습니다. 이 능력은 로봇이 주변에 있는 사물들을 감지하고 주어진 일과 관련지어 그것들을 분석할 수 있게 해줍니다. 마지막으로, 독립적인 행동을 할 수 있게 만들었습니다. 이것은 로봇이 자신이 수집하는 정보를 처리하고, 주어진 업무나 상황과 관련하여 어떻게 하라는 지시 없이 다음 행동을 결정할 수 있게 해줍니다.

Driscoll Robotics has developed a new system exclusively for the enhancement of Anthro One's "intelligence." This new system relies on visual, auditory, and tactile sensors to allow it to see, hear, and touch, much like the senses of a human. After evaluating the input, the robot then studies the information and its environment and comes up with an appropriate action for the situation. With this new technology, the robot can respond to the movements of people and the events in its surroundings.
Driscoll Robotics는 독점적으로 Anthro One의 "지능" 향상만을 위한 새로운 시스템을 개발했습니다. 이 새로운 시스템은 인간의 감각과 매우 비슷하게 보고, 듣고 그리고 만질 수 있게 해주는 시각, 청각, 촉각 센서에 의존합니다. 입력데이터를 평가한 뒤, 이 로봇은 정보와 환경을 연구하여 상황에 맞는 적절한 행동을 고안해냅니다. 이 신기술로, 로봇은 주변에서 발생하는 사람들의 움직임과 사건에 반응할 수 있습니다.

Studying human beings to understand how to

make better humanoid robots is one of our primary approaches. We have established a collective team of experts to handle the human and robotic aspects of our business. Even as we introduce Anthro One, the first in our line of humanoid robots, [38, 39] our research and development teams are already developing next-generation humanoid robots that will imitate human movements almost to perfection. [39] The practical applications of such robots in other fields are almost limitless.
더 나은 인간형 로봇을 만드는 방법을 알기 위해 인간을 연구하는 것은 저희 회사의 주요 접근법 중 하나입니다. 저희는 이 사업의 인간적인, 그리고 로봇적인 측면을 다루기 위해 전문가로 구성된 팀을 만들었습니다. 저희의 인간형 로봇 제품군 중 첫 번째인 Anthro One을 소개하고 있는 이 시점에도, 저희 연구 개발 팀은 인간의 움직임을 거의 완벽하게 흉내 낼 차세대 인간형 로봇을 이미 개발하고 있습니다. 다른 분야에서 이러한 로봇들을 실용적으로 응용할 수 있는 방법은 거의 무한합니다.

I hope you've found my talk to be both entertaining and educational. If you have time, please feel free to drop by our office and see Anthro One for yourself.
제 연설이 재미있고 교육적이었기를 바랍니다. 시간이 있으시다면, 언제든 저희 사무실에 방문하셔서 직접 Anthro One을 구경해보십시오.

어휘
humanoid **adj.** 인간형의
decade **n.** 십 년
waver **v.** 흔들리다
proceed **v.** 진행하다
enterprising **adj.** 진취적인
abandoned **adj.** 버려진
premise **n.** 부지
presence **n.** 진출
essential **adj.** 필수적인
postural **adj.** 자세의
recognition **n.** 인식
surrounding **n.** 주변, (주위) 환경
determine **v.** 결정하다
exclusively **ad.** 독점적으로
tactile **adj.** 촉각의
appropriate **adj.** 적절한, 적합한
primary **adj.** 주요한
practical **adj.** 실용적인
application **n.** 응용, 적용

34. 주제/목적
이 연설의 목적은 무엇인가?

(a) 기술의 발전에 대한 최신 정보를 알려주는 것
(b) 새 회사를 시작하기 위해
(c) 미래의 추세를 예측하기 위해
(d) 신제품을 소개하기 위해

해설 첫 번째 문단을 보면, Lou Carter가 Driscoll Robotics에서 만든 새 인간형 로봇인 Anthro One을 소개하러 왔다고(I'm here today to introduce the Anthro One, a new humanoid robot by Driscoll Robotics) 말하고 있으므로, 정답은 (d)이다.

정답 (d)

어휘
advance **v.** 발전
launch **v.** 시작하다, 출시하다
predict **v.** 예측하다

35. 세부사항
왜 Driscoll Robotics는 인간형 로봇을 만들었는가?

(a) 회사가 개발한 새로운 시스템을 사용할 방법을 찾길 원했다.
(b) 인간형 로봇에 대한 회사의 기술을 시험해보는 것을 목표로 했다.
(c) 회사의 상징물을 필요로 했다.
(d) 로봇으로 인간의 삶을 풍요롭게 하길 원했다.

해설 두 번째 문단을 보면, 삶을 개선시키려는 회사의 목표를 실현하기 위해, 인간형 로봇 연구 분야를 살펴봤고 Anthro One 인간형 로봇을 개발했다고(In order to realize our goal of bettering lives, we looked to the area of humanoid robotic research and we have developed the Anthro One humanoid robot.) 말하고 있으므로, 정답은 (d)이다.

정답 (d)

어휘
enrich **v.** 풍요롭게 하다, 질을 높이다

TEST 2

36. 특정정보

처음 회사를 시작했을 때 사무실이 어디에 있었는가?

(a) 뉴욕시의 오래된 건물 내
(b) 산업 단지 내
(c) 멕시코의 차고 내
(d) 오하이오주의 George Driscoll 소유의 낡지만 큰 건물

해설 세 번째 문단을 보면, Driscoll Robotics를 소개하며 이 회사가 브루클린에 있는 작고 버려진 1층짜리 건물에서 시작하였다고(Starting out in a small, abandoned, one-story building in Brooklyn, New York) 말하고 있으므로, 정답은 (a)이다.

정답 (a)

어휘
garage **n.** 차고
barn **n.** (낡지만) 큰 건물, 헛간,

37. 특정정보

화자에 따르면, 인간형 로봇을 최초의 로봇으로 만드는 것은 무엇인가?

(a) 인간과 닮은 모습
(b) 선택할 수 있는 능력
(c) 사전 프로그래밍된 작업
(d) 걸어다니는 능력

해설 네 번째 문단을 보면, 이 인간형 로봇은 실제로 결정을 내릴 수 있다는 점에서 유일무이한 최초의 로봇이라고(This humanoid robot is the first of its kind in that it can actually make decisions) 말하고 있으므로, 정답은 (b)이다.

정답 (b)

어휘
appearance **n.** 모습, 외모
ability **n.** 능력, 재능, 기량

38. 세부사항

연구진들이 차세대 로봇으로 성취하고자 하는 바는 무엇인가?

(a) 로봇이 정확히 인간처럼 기능하는 것
(b) 로봇이 Driscoll Robotics를 운영하는 것
(c) 로봇에게 더 정교한 전자 센서를 탑재하는 것
(d) 로봇이 다른 로봇과 소통하도록 설정하는 것

해설 여섯 번째 문단을 보면, 연구개발팀이 인간의 움직임을 거의 완벽하게 흉내 낼 차세대 인간형 로봇을 개발하고 있다고(Our research and development teams are already developing next-generation humanoid robots that will imitate human movements almost to perfection.) 말하고 있으므로, 정답은 (a)이다.

정답 (a)

어휘
function **v.** 기능하다
keen **adj.** 정교한, 예민한
program **v.** 설정하다, 프로그램을 짜다

39. 세부사항

이 연설에 따르면, 왜 인간형 로봇의 실용성이 거의 무한한가?

(a) 인간형 로봇들은 모든 활동에서 인간을 대체할 수 있다.
(b) 그들은 거의 모든 인간의 업무를 처리하도록 고안될 수 있다.
(c) 그들은 스스로 연구 및 개발을 수행할 수 있다.
(d) 미래의 로봇은 인간과 구분되지 않을 것이다.

해설 여섯 번째 문단을 보면, 연구 개발 팀이 인간의 움직임을 거의 완벽하게 흉내 낼 차세대 인간형 로봇을 개발하고 있다고(Our research and development teams are already developing next-generation humanoid robots that will imitate human movements almost to perfection.) 하며 다른 분야에서 이러한 로봇들을 실용적으로 응용할 수 있는 방법이 거의 무한하다고(The practical applications of such robots in other fields are almost limitless.) 말하고 있으므로, 로봇이 인간의 움직임을 완벽히 흉내 내어 거의 모든 업무를 처리하게끔 만들 수 있기 때문에 실용성이 무한한 것이라고 추론할 수 있다. 따라서 정답은 (b)이다.

정답 (b)

어휘
replace **v.** 대체하다
conduct **v.** 수행하다
indistinguishable **adj.** 구분되지 않는, 구분할 수 없는

Part 3 Q. 40-45

40: What did Jill receive from her father?
41: Which is an advantage of an electronic book?
42: According to John, why is it more worry-free to read a printed book than an e-book?
43: How can e-books be helpful to students?
44: Based on the conversation, why is book swapping not advisable with e-books?
45: What will Jill probably do right after the conversation?

F: Hey, John! I've got some good news!
F: 안녕, John! 좋은 소식이 있어!

M: Hey, Jill. You seem excited. What's the good news?
M: 안녕, Jill. 굉장히 신나 보이네. 좋은 소식이 뭐야?

F: 40) My dad gave me money to buy books by my favorite author, Divine Stuart. It's my reward for getting high grades this school term.
F: 내가 가장 좋아하는 작가인 Divine Stuart가 쓴 책을 살 수 있게 아버지께서 용돈을 주셨어. 이번 학기에 내가 높은 점수를 받은 데 대한 보상이야.

M: That's great! I know how much you like Stuart's novels. I remember last year you even saved up just to buy a copy of her book.
M: 잘됐다! 네가 얼마나 Stuart의 소설을 좋아하는지 내가 알지. 작년에 네가 그녀의 책 사본을 사려고 심지어 저축까지 했던 거 기억나.

F: You're right. And to finally own all ten of her books would be a dream come true for me. However, I haven't decided yet whether to purchase printed copies of her books, like paperbacks, or to get the electronic versions of the books. Could you help me decide?
F: 맞아. 그리고 그녀의 책 10권 모두를 마침내 갖게 된다는 건 내 꿈이 실현되는 거야. 그런데, 페이퍼백처럼 인쇄본으로 살지 아니면 전자책으로 살지를 아직 결정하지 않았어. 내가 결정할 수 있게 도와줄래?

M: Sure. Let us first weigh the pros and cons of each type. Electronic books, or e-books, can be quite handy. E-book readers, the handheld devices used to view e-books, are small and light enough to bring wherever you go.
M: 물론이지. 우선 각각의 장단점을 따져보자. 전자책, 혹은 이북(e-book)은 꽤 편리할 수 있어. 이북(e-book)을 볼 때 사용되는 휴대 기기인 이북(e-book) 리더기는 작고 가벼워서 네가 어디를 가든 가져갈 수 있지.

F: E-books really seem convenient to carry around.
F: 이북(e-book)은 정말 들고 다니기 편리한 것 같아.

M: Yes, moreover, 41) the screen has its own light so you can even read in the dark. And you can change the text's size according to your preference.
M: 그럼. 게다가, 화면에 조명이 있기 때문에 어두운 곳에서도 읽을 수 있어. 그리고 네가 선호하는 대로 글자의 크기를 변경할 수도 있지.

F: Those are really convenient features. But I think those who are not familiar with e-books will prefer paperbacks.
F: 정말 편리한 기능이네. 그런데 내 생각엔 이북(e-book)에 익숙하지 않은 사람들은 페이퍼백을 선호할 것 같아.

M: Yeah. An advantage of printed books is that you don't need an e-book reader to read them. You wouldn't need to buy a reader online and give out your credit card number, which can be risky. Also, 42) you won't have to worry about reader malfunctions or breakdowns. A paperback is relatively easy to buy as long as the title is in print.
M: 응. 종이책의 장점은 이북(e-book) 리더기가 없어도 책을 읽을 수 있다는 거야. 온라인으로 리더기를 살 필요도 없고 신용카드 번호를 제공할 필요도 없는게, 이런 것들이 위험할 수 있잖아. 또한, 리더기 기능 불량이나 고장에 대해서 걱정할 필요도 없을 거야. 페이퍼백은 해당 서적이 출판되어 있기만 한다면 상대적으로 구매하기가 쉬워.

F: I understand those points. But tell me more about e-books. Do they have any more advantages?
F: 그런 점들이 이해는 가. 그런데 이북(e-book)에 관해서 더 이야기해줘. 다른 장점은 없니?

M: Well, as you already know, printed books obviously occupy space and can be heavy to carry around. But 43) e-books, on the other hand, are convenient especially for students. One device can contain several e-books so there would be no need to lug around heavy textbooks in your backpack all day.
M: 음, 네가 이미 알다시피, 종이 책들은 분명히 공간을 차지하고 들고 다니기 무거울 수 있지. 반면에, 이북(e-book)은 특히 학생들에게 편리해. 하나의 기기에 여러 이북(e-book)을 담을 수 있기 때문에 하루 종일 가방에 무거운 교과서들을 힘들게 들고 돌아다닐 필요가 없을 거야.

F: That's really worth considering; carrying books can

really be a burden.

F: 그건 진짜 생각해볼 만한 가치가 있구나. 책들을 들고 다니는 건 정말 짐이 될 수 있잖아.

M: But printed books can also have very practical advantages. They can become valuable collector's editions. Or you can have them autographed by your favorite authors. Rare books can also fetch very high prices on the market.

M: 그런데 종이 책들도 매우 실용적인 장점을 지닐 수도 있어. 그 책들이 귀중한 수집가용 한정판이 될 수도 있잖아. 아니면 네가 가장 좋아하는 작가의 사인을 책에 받을 수도 있지. 희귀한 책들은 시장에서 고가에 판매될 수도 있어.

F: Correct. Besides, there is also something about holding a printed book that makes it more appealing to read at night. It's weird, but I also like smelling its pages.

F: 맞아. 게다가, 또 책을 가지고 있으면 밤에 읽는게 더 끌릴 때가 있어. 이상하긴 하지만, 나는 책 냄새 맡는 걸 좋아해.

M: Hey, I also do that! Ha-ha! Oh, 44) another drawback of e-books is that you cannot borrow or lend them without having to borrow or lend the reader as well.

M: 야, 나도 그러는데! 하하! 아, 이북(e-book)의 또 다른 단점은 리더기를 빌리거나 빌려주지 않고서는 이북(e-book) 역시 빌리거나 빌려줄 수 없다는 거야.

F: So 44) book swapping is not really a choice for e-books, huh?

F: 그러니까 책을 맞바꾸어 보는 건 이북(e-book)을 위한 선택은 아니겠구나, 응?

M: Right. But there's also the matter of availability for printed books. If a book you're looking for is not available in bookstores, you will have to find it online. This might be a little expensive because you'll also have to pay for shipping. On the other hand, there are many e-books online and some can even be downloaded for free.

M: 맞아. 그런데 종이 책의 구매 가능성에 대한 문제도 있어. 만약에 찾고 있는 책이 서점에 없으면, 온라인에서 찾아야 할 거야. 또한 배송비를 지불해야 하기 때문에 약간 비쌀지도 모르지. 반면에, 온라인상에는 많은 이북(e-book)이 있고 몇몇 이북(e-book)은 심지어 무료로 다운받을 수 있어.

F: Thanks for your help, John. I'm leaning towards buying printed books because I don't have an e-book reader. Besides, I want Divine Stuart to sign the books I'm going to buy.

F: 도와줘서 고마워, John. 나는 이북(e-book) 리더기가 없어서 종이 책을 구매하는 쪽으로 마음이 기울어지네. 게다가, 나는 Divine Stuart가 내가 살 책에 사인을 해주었으면 하거든.

M: That's great, Jill. Would you be willing to lend me the books after you read them?

M: 멋진데, Jill. 그 책들을 읽은 후에 나에게 빌려줄 수 있니?

F: Sure, John! Well, 45) I'd better go to the bookstore now. See you!

F: 물론이지, John! 자, 난 이제 서점에 가야겠어. 나중에 보자!

어휘
reward **n.** 보상
purchase **v.** 구매하다
paperback **n.** 페이퍼백, 표지가 종이로 된 책
weigh **v.** 따져보다, 저울질하다
handy **adj.** 편리한
preference **n.** 선호
feature **n.** 기능
malfunction **n.** 기능 불량
title **n.** 서적, 제목
occupy **v.** 차지하다
contain **v.** 포함하다
lug around **phr v.** 끌고 다니다
appealing **adj.** 매력적인
swap **v.** 맞바꾸다
availability **n.** (이용, 구매) 가능성
lean toward **phr v.** ~쪽으로 마음이 기울다

40. 세부사항

Jill이 아버지로부터 받은 것은 무엇인가?

(a) 사인이 되어있는 책
(b) 책을 구매할 돈
(c) 전자 책 리더기
(d) 전자 책 모음집

해설 Jill의 두 번째 대사를 보면, 자신이 가장 좋아하는 작가인 Divine Stuart가 쓴 책을 살 수 있게 아버지께서 용돈을 주셨다고(My dad gave me money to buy books by my favorite author, Divine Stuart.) 말하고 있으므로, 정답은 (b)이다.

정답 (b)

어휘
autographed **adj.** 사인 된, 서명이 있는
collection **n.** 모음집, 수집품

41. 특정정보

전자 책의 장점은 무엇인가?

(a) 배낭에 잘 맞는다.
(b) 서점에서 쉽게 구매할 수 있다.
(c) 친구한테 쉽게 빌릴 수 있다.
(d) 글자가 좀 더 보기 쉽다.

해설 John의 네 번째 대사를 보면, 이북(e-book) 리더기의 화면에 조명이 있기 때문에 어두운 곳에서도 읽을 수 있고(The screen has its own light so you can even read in the dark.), Jill이 원하는 대로 글자의 크기를 변경할 수도 있다고(And you can change the text's size according to your preference.) 했으므로, 정답은 (d)이다.

정답 (d)

> **어휘**
> readily **ad.** 쉽게

42. 세부사항

John에 의하면, 왜 이북(e-book)보다 종이책을 읽는 것이 걱정으로부터 더 자유로울까?

(a) 그것은 갑자기 작동을 멈추지 않는다.
(b) 그것은 절판되지 않는다.
(c) 그것은 큰 활자로 된 것을 구매할 수 있다.
(d) 그것은 자체적인 조명을 탑재하고 있다.

해설 John의 다섯 번째 대사를 보면, 종이 책을 읽을 경우 리더기의 기능 불량이나 고장에 대해서 걱정할 필요가 없다고(you won't have to worry about reader malfunctions or breakdowns.) 말하고 있으므로, 정답은 (a)이다.

정답 (a)

> **어휘**
> unexpectedly **ad.** 갑자기, 예상치 못하게

43. 추론

이북(e-book)이 학생들에게 어떻게 도움이 될 수 있는가?

(a) 대부분의 교과서를 이북(e-book)으로 이용한다.
(b) 교과서를 온라인으로 다운받는 것이 용이하다.
(c) 많은 교과서가 하나의 리더기에 들어갈 수 있다.
(d) 대부분의 선생님들이 학생들에게 학교에 이북(e-book)을 가져오라고 요구한다.

해설 John의 여섯 번째 대사를 보면, 이북(e-book)은 특히 학생들에게 편리하다고(e-books are convenient especially for students.)하며, 하나의 기기에 여러 이북(e-book)을 담을 수 있기 때문에 하루 종일 무거운 교과서들을 힘들게 들고 돌아다닐 필요가 없을 거라고(One device can contain several e-books so there would be no need to lug around heavy text-books in your backpack all day.) 말하고 있으므로, 많은 교과서가 하나의 리더기에 들어가기 때문에 학생들에게 도움이 된다는 것을 추론할 수 있다. 따라서 정답은 (c)이다.

정답 (c)

> **어휘**
> multiple **adj.** 많은, 다수의
> require **v.** 요구하다

44. 세부사항

이 대화에 따르면, 왜 이북(e-book)으로 책을 바꿔 읽는 것이 권장되지 않는가?

(a) 리더기 없이는 빌리거나 빌려줄 수 없다.
(b) 다운받거나 공유하기엔 너무 비싸다.
(c) 모든 이북(e-book) 리더기와 호환이 가능하지 않다.
(d) 주인이 이북(e-book)에 자신의 이름을 표시할 수 없다.

해설 John의 여덟 번째 대사를 보면, 이북(e-book)의 또 다른 단점은 리더기를 빌리거나 빌려주지 않고서는 책을 빌리거나 빌려줄 수 없다는 것이라고(another drawback of e-books is that you cannot borrow or lend them without having to borrow or lend the reader as well.) 하고, 이에 대해 Jill이 동의하며 책을 맞바꾸어 보는 건 이북(e-book)을 위한 선택은 아니라고(book swapping is not really a choice for e-books.) 말하고 있으므로, 정답은 (a)이다.

정답 (a)

> **어휘**
> compatible **adj.** 호환이 되는
> mark **v.** 표시하다

TEST 2

45. 추론

대화 직후에 Jill이 무엇을 할 것 같은가?

(a) Devine Stuart의 최신작 읽기
(b) John에게 책 한 권 빌려주기
(c) 서점에 Stuart의 책이 있는지 확인하기
(d) 아버지에게 선물에 대한 감사표시하기

해설 Jill의 마지막 대사를 보면, 서점에 가야겠다고(I'd better go to the bookstore now.) 말하고 있으므로, 서점에 본인이 살 Stuart의 책이 있는지 확인하러 가는 것이라고 추론할 수 있다. 따라서 정답은 (c)이다.

정답 (c)

어휘
latest **adj.** 최신의, 최근의

Part 4 Q. 46-52

46: Who is most likely to benefit from this talk?
47: What is the first thing to do when starting a baking business?
48: Why is it advisable to borrow money from friends and relatives?
49: Why most likely could supplying baked goods to restaurants establish one's name in the business?
50: According to the talk, how can one stay on top of one's costs?
51: According to the speaker, when can businesses get into trouble?
52: How can business owners stay ahead of the competition?

Good morning, everyone. Welcome to the livelihood seminar prepared by the Canyon Lake Chamber of Commerce. As your resource speaker today, 46) I'm going to discuss the steps involved in starting your own baking business. Running a bakery can be both a stressful and exciting activity, but it is one business that will always be in demand.
안녕하세요, 여러분. Canyon Lake 상공 회의소에서 준비한 민생 토론회에 오신 것을 환영합니다. 오늘 저는 해당 분야의 연설가로서, 여러분 자신의 제과 사업을 시작하는 것과 관련된 절차에 대해서 논할 예정입니다. 제과점을 운영하는 것은 스트레스가 많으면서 신나는 활동이 될 수도 있지만, 항상 수요가 있을 하나의 사업입니다.

47) The first thing to learn in setting up a bakery is the basics of its operation. Naturally, you will have to learn how to bake because baked goods are what you will be selling. You may join a regular baking class, or enroll in an online course. After learning the basics of producing essential baked goods, like breads and cakes, expand your list of products by becoming familiar with different ingredients and more advanced baking techniques.
제과점을 시작하는데 있어서 처음으로 배워야 할 것은 운영의 기본기입니다. 당연히, 제과제품들은 여러분들이 판매할 것이기 때문에 제과하는 방법을 배워야 할 것입니다. 정규 제과 수업에 참여하거나 온라인 수업에 등록하면 됩니다. 빵과 케이크 같은 기본적인 제과 제품을 생산하는 기본기를 배운 후, 다양한 재료와 더욱 고급의 제과 기술을 익히면서 제품 목록을 확장해보십시오.

The next step is to consider how you will finance your business. If you have enough money of your own to start with, then you're off to a good start. However, if you don't have the funds to jumpstart your business, then consider borrowing from relatives or friends.
다음 단계는 사업에 필요한 재원을 어떻게 마련할 것인지 생각해보는 것입니다. 여러분만의 사업을 시작할 수 있는 충분한 돈이 있다면, 아주 순조로운 출발을 하는 것입니다. 그러나, 사업을 시작할 자금을 가지고 있지 않다면, 친지나 친구들에게 빌리는 것을 고려해보십시오.

Another option to generate funds is to borrow from financial institutions like banks or lending companies. 48) Borrowing from people whom you are close to, however, would be better because you won't have the pressure of repaying your debts within a strict timeframe. Unlike borrowing from a bank, there would also be fewer documents to prepare, if at all, when borrowing from friends and relatives. In some cases, they will not require you to pay them back with interest.
자금을 마련하는 또 다른 방법은 은행이나 대부업체와 같은 금융기관으로부터 대출을 받는 것입니다. 그러나, 여러분과 가까운 관계의 사람들에게 빌리는 것은 빠듯한 기간 내에 빚을 상환해야 한다는 압박이 없을 것이기 때문에 더 나을 수 있습니다 은행에서 대출하는 것과는 다르게, 적어도 친구나 친지로부터 돈을 빌릴 때는 준비할 서류가 더 간소해질 것입니다. 경우에 따라서는, 그들이 이자와 함께 돈을 갚으라고 요청하지 않을 것입니다.

The third step is to apply for the necessary health and sanitary permits and business licenses. 51)

Starting a food business specifically requires a health permit to ensure that the workplace you will be operating is clean and your products are safe. In terms of registration, you will need a business license, sometimes called a business permit, for the proper identification of your business and for tax purposes.
세 번째 단계는 필요한 보건 혹은 위생 허가증과 사업자 등록증을 신청하는 것입니다. 요식업을 시작할 때는 운영하게 될 사업장이 청결하고 여러분의 제품이 안전하다는 것을 보장하기 위한 보건 허가증이 분명히 필요합니다. 등록에 있어서는, 올바른 사업 정보 증명과 세금 정산을 위해 사업 허가증이라고 불리기도 하는 사업자 등록증이 필요할 것입니다.

The fourth step is to market your products. Aside from the customers that you'll be attracting from your neighborhood, 49) approach restaurants, cafes, and other places that serve breads and pastries. 49) Supplying wholesome, quality products will not only establish your name as a reputable supplier of baked products, but it could also increase your customer base. Create promotional materials like brochures and flyers describing your products and company.
네 번째 단계는 여러분의 제품을 홍보하는 것입니다. 인근에서 끌어 모을 수 있는 고객들 이외에도, 레스토랑, 카페, 그리고 빵과 페이스트리를 제공하는 곳들에 접근해 보십시오. 건강하고 양질의 제품을 납품하는 것은 평판이 좋은 제과 제품 납품업자로서 여러분의 명성을 확고히 해줄 뿐만 아니라 고객층 또한 늘릴 수 있습니다. 여러분의 제품과 회사에 대해 설명하는 책자나 전단과 같은 홍보 자료를 만들어 보십시오.

50) The fifth step is to identify ways to stay on top of your costs. To get discounts, buy supplies in bulk as much as possible. Choose suppliers that offer quality ingredients and materials at reasonable prices. When selling your products, do not undervalue your merchandise just to encourage customers to buy. It's never a good business practice to sell way below the market price just to undercut the competition and make less profit in the process.
다섯 번째 단계는 사업비를 잘 관리하는 방법을 찾는 것입니다. 할인을 받기 위해, 가능한 한 재료를 대량으로 구매하십시오. 적당한 가격에 좋은 품질의 재료와 자재를 제공하는 납품 업체를 선택하십시오. 제품을 판매할 때, 단지 고객의 구매를 장려하겠다고 여러분 상품의 가격을 낮추지 마십시오. 단지 경쟁 상대보다 싸게 판매하기 위해 시가보다 훨씬 낮은 가격에 판매하고 그 과정에서 더 적은 이익을 취하는 것은 결코 좋은 사업 방식이 아닙니다.

The sixth step is to develop practices to maintain cleanliness in your workplace. All food-related businesses can get into trouble when the products' safety is put into question. 51) Keep your products uncontaminated, wholesome, and of high quality to prevent customers from getting food poisoning. Provide clear and detailed information on your packaging to inform customers who may be allergic to certain ingredients.
여섯 번째 단계는 사업장의 청결을 유지하는 관례를 만드는 것입니다. 모든 요식 관련 사업은 제품의 안전이 문제시 될 때 어려움에 처할 수 있습니다. 고객이 식중독에 걸리는 것을 방지하기 위해서 제품을 오염되지 않고, 건강에 좋고, 그리고 양질의 상태로 유지하십시오. 포장지에 명확하고 상세한 정보를 제공하여 특정 재료에 알레르기가 있을 수 있는 고객에게 안내할 수 있도록 하십시오.

Lastly, keep yourself ahead of the competition. 52) Always stay updated on the latest developments in baking. Join peer groups, surf the Internet, and remain aware of the most recent trends in the business.
마지막으로, 경쟁에서 앞서 나가십시오. 항상 제과 분야의 최근 동향을 파악하십시오. 동업 조합에 가입하고, 인터넷을 검색하고, 이 업계의 가장 최신의 경향을 파악하고 계십시오.

어휘
involved in **adj.** ~에 관련된
in demand **adj.** 수요가 많은
essential **adj.** 기본적인, 필수적인
expand **v.** 확장하다
ingredient **n.** 재료
advanced **adj.** 고급의, 진보한
finance **v.** 재원을 마련하다, 조달하다
generate **v.** 마련하다, 생성하다
institution **n.** 기관
pressure **n.** 압박, 압력
interest **n.** 이자
sanitary **adj.** 위생의, 청결한
identification **n.** 증명, 식별
establish **v.** 확고히 하다
promotional **adj.** 홍보의
undervalue **v.** (실제 가격보다) 낮게 평가하다
practice **n.** 방식, 관행
undercut **v.** (경쟁자보다) 싸게 팔다
uncontaminated **adj.** 오염되지 않은
wholesome **adj.** 건강한
development **n.** 동향, 정세

TEST 2

46. 추론

이 연설로 도움을 받을 수 있을 것 같은 사람은 누구인가?

(a) 사업을 시작하고자 하는 사람
(b) 제과 제품을 좋아하는 사람
(c) 사용하지 않은 제과 장비를 가지고 있는 사람
(d) 시간제 근무를 하고 싶은 사람

해설 첫 번째 문단을 보면, 연설자가 제과 사업 창업과 관련된 절차에 대해서 논할 예정이라고(I'm going to discuss the steps involved in starting your own baking business.) 하며 뒤이어 각 단계들을 설명하고 있으므로, 정답은 (a)이다.

정답 (a)

어휘
equipment **n.** 장비

47. 특정정보

제과 사업을 시작할 때 첫 번째로 해야 할 일은 무엇인가?

(a) 사업을 시작할 좋은 위치를 찾는 것
(b) 제과의 기본 기술을 배우는 것
(c) 모든 종류의 제과 제품을 만드는 법을 숙지하는 것
(d) 재료를 위해 좋은 납품 업체를 찾는 것

해설 두 번째 문단을 보면, 제과점을 시작하는데 있어서 처음으로 배워야 할 것은 운영의 기본기라고(The first thing to learn in setting up a bakery is the basics of its operation.) 하며, 제과 제품들을 판매할 것이기 때문에 당연히 제과하는 방법을 배워야 할 것이라고(Naturally, you will have to learn how to bake because baked goods are what you will be selling.) 말하고 있으므로, 정답은 (b)이다.

정답 (b)

어휘
location **n.** 위치

48. 특정정보

왜 친구나 친척에게 돈을 빌리는 것이 바람직한가?

(a) 큰 금액을 빌릴 수 있기 때문에
(b) 이자를 요청하지 않을 것이기 때문에
(c) 상환할 필요가 없을 것이기 때문에
(d) 상환할 시간을 더 줄 것이기 때문에

해설 네 번째 문단을 보면, 가까운 관계의 사람들에게 돈을 빌리는 것이 나을 수 있다고(Borrowing from people whom you are close to would be better) 하며 이는 빠듯한 기간 내에 빚을 상환해야 한다는 압박이 없을 것이기 때문이라고(because you won't have the pressure of repaying your debts within a strict timeframe.) 말하고 있으므로, 정답은 (d)이다.

정답 (d)

어휘
sum **n.** 돈, 합계

49. 추론

왜 레스토랑에 제과 제품을 납품하는 것이 업계에서 명성을 확고히 해줄 수 있는가?

(a) 대부분의 레스토랑이 믿을 수 있는 납품업체하고만 거래한다.
(b) 대부분의 사람들이 레스토랑에서 제과 제품을 구매한다.
(c) 레스토랑은 품질이 좋은 빵과 페이스트리를 판매한다.
(d) 레스토랑은 제과 제품의 주요 구매업체이다.

해설 여섯 번째 문단을 보면, 레스토랑, 카페, 그리고 빵과 페이스트리를 제공하는 곳들에 접근해 보라고(approach restaurants, cafes, and other places that serve breads and pastries.) 하며 건강에 좋고 양질의 제품을 납품하는 것은 평판이 좋은 제과 제품 납품업자로서 명성을 확고히 해줄 뿐만 아니라 고객층도 늘릴 수 있다고(Supplying wholesome, quality products will not only establish your name as a reputable supplier of baked products, but it could also increase your customer base.) 말하고 있으므로, 대부분의 레스토랑이 믿을 수 있는 납품업체하고만 거래를 한다는 것을 추론할 수 있다. 따라서 정답은 (a)이다.

정답 (a)

어휘
reliable **adj.** 믿을 수 있는

50. 특정정보

이 연설에 따르면, 어떻게 비용을 잘 관리할 수 있는가?

(a) 제품을 낮은 가격에 판매함으로써

(b) 비싼 재료를 공급하는 납품 업체를 고름으로써

(c) 대량으로 재료를 구매함으로써

(d) 대량으로 제과 제품을 생산함으로써

해설 일곱 번째 문단을 보면, 제과회사 창업과 관련된 다섯 번째 단계는 사업비를 잘 관리하는 방법을 찾는 것이라고(The fifth step is to identify ways to stay on top of your costs.) 소개하며, 할인을 받으려면 가능한 한 재료를 대량으로 구매하라고(To get discounts, buy supplies in bulk as much as possible.) 말하고 있으므로, 정답은 (c)이다.

정답 (c)

어휘
volume **n.** 양, 용량

51. 추론

화자에 따르면, 기업들은 언제 곤경에 처할 수 있는가?

(a) 제품이 너무 비싼 경우

(b) 작업장이 안전하지 않은 경우

(c) 성분이 알레르기 반응을 일으키는 경우

(d) 식품의 품질이 안전하지 않을 경우

해설 다섯 번째 문단을 보면, 요식업을 시작할 때는 운영하게 될 사업장이 청결하고 제품이 안전하다는 것을 보장하기 위한 보건 허가증이 분명히 필요하다고(Starting a food business specifically requires a health permit to ensure that the workplace you will be operating is clean and your products are safe.) 말하고 있으므로, 안전하지 않은 식품 보관이 보건 허가증이 취소되게 할 수 있음을 추론할 수 있다. 그리고 여덟 번째 문단을 보면, 고객이 식중독에 걸리는 것을 방지하기 위해서 제품을 오염되지 않고, 건강에 좋고, 그리고 양질의 상태로 유지하라고(Keep your products uncontaminated, wholesome, and of high quality to prevent customers from getting food poisoning.) 말하고 있으므로, 안전하지 않은 식품이 질병을 유발할 수 있다는 것을 추론할 수 있고, 그와 동시에 식품의 품질이 안 좋을 경우 기업을 곤경에 처할 수 있게 할 것이라고 추론할 수 있다. 따라서, 정답은 (d)이다.

정답 (d)

어휘
expensive **adj.** 비싼, 돈이 많이 드는
secure **adj.** 안전한, 안심하는
ingredient **n.** 성분, 재료

52. 세부사항

사업주는 어떻게 경쟁에서 앞서 나갈 수 있는가?

(a) 그들은 새로운 종류의 베이킹을 개발할 수 있다.

(b) 그들은 다른 사업체와 합병할 수 있다.

(c) 그들은 최신 정보를 배울 수 있다.

(d) 그들은 자신만의 웹사이트를 시작할 수 있다.

해설 마지막 문단을 보면, 제과 분야의 최근 동향을 알고 있으라 하며, 동업 조합에 가입하고, 인터넷을 검색하고, 이 업계의 최신 경향을 파악하고 있으라는(Always stay updated on the latest developments in baking. Join peer groups, surf the Internet, and remain aware of the most recent trends in the business.) 내용이 있으므로, 정답은 (c)이다.

정답 (c)

어휘
develop **v.** 개발하다, 성장(발달)하다
merge **v.** 합병(병합)하다, 합치다, (서로 구분이 안 되게) 어우러지다

TEST 2

Chapter 2
Listening

01 청취 모의고사 3회

27	(a)	28	(b)	29	(a)	30	(c)	31	(b)
32	(d)	33	(c)	34	(b)	35	(c)	36	(c)
37	(d)	38	(b)	39	(a)	40	(c)	41	(d)
42	(a)	43	(b)	44	(a)	45	(b)	46	(c)
47	(d)	48	(a)	49	(b)	50	(d)	51	(c)
52	(a)								

Part 1 Q. 27-33

27: What is the main topic of the conversation?
28: Why does Marie often choose to eat fast food?
29: What happens to the unused calories in one's body?
30: How do companies encourage people to eat fast food?
31: What does Marie rarely see in a fast food restaurant?
32: According to Marie, how can fast food cause hypertension?
33: What will Marie most likely do after the conversation?

M: Hi, Marie! What are your plans for dinner tonight?
M: 안녕, Marie! 오늘 밤 저녁 식사 계획이 어떻게 되니?

F: Hey, Raymond. I'll probably just order a burger and some fries for take-out tonight.
F: 안녕, Raymond. 오늘 밤에는 아마 햄버거랑 감자튀김을 포장해달라고 주문할 것 같아.

M: Fast food again? I just saw you having pizza for dinner the other night. 27) You are aware that eating too much fast food can be bad for you, right?
M: 또 패스트푸드야? 네가 다른 날 밤에도 저녁으로 피자를 먹는 걸 봤는데. 과다한 패스트푸드 섭취가 너에게 나쁠 수 있다는 것을 알고 있잖아, 그치?

F: Yes, I know it isn't the best option. It's just that I don't always have time to cook when I get home from work. And even if I do, I'm usually too tired to do anything else but rest. Meanwhile, 28) fast food is always available and less time-consuming than cooking a regular meal.
F: 응, 나는 그게 최상의 선택이 아니라는 건 알아. 단지 퇴근하고 집에 도착했을 때 요리할 시간이 항상 있는 게 아니라서 그럴 뿐이야. 그리고 심지어 시간이 있다고 해도, 보통 무언가 다른 것을 하기에는 너무 피곤해서 쉬는 것밖에 할 수 없어. 반면, 패스트푸드는 항상 이용 가능하고 일반적인 식사를 요리하는 것보다 시간이 더 적게 들잖아.

M: That may be true, but convenience almost never makes up for healthy eating. Fast food has lots of calories. One hamburger, for instance, can contain as much as one thousand five hundred calories, almost two-thirds of the recommended daily calorie intake for an average adult.
M: 그게 사실일지 모르지만, 편리함이 건강한 식사를 대신하는 일은 거의 없어. 패스트푸드는 칼로리가 높거든. 예를 들어, 햄버거 하나는 1,500 칼로리 정도를 함유하는데, 일반 성인을 위한 하루 칼로리 권장량의 거의 3분의 2에 해당해.

F: Really? Does that mean all the calories I get from other meals that day would put me over the daily recommended limit?
F: 정말? 그럼 내가 그날 다른 식사로 섭취하는 모든 칼로리가 하루 권장 제한을 넘기게 될 거라는 말이야?

M: That's correct. By eating a single serving of a burger with fries, you take in twice as many calories as you would if you ate a typical serving of pasta and salad.
M: 맞아. 햄버거와 감자튀김 1인분을 먹음으로써, 네가 보통 파스타와 샐러드를 먹었을 때보다 2배 더 많은 칼로리를 섭취하게 되는 거야.

F: So, 29) what happens to the extra calories in my body?
F: 그럼, 내 체내에 있는 여분의 칼로리에는 무슨 일이 벌어지는 거야?

M: 29) Those that are not converted into energy turn into fat, especially if you lead a sedentary lifestyle. That is, if you spend most of your day just sitting around reading, using the computer, or watching TV.
M: 에너지로 변하지 않는 칼로리들은 지방으로 변하게 돼, 특히 네가 주로 앉아서 지내는 생활을 한다면 말이야. 즉, 네가 하루의 대부분을 그저 책을 읽거나, 컴퓨터를 하거나, 텔레비전을 보면서 빈둥댄다면 말이지.

F: That sounds exactly like my lifestyle.
F: 그건 완전히 내 생활방식 같은데.

M: Well, if you keep eating fast food, you'll surely put on extra weight. Studies have shown that consumption of fast food is a leading cause of obesity. This is bad news for people who don't find the time to choose nutritious meals and just turn to fast food as a mainstay of their diet.
M: 음, 만일 네가 계속 패스트푸드를 먹는다면, 분명히 체중이 늘 거야. 연구들은 패스트푸드 섭취가 비만의 주요 원인이라고 밝혔어. 이건 영양가 높은 식사를 할 시간이 없어 주식으로 패스트푸드에 의지하는 사람들에게는 안 좋은 소식이지.

F: I agree, but it's hard to resist sometimes. I mean, 30) to entice more customers, many fast food chains are now offering larger portions for an additional charge of next to nothing. You just spend a few extra dollars to upgrade your meal.
F: 동의해. 하지만 때때로 거부하기가 힘들어. 내 말은, 요새 더 많은 고객을 유인하기 위해, 많은 패스트푸드 체인점이 아주 약간의 추가 금액만 내면 더 많은 양을 제공하고 있거든. 식사를 업그레이드하기 위해 단지 몇 달러만 더 내면 되는 거야.

M: It all sounds very enticing, especially to people who just want to eat without considering nutrition. 31) Fast food meals are very high in fats to improve taste, but low in the complex carbohydrates and vitamins and minerals that keep you healthy.
M: 모두 굉장히 유혹적으로 들리네, 특히 영양을 생각하지 않고 그저 먹기만 하고 싶어하는 사람들에게 말이야. 패스트푸드 식사는 맛을 좋게 하기 위한 지방이 매우 많은데, 건강함을 유지하게 해주는 복합 탄수화물, 비타민, 그리고 무기물이 적어.

F: Hmm··· No wonder 31) I rarely see fresh fruits, vegetables, or whole grains on a fast food restaurant's menu.
F: 음. 패스트푸드점 메뉴에서 신선한 과일, 야채, 또는 통밀을 거의 볼 수 없는 게 놀랄 일이 아니구나.

M: Yes, most fast food lacks natural ingredients and is usually prepared with artificial additives to enhance flavor, texture, and color. Also, a lot of salt is added to fast food items as a preservative. You can get your daily salt requirement from just one fast food meal!
M: 그렇지. 대부분의 패스트푸드는 자연 재료가 부족하고 맛, 식감, 그리고 색을 향상시키기 위해 인공 첨가물로 보통 만들어져. 또한, 패스트푸드 제품에는 방부제로 소금이 많이 첨가되기도 해. 패스트푸드 단 한 끼로 하루 필요 소금양을 섭취할 수 있어!

F: I didn't know that. And 32) doesn't too much salt cause hypertension?
F: 그건 몰랐어. 그리고 과다한 소금 섭취는 고혈압을 야기하지 않니?

M: Yes, not to mention heart disease and strokes.
M: 응, 심장병과 뇌졸중은 말할 것도 없지.

F: Well, fast food certainly comes with a lot of risks.
F: 이런, 패스트푸드는 정말로 많은 위험요소를 가지고 있구나.

M: 33) It's all right to indulge once in a while, Marie, but it won't hurt to put more effort into making healthier choices.
M: 어쩌다가 한번 마음껏 먹는 건 괜찮지만, Marie, 더 건강한 선택을 하는 데 노력을 더 기울이는 게 나쁠 건 없지.

F: 33) I'll take your advice seriously. Thanks a lot, Raymond!
F: 네 충고를 진지하게 받아들일게. 정말 고마워, Ray-

어휘
time-consuming **adj.** (많은)시간이 걸리는
convenience **n.** 편리함
contain **v.** 포함하다
average **adj.** 일반의, 평균의, 보통의
convert **v.** 변하게 하다, 전환시키다
sedentary **adj.** 주로 앉아서 하는
consumption **n.** 섭취, 소비
leading **adj.** 주요한, 가장 중요한
obesity **n.** 비만
nutritious **adj.** 영양가 높은
resist **v.** 거부하다
enticing **adj.** 유혹적인
ingredient **n.** 재료
artificial **adj.** 인공적인
preservative **n.** 방부제
requirement **n.** 필요(요건)
indulge **v.** 마음껏 하다

TEST 3

27. 주제

대화의 주요 주제는 무엇인가?

(a) 과다한 패스트푸드의 영향
(b) 칼로리 계산의 중요성
(c) 패스트푸드에 대한 Raymond의 불호
(d) Marie의 빡빡한 업무 일정

해설 Raymond의 두 번째 대사를 보면, Marie에게 과다한 패스트푸드 섭취가 너에게 나쁠 수 있다는 것을 알고 있지 않느냐고(You are aware that eating too much fast food can be bad for you) 하며 대화 전반에 패스트푸드의 악영향에 대해서 이야기하고 있으므로, 정답은 (a)이다.

정답 (a)

어휘
hectic **adj.** 빡빡한, 바쁜

28. 세부사항

왜 Marie는 종종 패스트푸드 먹는 것을 택하는가?

(a) 하루 칼로리 섭취량으로 가득 차 있기 때문에
(b) 그녀에게는 그렇게 하는 것이 편리하기 때문에
(c) 건강한 음식보다 더 포만감을 주기 때문에
(d) 집에서 요리한 음식보다 더 맛있기 때문에

해설 Marie의 두 번째 대사를 보면, 패스트푸드는 항상 이용할 수 있고 일반적인 식사를 요리하는 것보다 시간이 덜 든다고(fast food is always available and less time-consuming than cooking a regular meal.) 말하고 있으므로, 정답은 (b)이다.

정답 (b)

어휘
packed with **phr v.** ~로 꽉 찬
filling **adj.** 포만감을 주는

29. 세부사항

체내의 소비되지 않은 칼로리에 무슨 일이 생기는가?

(a) 체지방으로 변한다.
(b) 정적인 생활방식으로 이어진다.
(c) 영양의 흡수를 막는다.
(d) 여분의 에너지를 제공한다.

해설 Marie가 네 번째 대사에서 체내에 있는 여분의 칼로리에 무슨 일이 벌어지는 거냐고(what happens to the extra calories in my body?) 묻자, 그 다음 대사에서 Raymond가 에너지로 변하지 않은 칼로리는 지방으로 변한다고(Those that are not converted into energy turn into fat) 말하고 있으므로, 정답은 (a)이다.

정답 (a)

어휘
absorption **n.** 흡수

30. 세부사항

어떻게 회사가 사람들로 하여금 패스트푸드를 먹도록 하는가?

(a) 더 맛있는 식사를 제공함으로써
(b) 더 많은 영양분을 제공함으로써
(c) 더 많은 양을 제공함으로써
(d) 서비스를 향상시킴으로써

해설 Marie의 여섯 번째 대사를 보면, 더 많은 고객을 유인하기 위해 많은 패스트푸드 체인점이 아주 약간의 추가 금액만 내면 더 많은 양을 제공하고 있다고(to entice more customers, many fast food chains are now offering larger portions for an additional charge of next to nothing.) 말하고 있으므로, 정답은 (c)이다.

정답 (c)

어휘
nutrition **n.** 영양분, 영양

31. 특정정보

Marie가 패스트푸드 식당에서 거의 볼 수 없는 것은 무엇인가?

(a) 메뉴의 영양 정보
(b) 식품의 건강한 성분
(c) 정말 맛있는 식사
(d) 자연의 맛을 즐기는 사람

해설 Raymond의 일곱 번째 대사를 보면, 패스트푸드 식사는 맛을 좋게 하기 위한 지방이 매우 많은 반면 건강함을 유지하게 해주는 복합 탄수화물, 비타민과 무기물이 적다고(Fast food meals are very high in fats to improve taste, but low in the complex carbohydrates and vitamins and minerals that keep you healthy.) 말하고 있으며, 패스트푸드점 메뉴에서 신선한 과일, 야채, 그리고 통곡물을 거의 볼 수 없는 게 놀랄 일이 아니라고(I rarely see fresh fruits, vegetables, or whole grains on a fast food restaurant's menu.) 말하고 있으므로 건강한 성분이 거의 없다는 것을 알 수 있다. 따라서 정답은 (b)이다.

정답 (b)

어휘
nutrient **n.** 영양소

32. 세부사항

Marie에 따르면, 어떻게 패스트푸드가 고혈압을 야기할 수 있는가?

(a) 체내의 무기물을 제거한다.
(b) 비타민이 부족하다.
(c) 인공 첨가물이 있다.
(d) 소금이 너무 많이 함유되어 있다.

해설 Marie의 여덟 번째 대사를 보면, 과다한 소금 섭취가 고혈압을 야기하지 않느냐고(doesn't too much salt cause hypertension?) 말하고 있으므로, 정답은 (d)이다.

정답 (d)

어휘
additive **n.** 첨가물

33. 추론

대화 후에 Marie는 무엇을 할 것 같은가?

(a) 패스트푸드 식사 업그레이드하지 않기
(b) 칼로리를 태우기 위해 운동 시작하기
(c) 패스트푸드 섭취 줄이기
(d) 하루 칼로리 섭취량 관찰 시작하기

해설 Raymond와 Marie의 마지막 대화를 보면, 패스트푸드를 어쩌다가 한번 먹는 건 괜찮지만 더 건강한 선택을 하는 데 노력을 기울여서 나쁠 게 없다는(It's all right to indulge once in a while, Marie, but it won't hurt to put more effort into making healthier choices.) Raymond의 말에 Marie가 그의 충고를 진지하게 받아들일 것이라고(I'll take your advice seriously.) 말하고 있으므로, 정답은 (c)이다.

정답 (c)

어휘
monitor **v.** 관찰하다, 감시하다

Part 2 Q. 34-39

34: What is Sally Morgan mainly discussing in her talk?
35: Aside from a busy work schedule, why are some parents unable to have an active social life?
36: What guarantees customers that Busy Bee babysitters are reliable and trustworthy?
37: According to the speaker, which requires a second babysitter?
38: How can parents get a visit from a consultant?
39: Who are most likely to be interested in the talk?

Good morning! My name is Sally Morgan, and I am the general manager of Busy Bee Babysitting Services. 34) Aside from our company being a leader in providing parents with quality childcare, we help children explore their artistic skills and get in touch with the artists within.
좋은 아침입니다! 제 이름은 Sally Morgan이고, Busy Bee 위탁 보육 서비스의 총괄 매니저입니다. 당사는 부모에게 우수한 보육 서비스를 제공하는 데 있어서 선도적인 기업일 뿐만 아니라, 아이들이 자신의 예술적 능력을 탐구하고 내면의 예술가를 만날 수 있도록 도와주기도 합니다.

We understand that finding quality childcare is a top priority for you as a parent. 35, 39) With a hectic work schedule plus the responsibility of caring for your children, it may seem impossible for you to enjoy a healthy and active social life. As a parent,

it can also be difficult to find the right people to tend to your kids in your absence. But with Busy Bee, not only can you trust our highly competent babysitters to take care of your children, you can also rest assured that they will give them a fun learning experience.
당사는 우수한 보육 서비스를 찾는 것이 부모로서의 여러분에게 최우선 순위라는 것을 알고 있습니다. 바쁜 업무 일정과 아이를 돌봐야 하는 책임감이 더해지면, 건강하고 활발한 사회생활을 즐기는 것은 여러분에게 불가능해 보일지도 모릅니다. 부모로서, 부재 시 아이들을 돌봐 줄 적절한 사람을 찾는 것 역시 어려울 수 있죠. 그러나 Busy Bee와 함께하면, 여러분의 아이들을 돌봐 줄 굉장히 유능한 저희 보육사를 신뢰할 수 있을 뿐만 아니라, 그들이 아이들에게 재미있는 학습 경험을 제공할 테니 안심하셔도 됩니다.

In addition to being certified childcare providers, our babysitters are also artists from many different fields. Their talents range from acting, singing and dancing to creative writing, photography, and the graphic arts. They use their skills to engage a child in activities that match his or her interests. We take pride in our interactive childcare model that allows children to actively take part in skill-building exercises. During the babysitting sessions, our childcare providers enforce a "no television" policy to ensure that creative goals are reached by the end of each session.
당사의 보육사는 검증된 보육 서비스 제공자일 뿐만 아니라, 많은 다양한 분야의 예술가이기도 합니다. 그들의 재능은 연기, 노래, 춤부터 문예창작, 사진, 그리고 그래픽 아트까지 다양합니다. 그들은 자신의 기술을 사용하여 아이가 각자의 흥미에 맞는 활동에 참여하게끔 합니다. 당사는 아이가 실력 쌓기 활동에 능동적으로 참여하게 해주는 상호 보육 서비스 모델에 대한 자부심이 있습니다. 매 수업 시간이 끝날 때 창의적인 목표를 달성할 수 있도록 하기 위해, 당사의 보육사는 보육 수업 동안 "텔레비전 금지" 정책을 시행합니다.

36) Rest assured that all of our childcare providers have good reputations. We perform thorough background checks on each babysitter before hiring them. We solicit references from all of their previous employers to get a complete picture of the candidate's character and employment history. After being hired, they undergo our childcare courses so they understand the company's standards and methods for creative childcare. They also complete training in basic first aid so they are able to handle emergency situations safely and quickly.
당사의 보육 제공자들 전부 좋은 평판을 보유하고 있으니 안심하세요. 당사는 보육사를 고용하기 전에 각 보육사에 대한 철저한 신원 조사를 실시합니다. 지원자의 성격이나 경력을 완벽하게 파악하기 위해 모든 그들의 이전 고용주에게 추천서를 요청합니다. 고용 후, 보육사들은 창의적 보육에 대한 당사의 기준과 방법을 이해하기 위해 보육 관련 수업을 받습니다. 그들은 또한 응급 상황을 안전하고 신속하게 해결할 수 있도록 기본 응급 처치 훈련도 수료합니다.

Our babysitters are available for very reasonable prices anytime you need them, everything from the occasional night out to a regular weekly babysitting schedule. 37) If you have more than four children, or more than two children under three years of age, a second babysitter is required for the session. Our rates start at $15 per hour with a minimum of three hours per session.
간헐적 야간 외출부터 정기 주간 돌봄 스케줄까지 모든 것을 포함하여, 여러분이 필요한 시간이라면 언제든 상관없이 당사의 보육사들을 굉장히 합리적인 비용에 이용할 수 있습니다. 자녀가 4명 이상이거나 3살 미만의 아이가 2명 이상이라면, 해당 수업 시간에 두 번째 보육사가 필요합니다. 비용은 수업 당 최소 3시간으로 시간 당 15달러부터 시작합니다.

Payment shall be made to the babysitter in cash at the end of each session. Standard hourly rates apply until 10:00 p.m. Any babysitter who stays beyond 10:00 p.m. is entitled to a transportation allowance on top of overtime pay, which is 1.5 times the standard rate. Sessions should be scheduled at least one day in advance. In the event of a cancellation, our office must be notified at least 24 hours prior to the session.
비용은 매 수업이 끝날 때 보육사에게 현금으로 지불해야 합니다. 기본 시급은 밤 10시까지 적용됩니다. 밤 10시를 초과해서 근무하는 모든 보육사는 기본 시급의 1.5배인 초과 근무 수당 외에 교통비도 적용받습니다. 수업은 적어도 하루 전에 미리 예약해야 합니다. 취소 시에는, 늦어도 수업 24시간 전에 저희 사무실에 알려주어야 합니다.

38) Once you decide to hire our company, one of our consultants will visit you at home to discuss both your babysitting needs and the dynamics of

your family. This in-home consultation will cover all the necessary information regarding costs, schedules, choice of babysitters, and any other concerns you may have. At the end of this visit, you will be asked to sign our service agreement contract.
당사를 이용하기로 결정하면, 여러분의 위탁 보육 요구 조건과 가족이 소통하는 방식환경에 대해 논의하기 위해 상담사 중 한 명이 집을 방문할 것입니다. 이 가정 방문 상담은 비용, 일정, 보육사 선택, 그리고 여러분이 갖고 있을지도 모르는 다른 우려 사항들에 관련된 모든 필수 정보를 다룰 것입니다. 방문이 끝날 때, 여러분은 서비스 이용 동의 계약서에 서명하라는 요청을 받을 것입니다.

[39] Let Busy Bee Babysitting Services bring out the creativity in your children, and put time back into your social life. Please call us at 555-0159 or send us an email.
Busy Bee 위탁 보육 서비스가 여러분의 아이에게 내재되어 있는 창의성을 끌어내 주고, 여러분이 사회생활을 즐길 시간을 돌려주겠습니다. 저희에게 555-0159로 전화 주시거나 이메일을 보내주십시오.

어휘
explore **v.** 탐구하다, 찾다
priority **n.** 우선 순위
hectic **adj.** 바쁜, 빡빡한
tend to **phr v.** ~를 보살피다
absence **n.** 부재
competent **adj.** 유능한, 능력 있는
rest assured **phr v.** 안심해도 된다, ~를 믿어도 된다
interactive **adj.** 상호적인
reputation **n.** 평판, 명성
thorough **adj.** 철저한
solicit **v.** 요청하다, 간청하다
reference **n.** 추천서
candidate **n.** 지원자
undergo **v.** 받다, 겪다
reasonable **adj.** 합리적인, 적당한
occasional **adj.** 간헐적인, 가끔의
allowance **n.** 비용, 수당
notify **v.** 알리다, 고지하다
dynamics **n.** 소통하는/영향을 미치는 방식

34. 주제

Sally Morgan이 연설에서 주로 이야기하고 있는 것은?

(a) 적절한 위탁 보육의 중요성
(b) 위탁 보육 회사의 서비스
(c) 부모 됨의 어려움
(d) 예술 탐구의 이점

해설 첫 번째 문단을 보면, 자신의 회사가 부모에게 우수한 보육 서비스를 제공하는 데 있어서 선도적인 기업일 뿐만 아니라, 아이가 예술적 능력을 찾고 자신 안에 있는 예술가를 만날 수 있도록 도와주기도 한다고(Aside from our company being a leader in providing parents with quality childcare, we help children explore their artistic skills and get in touch with the artists within.) 소개하며, 연설 내내 회사가 제공하는 보육 서비스에 대한 설명을 하고 있으므로, 정답은 (b)이다.

정답 (b)

어휘
benefit **n.** 이점
exploration **n.** 탐구

35. 세부사항

바쁜 업무 일정 이외에, 왜 몇몇 부모가 활발한 사회생활을 할 수 없는가?

(a) 보육사를 신뢰하지 않기 때문에
(b) 보육사를 고용할 여유가 없기 때문에
(c) 아이를 돌봐야 하기 때문에
(d) 보통 오랜 시간 근무하기 때문에

해설 두 번째 문단을 보면, 바쁜 업무 일정과 아이를 돌봐야 하는 책임감이 더해지면 건강하고 활발한 사회생활을 즐기는 것이 불가능해 보인다고(With a hectic work schedule plus the responsibility of caring for your children, it may seem impossible for you to enjoy a healthy and active social life.) 말하고 있으므로, 정답은 (c)이다.

정답 (c)

어휘
afford **v.** ~할 여유가 되다

TEST 3

36. 특정정보

무엇이 고객들에게 Busy Bee 보육사들이 믿을 만하고 신뢰할 수 있다고 보장해주는가?

(a) 예술 분야에 있어서 엄격한 교육
(b) 보육 분야에서의 수년간 실무 경험
(c) 고용 전 자세히 확인된 개인 이력
(d) 응급 처치에 관한 고도의 지식

해설 네 번째 문단을 보면, 회사의 보육사 전부가 좋은 평판을 보유하고 있으니 안심해도 된다고(Rest assured that all of our childcare providers have good reputations.) 하며, 보육사를 고용하기 전에 철저한 신원 조사를 실시한다고(We perform thorough background checks on each babysitter before hiring them.) 말하고 있으므로, 정답은 (c)이다.

정답 (c)

어휘
rigid **adj.** 엄격한
advanced **adj.** 고도의, 고급의,

37. 세부사항

연설자에 따르면, 다음 중 어느 경우에 두 번째 보육사가 필요한가?

(a) 가정의 자녀가 4명 미만
(b) 특별한 주의가 필요한 아이
(c) 밤 10시를 넘기는 수업
(d) 2명 이상의 3살 미만 아이들

해설 다섯 번째 문단을 보면, 자녀가 4명 이상이거나 3살 미만의 아이가 2명 이상이라면 해당 수업 시간에 두 번째 보육사가 필요하다고(If you have more than four children, or more than two children under three years of age, a second babysitter is required for the session.) 말하고 있으므로, 정답은 (d)이다.

정답 (d)

어휘
require **v.** 필요하다, 요구하다

38. 세부사항

어떻게 부모들은 상담사로부터 방문을 받을 수 있는가?

(a) 서비스에 대한 우려를 표명함으로써
(b) 서비스 가입을 선택함으로써
(c) 계약 파기를 결정함으로써
(d) 추가 상담 비용 지불을 함으로써

해설 당사를 이용하기로 결정하면, 위탁 보육 요구 조건과 가정환경에 대해 논의하기 위해 상담사 중 한 명이 집을 방문할 것이라는(Once you decide to hire our company, one of our consultants will visit you at home to discuss both your babysitting needs and the dynamics of your family.) 내용이 나와 있으므로 서비스 가입 선택 시 상담사가 방문한다는 것을 알 수 있다. 따라서 정답은 (b)이다.

정답 (b)

어휘
require **v.** 필요하다, 요구하다

39. 추론

누가 이 연설에 흥미를 가질 것 같은가?

(a) 맞벌이 부모들
(b) 장차 보육사가 되려는 사람들
(c) 전문 예술가들
(d) 간호학과 학생들

해설 두 번째 문단을 보면, 바쁜 업무 일정과 아이를 돌봐야하는 책임감이 더해지면 건강하고 활발한 사회생활을 즐기는 것이 불가능해 보인다고(With a hectic work schedule plus the responsibility of caring for your children, it may seem impossible for you to enjoy a healthy and active social life.) 말하고 있고, 마지막 문단에서 Busy Bee 위탁 보육 서비스가 아이에게 내재되어 있는 창의성을 끌어내 주고, 사회생활을 즐길 시간을 돌려주겠다고(Let Busy Bee Babysitting Services bring out the creativity in your children, and put time back into your social life.) 말하고 있으므로, 이 연설에 흥미를 가질 것 같은 사람은 일하느라 바쁜 맞벌이 부모들이라는 것을 추론할 수 있다. 따라서 정답은 (a)이다.

정답 (a)

어휘
aspiring **adj.** 장차 ~가 되려고 하는

Part 3 Q. 40-45

40: What are Kim and Jesse discussing?
41: Which is true about the tuition fees for online universities?
42: Why is online education ideal for working individuals?
43: Why does Kim prefer an online classroom over a traditional one?
44: Why most likely does Jesse think a traditional classroom offers a better learning experience?
45: What will Kim most likely do after the conversation?

M: Hi, Kim! Congratulations on graduating from college! It must be a big relief to finally be done with school.
M: 안녕, Kim! 대학교 졸업을 축하해! 마침내 학교 공부를 다 마쳐서 한시름 놓았겠구나.

F: Thanks, Jesse! Actually, I don't think I'm quite done yet. I might start on a master's degree in September.
F: 고마워, Jesse! 사실, 아직 다 끝마친 것 같진 않아. 9월에 석사 과정을 시작할 지도 몰라.

M: Really? Where will you be studying this time?
M: 정말? 이번에는 어디서 공부할 예정이니?

F: 40) I want to try my luck with an online university. I haven't picked one yet, but it's nice to think that my campus, so to speak, could be a place with the nearest Internet connection.
F: 온라인 대학교에서 내 운을 시험해 보고 싶어. 아직 학교를 선택하진 않았지만, 소위 말하는 내 캠퍼스가 가장 가까운 인터넷 연결이 가능한 장소가 될 수 있다고 생각하니 좋아.

M: Yeah, but is it true that the tuition for most online universities is higher than that of regular schools?
M: 그래, 근데 대부분의 온라인 대학교 등록금이 보통 학교의 등록금보다 더 비싸다는게 사실이야?

F: Not at all. Many of the most expensive and prestigious colleges are starting to put their courses online at a fraction of the cost. Also, 41) in an online university, the price of course materials is usually included in the tuition, so there are no unexpected expenses. You can even apply for financial aid from the school.
F: 전혀 그렇지 않아. 등록금이 비싸고 유명한 대학교 중 다수가 적은 비용에 온라인으로 수업을 제공하기 시작하고 있어. 또한, 온라인 대학교에서는, 교재비가 보통 등록금에 포함되어 있어서, 예상치 못한 비용이 발생하지 않아. 심지어 학교에 재정적인 지원을 요청할 수도 있어.

M: Well, online universities do sound convenient. You won't have to worry about transportation costs, travel time, or parking fees, either.
M: 그렇구나, 온라인 대학교가 정말 편리해 보이네. 교통비, 통학 시간이나 주차 비용 같은 걸 걱정할 필요도 없을 거야.

F: Exactly. 42) I also plan to work part-time while studying. Online education seems ideal because I'll be able to take courses at my own pace. I can choose the number of classes to take in a given term. And even if I can only spend a limited time on schoolwork, I'll still get my degree eventually.
F: 맞아. 그리고 나는 공부하면서 시간제로 근무할 계획이야. 나만의 속도에 맞춰 수업을 들을 수 있을 것이기 때문에 온라인 교육이 이상적인 것 같아. 정해진 학기에 수강할 수업 수를 선택할 수 있거든. 그리고 학교 공부에 한정된 시간만을 쓰게 되더라도 결국엔 학위를 받게 될 거야.

M: Doing schoolwork on your own schedule is a nice perk, but you'll need discipline to finish assignments, especially those with deadlines in place. That could be difficult if you work 40 hours a week.
M: 네 일정에 맞춰서 학교 공부를 하는 건 좋은 특전이긴 한데, 과제를 마치기 위해선 훈련이 필요할 거야. 특히 마감이 있는 과제의 경우에 말이야. 만일 네가 일주일에 40시간을 일한다면 힘들 수 있어.

F: Well, I think it will depend on how hard I work and how well I manage my time. Anyway, another reason I'm considering an online program is to avoid scheduling conflicts. For instance, if one of the courses I need is only offered during the day, it would be regrettable if I had to give up my job just for one class.
F: 음, 그건 내가 얼마나 열심히 일하고 내 시간을 얼마나 잘 관리하느냐에 달릴 것 같아. 어쨌든, 내가 온라인 과정을 고려하는 또 다른 이유는 일정이 겹치는 걸 피하기 위해서야. 예를 들어, 만일 내가 필요로 하는 수업 중 하나가 낮에만 제공된다면, 그 한 수업을 위해서 내 일을 포기해야 하는 게 후회스러울 거야.

M: I understand that, Kim. However, an online program won't give you the college experience that comes from interacting with other students. I

TEST 3

mean, 43) you'll still be able to communicate with other people, but it will only be virtually, that is, through chat rooms and discussion threads on the Internet. That won't be as exciting as actual classroom interaction.

M: 그건 이해해, Kim. 하지만, 온라인 과정은 다른 학생들과 교류하는 데서 오는 대학교 경험을 주지는 못할거야. 내 말은, 네가 여전히 다른 사람과 소통할 수는 있겠지만, 그건 인터넷상의 채팅방이나 토론 게시판 의견을 통해 가상으로만 가능할테고. 실제 강의실에서의 상호작용만큼 재미있지는 않을거야.

F: 43) Honestly, I'd prefer it that way. It'd be easier to concentrate on schoolwork. In a regular classroom, I would probably get easily distracted by unruly students.

F: 솔직히, 나는 그 방식이 더 좋아. 학교 수업에 집중하기가 더 쉬울 거야. 일반적인 교실에서는, 제멋대로 구는 학생에 의해 아마도 쉽게 산만해질 것 같아.

M: Well, 44) I think it's still better to be taught by someone who can both explain the lessons and answer your questions in person. With online schooling, you only get to view recordings of lectures when you sign into a website, and you can only discuss things with the class in chat rooms.

M: 음, 그래도 나는 여전히 직접 수업 내용을 설명하고 네 질문에 답해줄 수 있는 누군가에게 배우는 게 더 좋은 것 같아. 온라인 수업으로, 너는 겨우 웹사이트에 접속해서 강의 녹화 영상만 볼 수 있고, 그리고 수업의 채팅방에서만 토론할 수 있는 거잖아.

F: I don't really mind that, Jesse. Besides, another advantage of online classes is that there are usually records of the important references on the website, and discussion threads are often saved. Lectures and assignments are accessible in video or text formats and can be downloaded at any time. If I miss a session or didn't catch important points during a lecture, I can always go back and review.

F: 난 그 부분에 대해서는 정말 상관 안 해, Jesse. 게다가, 온라인 수업의 또 다른 이점은 보통 그 웹사이트에 중요한 참고 문헌 기록이 있고, 토론 게시판 의견이 자주 저장된다는 거야. 강의와 과제는 비디오나 문서 형식으로 이용 가능하고, 아무 때나 다운받을 수 있어. 내가 수업을 놓치거나 강의 시간에 중요한 내용을 파악하지 못했더라도, 항상 다시 가서 복습할 수 있지.

M: I can't argue with that. Well, 45) it seems you've really got your mind set on an online university. I hope you find the right one for you.

M: 그건 반박할 수가 없네. 그래, 네가 정말 온라인 대학교로 마음을 굳힌 것 같구나. 너한테 딱 맞는 곳을 찾길 바랄게.

F: 45) I hope so, too. Thanks, Jesse!

F: 나도 그러길 바라. 고마워, Jesse!

M: You're welcome, Kim. Good luck!

M: 천만에, Kim. 행운을 빌어!

어휘

relief **n.** 안도감, 안심
fraction **n.** 적은 비용
unexpected **adj.** 예상치 못한, 예상 밖의
financial **adj.** 재정적인
perk **n.** 특전
discipline **n.** 훈련, 단련, 규율
assignment **n.** 과제
conflict **n.** 겹침, 갈등
regrettable **adj.** 후회스러운, 유감스러운
virtually **ad.** 가상으로
distracted **adj.** 산만한
unruly **adj.** 제멋대로 구는
reference **n.** 참고 문헌
discussion thread **n.** 토론 게시판에 올라온 일련의 의견

40. 주제

Kim과 Jesse가 이야기하고 있는 것은 무엇인가?

(a) 전통적인 대학교에서 Jesse가 한 경험
(b) 석사 학위를 받는 것에 대한 Jesse의 관심
(c) 온라인 대학교에 등록하려는 Kim의 계획
(d) 대학원 교육과정을 위한 Kim의 예산

해설 Kim의 두 번째 대사를 보면, 온라인 대학교에서 내 운을 시험해 보고 싶다고(I want to try my luck with an online university.)하며, 대화 전반에서 Kim의 계획 및 온라인 대학교의 장단점에 대해 이야기하고 있으므로, 정답은 (c)이다.

정답 (c)

어휘

enroll **v.** 등록하다
budget **n.** 예산

41. 사실확인

온라인 대학교 등록금에 대한 설명으로 바른 것은?

(a) 숨겨진 비용이 많다.
(b) 전통적인 학교의 등록금보다 비싸다.
(c) 학생들은 등록금을 충당하기 위한 장학금에 지원할 수 없다.
(d) 등록금의 일부가 교육 자료 비용이다.

해설 Kim의 세 번째 대사를 보면, 온라인 대학교에서는 보통 등록금에 수업 교재비가 포함되어 있어서 예상치 못한 비용이 발생하지 않는다고(in an online university, the price of course materials is usually included in the tuition, so there are no unexpected expenses.) 말하고 있으므로, 정답은 (d)이다.

정답 (d)

어휘
charge **n.** 비용, 요금

42. 세부사항

왜 온라인 교육이 일하는 사람에게 이상적인가?

(a) 더 유동적인 일정을 제공하기 때문에
(b) 보통 학생과 비교했을 때 수업을 들을 여유가 있기 때문에
(c) 학생 장학금을 신청할 수 있게 해주기 때문에
(d) 학교 과제를 덜 내주기 때문에

해설 Kim의 네 번째 대사를 보면, 공부하면서 시간제로 근무할 계획이라고(I also plan to work part-time while studying.) 하며 자신만의 속도에 맞춰 수업을 들을 수 있기 때문에 온라인 교육이 이상적인 것 같다고(Online education seems ideal because I'll be able to take courses at my own pace.) 말하고 있으므로, 정답은 (a)이다.

정답 (a)

어휘
flexible **adj.** 유동적인, 유연한, 융통성 있는
assign **v.** (일, 과제 등을) 내다

43. 세부사항

왜 Kim이 전통적인 교실보다 온라인 교실을 선호하는가?

(a) 다른 사람과 공부해야 하는 것으로부터 피하게 해준다.
(b) 수업에 더 집중할 수 있게 해준다.
(c) 언제든지 강의에 빠질 수 있다.
(d) 온라인으로 소통하는 것을 즐긴다.

해설 Jesse가 여섯 번째 대사에서 Kim이 온라인 수업을 듣는다면 다른 사람과 소통할 수는 있겠지만 인터넷상의 채팅방이나 토론 게시판 의견 교환처럼 가상으로만 가능할 뿐이라고(you'll still be able to communicate with other people, but it will only be virtually, that is, through chat rooms and discussion threads on the Internet.) 하자, 그 다음 대사에서 Kim이 솔직히 그 방식이 더 좋다고(Honestly, I'd prefer it that way.) 하며 학교 수업에 집중하기가 더 쉬울 거라고(It'd be easier to concentrate on schoolwork.) 말하고 있으므로, 정답은 (b)이다.

정답 (b)

어휘
skip **v.** 빠지다, 거르다

44. 추론

왜 Jesse는 전통적인 교실이 더 나은 학습 경험을 제공한다고 생각하는가?

(a) 대면 교육이 온라인 교육보다 더 직접적이다.
(b) 전통적인 교실이 학습에 더 좋은 환경이다.
(c) 더 잘 배우기 위해서는 학생이 서로를 만나야 한다.
(d) 전통적인 교실 선생님이 더 똑똑하다.

해설 Jesse의 일곱 번째 대사를 보면, 직접 수업 내용을 설명하고 질문에 답해줄 수 있는 누군가에게 배우는 게 더 좋은 것 같다고(I think it's still better to be taught by someone who can both explain the lessons and answer your questions in person.) 말하고 있으므로, 정답은 (a)이다.

정답 (a)

어휘
environment **n.** 환경

TEST 3

45. 추론
대화 후에 Kim은 무엇을 할 것 같은가?

(a) 학사 학위 과정 마치기
(b) 온라인 대학교에 등록할 준비하기
(c) 전통적인 대학원 수업 프로그램에 등록하기
(d) 온라인 대학교 수업에 대해 더 알아보기

해설 Jesse와 Kim의 마지막 대화를 보면, Jesse가 Kim에게 온라인 대학교로 마음을 굳힌 것 같아 보인다며(it seems you've really got your mind set on an online university.) 딱 맞는 곳을 찾길 바란다고(I hope you find the right one for you.) 하자, 이에 Kim이 자신도 그러길 바란다고(I hope so, too.) 말하고 있으므로, 곧 온라인 대학교 등록 준비를 할 예정이라는 것을 추론할 수 있다. 따라서 정답은 (b)이다.

정답 (b)

어휘
prepare **v.** 준비하다

Part 4 Q. 46-52

46: Why did Carl Heisenberg address the audience?
47: Based on the talk, why is photography relatively easy to learn?
48: What should be done to prevent an image from being confusing?
49: How can following the "rule of thirds" improve a photograph?
50: Why should subjects be photographed from an angle?
51: How can photographers add drama to an ordinary photograph?
52: Based on the talk, what is most likely the importance of understanding composition in photography?

Hello, everyone. Welcome to the Shutterbugs Basic Photography Workshop. My name is Carl Heisenberg, and 46) I am here to talk about photography technique. One of the many appeals of photography is that it is relatively easy to pick up. 47) While painting, sculpture, and other artistic fields may require years of training, almost anyone can learn how to take a picture easily.
안녕하세요, 여러분, Shutterbugs 기초 사진 촬영 워크숍에 오신 것을 환영합니다. 제 이름은 Carl Heisenberg이고, 이곳에 사진 촬영 기술에 대해 이야기하러 왔습니다. 사진 촬영의 많은 매력 중 하나는 상대적으로 익히기 쉽다는 것입니다. 그림, 조각, 그리고 다른 예술 분야는 수년간의 훈련을 필요로 할지 모르지만, 사진 촬영하는 방법은 거의 모든 사람이 쉽게 배울 수 있습니다.

Each year, a wide array of new cameras enters the market, and millions of photographs are taken. Even so, a good picture is seldom created by chance. We must first understand one of most important elements of photography: composition.
매년, 다수의 신형 카메라가 시장에 출시되고, 수백만 장의 사진이 찍힙니다. 그럼에도 불구하고, 좋은 사진은 우연히 찍히는 경우가 거의 없습니다. 우리는 사진 촬영의 가장 중요한 요소 중 하나인 구도에 대해 우선 배워야 합니다.

Composition is the arrangement of the visual elements in an image. The first thing to remember about composition is that 48) a picture should have only one subject or main center of interest. The other elements in the picture should support and focus the viewer's attention on the subject of the image. 48) A picture with more than one center of interest can be puzzling, leaving the viewer wondering what the picture is about. In contrast, an image with a single subject that boldly stands out, such as a white sailboat against a background of dark water, is immediately understood.
구도는 사진에서 시각적 요소의 배치를 의미합니다. 구도에 대해서 첫 번째로 기억해야 할 것은 사진에는 단 하나의 피사체 혹은 흥미를 끄는 주요 요소가 있어야 한다는 것입니다. 사진의 나머지 요소는 보는 이가 사진의 피사체에 집중하게끔 도와주어야 합니다. 흥미를 끄는 요소가 하나 이상인 사진은 혼란스러울 수 있고, 보는 이가 사진이 무엇에 관한 것인지 의아하게끔 만듭니다. 반면에, 어두운 물을 배경으로 한 하얀색 범선 같이, 과감하게 돋보이는 단 하나의 피사체가 있는 사진은 즉각적으로 이해됩니다.

Next, keep your subject simple. Simplicity is the key to good photographs. The more direct a picture is, the clearer and stronger its story or message becomes. Select a subject that lends itself to a simple arrangement. For example, instead of photographing an entire area, focus on an important object within the area. Make sure the material in the picture is just enough to convey a single idea. Although a picture may be composed of many contributing elements, none should attract more attention than the main object.

다음으로, 피사체를 단순하게 만드십시오. 단순함은 좋은 사진의 비결입니다. 사진이 더 직접적일수록, 이야기나 메시지가 더 분명해지고 강해집니다. 단순한 배치에 적합한 피사체를 선택하십시오. 예를 들어, 구역 전체를 찍는 대신에, 그 구역 안에서 중요한 하나의 대상에 초점을 맞추십시오. 사진에 있는 그 소재가 반드시 하나의 생각을 충분히 전달하도록 하십시오. 비록 사진이 수많은 기여 요소로 구성되어 있을지 몰라도, 그 중 어느 것도 주요 대상보다 더 많은 주의를 끌어서는 안 됩니다.

The third step is to consider the best placement of your subject. Sometimes, good composition is achieved by placing the subject in the center of the picture. However, it's not always a good idea to center the subject because it divides the picture into equal halves and makes it uninteresting. The general guideline for choosing the best location for the center of interest is called the "rule of thirds." 49) To create a feeling of balance in the composition, divide the picture's area into thirds, both vertically and horizontally, and place the subject at one of the intersections of the imaginary lines.
세 번째 단계는 여러분이 정한 피사체의 가장 좋은 위치를 생각해보는 것입니다. 때때로, 좋은 구도는 대상을 사진 가운데에 놓음으로써 이루어지기도 합니다. 그러나, 대상을 가운데에 두는 것이 항상 좋은 생각은 아닌데, 그 대상이 사진을 균일하게 반으로 나누어 대상이 자칫 지루해 보이게 만들기 때문입니다. 흥미를 끄는 요소의 최적 위치를 선택하는 일반적인 지침은 "삼등분의 법칙"이라고 불립니다. 구도의 균형감을 조성하기 위해, 사진의 구역을 수직 및 수평으로 각각 삼등분하고, 가상의 선들이 서로 교차하는 지점 중 하나에 피사체를 두는 것입니다.

Lastly, choose the best viewpoint for your image. 50) A proper viewpoint or camera angle is an important factor in good composition. Photographing from an unusual camera angle can bring out a unique feature of the subject. Most photography subjects are three-dimensional and should be photographed from an angle to show more than one of its sides.
마지막으로, 사진을 위한 최상의 각도를 선택하는 것입니다. 적합한 각도 혹은 촬영 각도는 좋은 구도의 중요한 요소입니다. 특이한 촬영 각도에서 사진을 찍는 것은 대상의 독특한 특징을 돋보이게 할 수 있습니다. 대부분의 피사체는 입체적이고, 한 면 이상을 보여주는 각도에서 촬영되어야 합니다.

51) A low camera angle can add drama and interest to an ordinary photograph. It can also give the subject strength and authority. To achieve a low angle, place the camera below the subject and point upward. Meanwhile, a high camera angle shows more of the relationships among the elements in the picture by playing down the strength of the subject. This is achieved by shooting from an elevated position.
로 앵글은 평범한 사진에 극적인 효과와 흥미를 더해줍니다. 또한 피사체에게 힘과 권위를 부여합니다. 로 앵글을 맞추기 위해서는, 카메라를 피사체보다 아래에 두고 위쪽으로 초점을 맞추십시오. 반면에, 하이 앵글은 피사체의 힘을 줄임으로써 사진 내 요소들 간의 관계를 더 보여줍니다. 이 각도는 높은 위치에서 촬영함으로써 맞출 수 있습니다.

The next time you take a picture, try applying these tips I have shared. 52) Once you have mastered the principles of photographic composition, you can capture interesting effects in your pictures with ease, and start shooting more professional photographs.
다음에 사진을 촬영할 때, 제가 공유해드린 이 조언을 적용해보십시오. 사진 구도의 원칙을 습득하고 나면, 여러분의 사진 속에 흥미로운 효과를 쉽게 포착할 수 있고, 더 전문적인 사진을 찍는 것을 시작할 수 있습니다.

어휘
photography **n.** 사진 촬영
appeal **n.** 매력
relatively **ad.** 상대적으로
a wide array of **adj.** 다수의
element **n.** 요소
composition **n.** 구도
lend itself to sth **phr.** ~에 적합하다
arrangement **n.** 배치, 정돈
puzzling **adj.** 혼란스러운
stand out **phr v.** 돋보이다, 눈에 띄다
subject **n.** 피사체
contributing **adj.** 기여하는, 보조하는
intersection **n.** 교차하는 지점
imaginary **adj.** 가상의
unique **adj.** 독특한
feature **n.** 특징
ordinary **adj.** 평범한
elevated **adj.** 높은
apply **v.** 적용하다
principle **n.** 원칙, 원리
capture **v.** 포착하다

TEST 3

46. 주제
왜 Carl Heisenberg는 청중에게 연설했는가?

(a) 사진 촬영 동호회에 가입하라고 초대하기 위해
(b) 사진의 피사체를 선정하는데 조언을 해주기 위해
(c) 사진의 구도를 잡는 것에 대해 이야기하기 위해
(d) 카메라 구매에 관한 조언을 해주기 위해

해설 첫 번째 문단을 보면, 사진 촬영 기술에 대해 이야기하러 왔다고(I am here to talk about photography technique) 하며, 전반적으로 구도(composition)에 대해서 이야기하고 있으므로, 정답은 (c)이다.

정답 (c)

어휘
compose **v.** (사진, 그림 등의) 구도를 잡다

47. 세부사항
연설에 따르면, 왜 사진 촬영이 상대적으로 배우기 쉬운가?

(a) 그림을 그리는 것과 비슷하기 때문에
(b) 카메라를 저렴하게 구매할 수 있게 때문에
(c) 사진을 수정하기가 쉽기 때문에
(d) 집중 학습을 요구하지 않기 때문에

해설 첫 번째 문단을 보면, 그림, 조각 및 다른 예술 분야는 수년간의 훈련을 필요로 할 지 모르지만, 사진 촬영하는 방법은 거의 모든 사람이 쉽게 배울 수 있다고(While painting, sculpture, and other artistic fields may require years of training, almost anyone can learn how to take a picture easily.) 말하고 있으므로, 정답은 (d)이다.

정답 (d)

어휘
intensive **adj.** 집중적인

48. 특정정보
사진이 혼란스럽게 되는 것을 방지하려면 무엇을 해야 하는가?

(a) 오직 하나의 피사체를 사용할 것
(b) 평범한 피사체를 선택할 것
(c) 사진에 다양한 요소를 추가할 것
(d) 다양한 피사체를 동등하게 강조할 것

해설 세 번째 문단을 보면, 사진에는 단 하나의 피사체 혹은 흥미를 끄는 요소가 있어야 한다고(a picture should have only one subject or main center of interest.) 하며, 흥미를 끄는 요소가 하나 이상인 사진은 혼란스러울 수 있다고(A picture with more than one center of interest can be puzzling) 말하고 있으므로, 정답은 (a)이다.

정답 (a)

어휘
plain **adj.** 평범한
emphasize **v.** 강조하다

49. 세부사항
어떻게 "삼등분의 법칙"을 따르는 것이 사진을 개선할 수 있는가?

(a) 사진의 요소를 홀수로 보장함으로써
(b) 사진에 균형감을 부여함으로써
(c) 피사체를 가운데에 배치함으로써
(d) 하나 이상의 피사체를 위한 공간을 제공함으로써

해설 다섯 번째 문단을 보면, 구도의 균형감을 조성하기 위해서는 사진의 구역을 수직 및 수평으로 각각 삼등분하라고(To create a feeling of balance in the composition, divide the picture's area into thirds, both vertically and horizontally) 말하고 있으므로, 정답은 (b)이다.

정답 (b)

어휘
ensure **v.** 보장하다

50. 추론
왜 피사체가 한 각도에서 촬영되어야 하는가?

(a) 피사체를 특이하게 보이게 하기 위해
(b) 보는 이의 감정을 변화시키기 위해
(c) 가장 고유한 특징을 숨기기 위해
(d) 다른 관점을 보여주기 위해

해설 여섯 번째 문단을 보면, 적합한 각도 혹은 촬영 각도는 좋은 구도의 중요한 요소이며(A proper viewpoint or camera angle is an important factor in good composition.), 대부분의 피사체는 입체적이고, 한 면 이상을 보여주는 각도에서 촬영되어야 한다는(Most photography subjects are three-dimensional and should be photographed from an angle to show more than one of its sides.) 문장을 통해 다른 관점을 보여주기 위해 각도를 잡고 사진을 찍어야 한다고 추측할 수 있다. 따라서 정답은 (d)이다.

정답 (d)

어휘
impact **n.** 효과

51. 추론
어떻게 사진작가들은 평범한 사진에 극적인 효과를 더할 수 있을까?

(a) 권위가 있는 피사체를 선정할 수 있다.
(b) 카메라를 높은 곳에 둘 수 있다.
(c) 피사체를 아래에서 촬영할 수 있다.
(d) 개인적인 관계에 집중할 수 있다.

해설 일곱 번째 문단을 보면, 로 앵글은 평범한 사진에 극적인 효과와 흥미를 더할 수 있고, 또한 피사체에게 힘과 권위를 부여한다고(A low camera angle can add drama and interest to an ordinary photograph. It can also give the subject strength and authority) 말하고 있으며, 로 앵글을 맞추기 위해 카메라를 피사체보다 아래에 두고 위를 향하게 하라고(To achieve a low angle, place the camera below the subject and point upward.) 나와있으므로, 정답은 (c)이다.

정답 (c)

어휘
authority **n.** 권위, 권한
elevation **n.** 높은 곳, 고도

52. 추론
이 연설에 따르면, 사진 촬영에 있어서 구도 이해의 중요성은 무엇일 것 같은가?

(a) 고품질의 사진을 촬영할 수 있게 도와준다.
(b) 모든 각도에서 촬영할 수 있게 해준다.
(c) 사진 촬영에 대해 흥미를 개발해준다.
(d) 전문 사진작가가 되도록 영감을 준다.

해설 마지막 문단을 보면, 사진 구도의 원칙을 습득하면 사진 속에 흥미로운 효과를 쉽게 담아낼 수 있고, 더 전문적인 사진을 찍을 수 있게 된다고(Once you have mastered the principles of photographic composition, you can capture interesting effects in your pictures with ease, and start shooting more professional photographs.) 말하고 있으므로 구도를 이해하게 되면 고품질의 사진을 촬영할 수 있다는 것을 추측할 수 있다. 따라서 정답은 (a)이다.

정답 (a)

어휘
inspire **v.** 영감을 주다, 고무하다

TEST 3

Chapter 3

Reading & Vocabulary

01 독해 모의고사 1회

53	(b)	54	(a)	55	(c)	56	(d)	57	(a)
58	(c)	59	(d)	60	(a)	61	(b)	62	(d)
63	(c)	64	(a)	65	(c)	66	(b)	67	(c)
68	(a)	69	(b)	70	(d)	71	(a)	72	(b)
73	(d)	74	(c)	75	(d)	76	(a)	77	(b)
78	(c)	79	(a)	80	(b)				

Part 1 Q. 53-59

H.G. WELLS
H.G. 웰스

53) Herbert George Wells was an English historian and novelist who gained worldwide acclaim for his science fiction novels. He is perhaps best known for his novel *The War of the Worlds* which was adapted for the radio in 1938 and then twice for film, first in 1953 and again in 2005. For his important contributions to the genre, Wells is often called the 'Father of Science Fiction.'
Herbert George Wells는 공상과학소설로 세계적인 찬사를 받았던 영국의 역사가이자 소설가였다. 아마도 그는 1938년 라디오 방송으로, 그리고 1953년에 처음, 그 다음 2005년에, 이렇게 두 차례 영화로 각색되었던 그의 소설 <The War of the Worlds>로 가장 잘 알려져 있을 것이다. 장르에 대한 그의 중요한 공헌 때문에, Wells는 종종 '공상과학소설의 아버지'로 불린다.

Herbert George Wells was born in Kent, England on September 21, 1866. His parents were Joseph Wells and Sarah Neal. 54) At eight years old, Wells suffered from an accident that confined him to bed for many months. He spent his time reading books, which started his interest in other worlds and lives and developed his passion for writing. He received basic education at a local school and became a pupil-teacher at Midhurst Grammar School in 1879. Wells won a scholarship to the Normal School of Science at Midhurst. His biology teacher was the famous English biologist, T. H. Huxley.
Herbert George Wells 는 1866년 9월 21일에 영국의 Kent 주에서 태어났다. 그의 부모는 Joseph Wells와 Sarah Neal이었다. 8살에 Wells는 수개월 동안 그를 병상에 눕게 만들었던 사고를 겪었다. 그는 책을 읽으며 시간을 보냈는데, 이것이 다른 세상과 삶에 대한 그의 흥미를 불러일으켰고 글쓰기에 대한 열정을 키우게 했다. 그는 지역 학교에서 기초 교육을 받았고, 1879년에 Midhurst 중등학교의 교생이 되었다. Wells는 장학금을 받아 Midhurst에 있는 과학 사범학교에 입학했다. 그의 생물학 선생님은 유명 영국 생물학자인 T.H. Huxley였다.

Wells moved to London and earned money by writing for weekly newspapers. 55) While studying at London University, he became a science master at the Henley House School where he taught the future renowned poet, A. A. Milne. He received his degree in zoology in 1890.
Wells는 런던으로 이사를 갔고, 주간 신문에 기고함으로써 돈을 벌었다. 런던 대학교에서 공부를 하는 동안, Henley House 학교의 과학 선생이 되었는데, 그곳에서 그는 이후 저명한 시인이 된 A.A. Milne를 가르쳤다. 그는 1890년에 동물학 학위를 받았다.

56) In 1895, Wells came out with his first successful science fiction novel, *The Time Machine*. This was followed by three more successful science fiction stories: *The Island of Dr. Moreau*, *The Invisible Man*, and *The War of the Worlds*. He also began writing non-fiction books and commentaries about society, politics, and technology. 56) His first non-fiction work, subtitled *An Experiment in Prophecy*, was a collection of his predictions for the future.
1895년에 Wells는 그의 첫 번째 성공적인 공상과학소설인 <The Time Machine>을 발표하였다. 이 소설에 뒤이어 <The Island of Dr. Moreau>, <The Invisible Man>, 그리고 <The War of the Worlds>, 이렇게 성공적인 공상과학소설 세 편이 더 나왔다. 그는 또한 비소설 서적과 사회, 정치 및 기술에 관한 논평을 쓰기 시작했다. <An Experiment in Prophecy>라는 부제가 달린 그의 첫 번째 비소설 작품은 미래에 대한 그의 예측들을 모은 것이었다.

Wells advocated a utopian world where society is better organized and people live more contentedly. This ideal was at the center of his 1905 novel,

A Modern Utopia, which depicts a "world state" where people live in happiness. 57) In his utopian novels, Wells also predicted catastrophic events like the Second World War in *The Shape of Things to Come*, and the rise of dictators in *The Holy Terror*.
Wells는 사회가 더 체계화되고 사람들이 더 행복하게 사는 유토피아적인 세상을 지지했다. 이러한 이상은 그의 1905년작 소설인 <A Modern Utopia>의 중점이었고, 이 소설은 사람들이 행복 속에서 사는 "세계 국"을 묘사한다. Wells는 <The Shape of Things to Come>에 나오는 제2차 세계대전, <The Holy Terror>에 나오는 독재자들의 발흥과 같이 그의 유토피안 소설에서 비극적인 사건들을 예측하기도 하였다.

H.G. Wells traveled to France between the first and second world wars. He moved back to London in 1933 and, refusing to flee the German attacks on the city, continued to live there throughout the war. He died of complications from diabetes in 1946.
H.G. Wells는 제1차 세계대전과 2차 세계대전 사이에 프랑스로 갔다. 그는 1933년에 런던으로 다시 이사 왔고, 그 도시에 가해진 독일의 공격으로부터 도망가는 것을 거부하며, 전쟁 내내 그곳에서 계속해서 살았다. 그는 1946년에 당뇨병 합병증으로 인해 사망했다.

어휘
gain acclaim for **phr.** 찬사를 받다
adapt **v.** 각색하다, 맞추다
contribution **n.** 공헌, 기여
fiction **n.** 소설, 허구
suffer **v.** (안 좋은 일을) 겪다, (질병 등에) 시달리다
confine **v.** (질병 등으로) 얽매이게 하다
master **n.** (구) 남자 선생
renowned **adj.** 유명한
degree **n.** 학위
non-fiction **n.** 비소설, 실화
commentary **n.** 논평, 논의
subtitle **v.** 부제를 달다
prediction **n.** 예측, 예견
advocate **v.** 지지하다, 옹호하다
contentedly **ad.** 행복하게
ideal **n.** 이상, 이상적인 것
depict **v.** 묘사하다, 그리다
catastrophic **adj.** 비극적인, 파멸의
event **n.** 사건
rise **n.** 발흥, 증가
dictator **n.** 독재자
refuse **v.** 거부하다
flee **v.** 도망치다
complication **n.** (의학) 합병증
diabetes **n.** 당뇨

53. 세부사항
H.G Wells는 무엇으로 유명한가?

(a) 영화 감독으로서 그의 재능의 범위
(b) 공상과학 장르에서의 그의 작품
(c) 라디오 쇼에서 그의 이야기 전달 기술
(d) 그의 광범위한 역사 지식

해설 첫 번째 문단의 첫 번째 문장에서 그가 공상과학 작품으로 세계적인 찬사를 받았다고(H.G. Wells was an English historian and novelist who gained worldwide acclaim for his science fiction novels.) 하였으므로, 정답은 (b)이다.

정답 (b)

어휘
accurate **adj.** 정확한
unrealistic **adj.** 비현실적인
view **n.** 견해, 관점

54. 세부사항
Wells는 언제 글쓰기에 대한 흥미를 기르기 시작하였는가?

(a) 어릴 때 책을 읽는 습관이 생겼을 때
(b) 지역 학교에 다녔을 때
(c) 중등학교에서 가르치고 있었을 때
(d) 런던 대학교에 다녔을 때

해설 두 번째 문단에서 두 번째 및 세 번째 문장을 보면 Wells가 8살에 사고로 인해 수개월 간 병상에 있었다고(At eight years old, Wells suffered from an accident that confined him to bed for many months.) 하였고, 독서에 시간을 보냈으며 이것이 다른 세상과 삶에 대한 그의 관심과 글쓰기에 대한 열정을 길렀다고(He spent his time reading books, which started his interest in other worlds and lives and developed his passion for writing.) 하였으므로, 정답은 (a)이다.

정답 (a)

어휘
take to sth **phr.** ~하는 습관이 생기다, ~를 좋아하기 시작하다
attend **v.** (학교 등에) 다니다, 출석하다
grammar school **n.** (과거 영국의) 중등학교

TEST 1

55. 세부사항
Wells는 런던 대학교에 다니는 동안 무엇을 했는가?

(a) 기숙사 사감이 되었다.
(b) 신문을 출판했다.
(c) 곧 위대해질 문학적 인물을 가르쳤다.
(d) 동물학과 교수진에 합류했다.

해설 세 번째 문단의 두 번째 문장을 보면, 런던 대학교에서 공부하면서 헨리 하우스 학교의 과학 선생님이 되었다고(While studying at London University, he became a science master at the Henley House School) 하였고, 이 학교에서 이후 유명한 시인이 된 A.A. Milne를 가르쳤다고(where he taught the future renowned poet, A. A. Milne.) 하였으므로, 정답은 (c)이다.

정답 (c)

어휘
resident assistant **n.** 기숙사 사감
literary **adj.** 문학의, 문학과 관련된
figure **n.** 인물
faculty **n.** 교수진
department **n.** (학)과

56. 특정정보
다음 중 Wells의 공상과학소설이 아닌 것은?

(a) *The War of the Worlds*
(b) *The Time Machine*
(c) *The Invisible Man*
(d) *An Experiment in Prophecy*

해설 네 번째 문단의 첫 번째 및 두 번째 문장을 보면, Wells가 1985년에 첫 공상과학소설인 *The Time Machine*을 출판했다고(In 1895, Wells came out with his first successful science fiction novel, The Time Machine.) 하였고, 이 후에 The Island of Dr. Moreau, The Invisible Man, The War of the Worlds 이렇게 세 편의 성공적인 공상과학소설이 나왔다고(This was followed by three more successful science fiction stories, *The Island of Dr. Moreau, The Invisible Man, and The War of the Worlds.*) 하였으므로, (a), (b), (c)는 그의 공상과학소설이 맞다.
그러나 마지막 문장을 보면, *An Experiment in Prophecy*라고 부제가 달린 Wells의 첫 번째 비소설 작품은 미래에 대한 그의 예측들을 모아놓은 것이라고(His first non-fiction work, subtitled *An Experiment in Prophecy*, was a collection of his predictions for the future.) 하였으므로, 이 작품은 그의 공상과학소설이 아니다. 따라서 정답은 (d)이다.

정답 (d)

어휘
invisible **adj.** 보이지 않는
experiment **n.** 실험
prophecy **n.** 예언

57. 추론

이 기사에 따르면, H.G. Wells의 유토피안 소설들은 어떻게 가장 정확하게 묘사될 수 있는가?

(a) 어느 정도 예지력이 있었다.
(b) 불만스러운 느낌을 조장했다.
(c) 20세기 이전에 출판되었다.
(d) 전쟁들 사이에 쓰였다.

해설 다섯 번째 문단의 세 번째 문장을 보면, 유토피안 소설 속에서 Wells가 The Shape of Things to Come에 나오는 제2차 세계대전, The Holy Terror에 나오는 독재자들의 발흥과 같이 비극적인 사건들을 예측하기도 했다고(In his utopian novels, Wells also predicted catastrophic events like the Second World War in *The Shape of Things to Come*, and the rise of dictators in *The Holy Terror*.) 하였으므로, 그의 유토피안 소설들이 어느 정도 예지력이 있었다는 것을 추론할 수 있다. 따라서 정답은 (a)이다.

정답 (a)

어휘
visionary **adj.** 예지력이 있는
promote **v.** (분위기, 생각 등을) 조장하다
discontent **n.** 불만

58. 동의어

해당 구절의 문맥 상, confined는(은) ______을(를) 의미한다.

(a) 포착된
(b) 갇힌
(c) 제한된
(d) 수감된

해설 해당 단어가 포함된 부분은 '수개월 동안 병상에 눕게 만들었다'는 것을 의미한다. 즉, '병상에 있기 때문에 다른 활동이 제한되었다' 라는 의미로도 해석이 가능하므로, 정답은 (c)이다.

정답 (c)

59. 동의어

해당 구절의 문맥 상, utopian은(는) ________을(를) 의미한다.

(a) 가상의
(b) 현실적인
(c) 로맨틱한
(d) 이상주의적인

해설 해당 단어가 포함된 부분은 Wells가 사회가 더 잘 조직되고 사람들이 더 행복하게 사는 '유토피아적인' 세계를 지지했다는 것을 의미한다. 이는 가장 완전하다고 여겨지는 '이상주의적인' 세계를 지지했다고도 표현될 수 있으므로, 정답은 (d)이다.

정답 (d)

Part 2 **Q. 60-66**

SCIENTISTS DISCOVER REMAINS OF ANCIENT FRESHWATER "MONSTER"
과학자들이 고대 담수 "괴물"의 잔해를 발견하다

A team of paleontologists have discovered the fossils of an 84-million-year-old freshwater "sea monster." 60) The creature belongs to a family of ancient marine reptiles known as "mosasaurs." Not technically dinosaurs, the mosasaurs were related to monitor lizards and snakes, and most of them looked like a cross between a whale and a crocodile.
한 고생물학자 팀이 8천 4백만년 된 담수 "바다 괴물"의 화석들을 발견했다. 이 생물체는 "모사사우루스"라고 알려진 고대 해양 파충류 과에 속한다. 엄밀히 따지자면 공룡은 아닌 모사사우루스는 왕 도마뱀 및 뱀과 동족 관계였으며(같은 과에 속했으며), 그들 중 대부분은 고래와 악어의 잡종처럼 생겼었다.

The fossils were discovered in the waste dump of a coal mine in the Bakony Hills of Western Hungary. 60, 63) Named *Pannoniasaurus inexpectatus*, the newly discovered species is 61) the first that is assumed to have adapted to and lived entirely in freshwaters. Previous species of mosasaurs are known to have lived exclusively in saltwater.
그 화석들은 헝가리 서부의 Bakony 언덕에 있는 탄광의 쓰레기 더미에서 발견되었다. Pannoniasaurus inexpectatus라고 명명된, 새롭게 발견된 이 종족은 담수에 적응하여 그 속에서만 살았다고 추정되는 첫 번째 종족이다. 모사사우루스의 이전 종족들은 오로지 해수에서만 살았던 것으로 알려져 있다.

TEST 1

The researchers uncovered thousands of *Pannoniasaurus fossils* in the area. 62) The concentration of so many specimens at one site suggests that the creature was a true freshwater dweller and not just a saltwater animal that swam into rivers the way some sharks do. 63) The area was part of a chain of islands in the middle of a big freshwater seaway that separated Africa and Southern Europe. Its small sharp teeth suggest that *Pannoniasaurus* probably preyed on the other forms of life that dwelled in the rivers running through the islands.
그 연구진들은 그 지역에서 수천 개의 Pannoniasaurus 화석을 발견했다. 한 지역에 그렇게 많은 표본들이 밀집되어 있다는 것은 그 생물체가 진정 담수에서만 사는 동물이었고, 일부 상어들처럼 강을 헤엄쳐 들어온 해수 동물이 아니었다는 점을 시사한다. 그 지역은 아프리카와 남부 유럽을 가르고 있었던 거대한 담수로의 중간 부분에 있는 군도의 일부분이었다. Pannoniasaurus의 작고 날카로운 이빨은 그것이 아마 그 섬들을 가로지르는 강들에 서식하는 다른 형태의 생명체들을 잡아먹었을 것이라는 점을 시사한다.

The fossils range from three feet to thirteen feet in length and are representative of specimens of varying ages. According to Michael Caldwell, a mosasaur expert at the University of Alberta, scientists usually discover big mosasaurs and rarely find young ones. The research also showed that, unlike other mosasaurs that swam with flippers, the *Pannoniasaurus* had limbs that resemble legs, suggesting that they occasionally traveled on land. 64) Paleontologists believe that they may have behaved like crocodiles, spending a lot of time in cold water, but sometimes crawling inland to regulate their body temperature.
그 화석들은 길이가 3피트(약 91센티미터)에서 13피트(약 3미터 96센티미터) 사이이며, 다양한 나이의 표본들을 대표한다. Alberta 대학교의 모사사우루스 전문가인 Michael Caldwell에 따르면, 과학자들은 보통 큰 모사사우루스들을 발견하고 어린 것들은 거의 찾지 못한다. 그 연구는 또한, 지느러미 발로 헤엄을 쳤던 다른 모사사우루스들과는 달리, Pannoniasaurus는 그들이 가끔 육지로 이동했다는 것을 시사하는 다리와 유사한 사지를 가지고 있었다는 것도 보여주었다. 고생물학자들은 그것들이 차가운 물에서 많은 시간을 보내지만 때때로 체온을 조절하기 위해 내륙 쪽으로 기어가며, 악어처럼 행동했을 지도 모른다고 생각한다.

Caldwell believes that *Pannoniasaurus* is not the only ancient marine reptile to successfully adapt to freshwater. He is certain that there are other ancient marine species that were also able to make the same transition. These species just have yet to be discovered.
Caldwell은 Pannoniasaurus가 담수에 성공적으로 적응한 유일한 고대 해양 파충류가 아니라고 생각한다. 그는 같은 방식으로 전이할 수 있었던 다른 고대 해양 종족들이 있을 거라고 확신한다. 이러한 종족들은 아직 발견되지 않았을 뿐이다.

어휘

remain **n.** 잔해, 유해
freshwater **adj.** 담수의, 민물의
paleontologist **n.** 고생물학자
ancient **adj.** 고대의
marine **adj.** 해양의
reptile **n.** 파충류
technically **ad.** 엄밀히 말하면
related **adj.** (동물 등이) 같은 과에 속한, 동족인
cross **n.** 잡종
fossil **n.** 화석
species **n.** 종(족), 종(족)들
assume **v.** 추정하다
adapt (to) **v.** (상황에) 적응하다
exclusively **ad.** 오로지, 독점적으로
uncover **v.** 발견하다, 알아내다
concentration **n.** 밀집, 집중
suggest **v.** 시사하다
dwell **v.** 서식하다, 살다
separate **v.** 가르다, 분리하다
range from A to B **phr v.** (범위가) A에서 B까지 다양하다
representative **adj.** 대표하는
specimen **n.** 표본
flipper **n.** (물개 등의) 지느러미 발
resemble **v.** 유사하다
occasionally **ad.** 가끔
behave **v.** 행동하다
crawl **v.** 기어가다
inland **ad.** 육지로
regulate **v.** 조절하다
temperature **n.** 온도
transition **n.** 전이

60. 추론

Pannoniasaurus는 어떻게 분류될 수 있는가?

(a) 다른 종의 파충류와 관련이 있다.
(b) 두 개의 수생동물 사이의 교차점이 다.
(c) 헝가리의 토착종이다.
(d) 이것은 새로 진화한 공룡이다.

해설 첫 번째 문단의 두 번째 및 세 번째 문장을 보면, 새로 발견된 화석의 생명체가 "모사사우루스"라고 알려진 고대 해양 파충류 과에 속한다고(The creature belongs to a family of ancient marine reptiles known as "mosasaurs.") 하였고, 모사사우루스는 엄밀히 따지자면 공룡은 아니고 왕 도마뱀 및 뱀과 동족 관계라고(Not technically dinosaurs, the mosasaurs were related to monitor lizards and snakes.) 하였다. 이후 두 번째 문단에서 새롭게 발견된 화석의 종족이 Pannoniasaurus inexpectatus라고 명명되었다고(Named *Pannoniasaurus inexpectatus*) 하였으므로, Pannoniasaurus는 모사사우루스의 일종으로 왕 도마뱀 및 뱀, 즉 파충류와 관계가 있다는 것을 추론할 수 있다. 따라서 정답은 (a)이다.

정답 (a)

어휘
classify **v.** 분류하다
modern-day **adj.** 현대의, 현재의
aquatic **adj.** 수생의, 수중의
evolve **v.** 진화하다, 진화 시키다

61. 특정정보

무엇이 다른 모사사우루스와 달리 Pannoniasaurus를 특별하게 만드는가?

(a) 다른 바다 생물체에 대한 기호
(b) 담수에 대한 성공적인 적응
(c) 상어의 행동을 모방하려는 경향
(d) 담수 및 해수에서 살 수 있는 능력

해설 두 번째 문단의 두 번째 및 세 번째 문장을 보면, Pannoniasaurus가 담수에 적응하여 그 속에서만 살았다고 추정되는 첫 번째 종족이며(the first that is assumed to have adapted to and lived entirely in freshwaters), 모사사우루스의 예전 종족들은 오로지 해수에서만 살았던 것으로 알려져 있다고(Previous species of mosasaurs are known to have lived exclusively in saltwater.) 하였으므로, 정답은 (b)이다.

정답 (b)

어휘
unique **adj.** 특별한, 독특한
fondness **n.** 기호
adaptation **n.** 적응
tendency **n.** 경향
imitate **v.** 모방하다

62. 추론

그 지역에 화석들이 밀집되어 있는 것은 무엇을 시사하는 것 같은가?

(a) 무리 지어 먹이를 섭취하는 것
(b) 이전에 바다에서 살았다는 것
(c) 그들이 육지로 이동해 살았다는 것
(d) 민물 밖에서 살지 않았다는 것

해설 세 번째 문단의 두 번째 문장을 보면, 한 지역에 그렇게 많은 표본들이 밀집되어 있다는 것은 그 생물체가 진정으로 담수에서 서식하는 동물이었고, 몇몇 상어들이 하는 것처럼 강으로 헤엄쳐 갔던 해수 동물이 아니었다는 것을 시사한다고(The concentration of so many specimens at one site suggests that the creature was a true freshwater dweller and not just a saltwater animal that swam into rivers the way some sharks do.) 하였으므로, Pannoniasaurus가 담수가 아닌 다른 곳에서는 살지 않았다는 것을 추론할 수 있다. 따라서 정답은 (d)이다.

정답 (d)

어휘
collectively **ad.** 집합적으로

TEST 1

63. 사실확인

새롭게 발견된 모사사우루스가 살았던 방식으로 사실이 아닌 것은?

(a) 그들은 섬 지역에 살았다.
(b) 그들은 다른 강물 생물들을 먹이로 삼았다.
(c) 그들은 남유럽의 바다에서 살았다.
(d) 그 인구는 한 지역에 집결하였다.

해설 두 번째 문단의 두 번째 문장을 보면, Pannoniasaurus inexpectatus라고 명명된, 새롭게 발견된 이 종족은 담수에 적응하여 그 속에서만 살았다고 추정되는 첫 번째 종족이라고(Named *Pannoniasaurus inexpectatus*, the newly-discovered species is the first that is assumed to have adapted to and lived entirely in freshwaters.) 하였고, 또 화석이 집중적으로 발견된 지역이 예전에는 아프리카와 남부 유럽을 가르고 있었던 거대한 담수로의 중간 부분에 있는 군도의 일부분이었다고(The area was part of a chain of islands in the middle of a big freshwater seaway that separated Africa and Southern Europe) 하였으므로, 이들이 바다에서 살았다는 것은 사실이 아니다. 따라서 정답은 (c)이다.

정답 (c)

어휘
inhabit **v.** 서식하다
divide **v.** 가르다, 나누다
converge **v.** 집중되다

64. 추론

이 글에 따르면, Pannoniasaurus가 사지를 이용하여 육지로 기어갔을 이유로 가장 적절한 것은 무엇인가?

(a) 체온을 높이기 위해
(b) 섬 사이를 이동하기 위해
(c) 육지 동물을 사냥하기 위해
(d) 육지 서식 동물로 진화하기 위해

해설 네 번째 문단의 마지막 문장을 보면, 고생물학자들은 Pannoniasaurus가 차가운 물에서 많은 시간을 보내지만 때때로 체온을 조절하기 위해 내륙 쪽으로 기어가며, 악어처럼 행동했을 지도 모른다고 생각한다고(Paleontologists believe that they may have behaved like crocodiles, spending a lot of time in cold water, but sometimes crawling inland to regulate their body temperature.) 하였으므로, Pannoniasaurus가 체온을 높이기 위해 육지로 가끔 기어갔을 수도 있다는 것을 추론할 수 있다. 따라서 정답은 (a)이다.

정답 (a)

어휘
increase **v.** 높이다, 늘리다

65. 동의어

해당 구절의 문맥 상, <u>separated</u>은(는) ________을(를) 의미한다.

(a) 출발했다
(b) 멀어지게 했다
(c) 나누었다
(d) 합쳤다

해설 해당 단어가 포함된 부분은 큰 담수로가 아프리카와 남부 유럽을 '<u>가르고 있었다</u>'는 것을 의미한다. 이는 담수로가 경계가 되어 아프리카와 남부 유럽을 '나누었다'고도 표현될 수 있으므로, 정답은 (c)이다.

정답 (c)

66. 동의어

해당 구절의 문맥 상, behaved은(는) ________ 을(를) 의미한다.

(a) 일했다
(b) 행동했다
(c) 달랐다
(d) ~처럼 보였다

해설 해당 단어가 포함된 부분은 Pannoniasaurus가 악어처럼 '행동했다'는 것을 의미하므로, 정답은 (b)이다.

정답 (b)

Part 3 Q. 67-73

THE GREAT BARRIER REEF
호주의 대보초

The Great Barrier Reef is the largest coral reef system in the world. This natural structure is located off the coast of Queensland, Australia, and consists of 2,900 individual reefs and 900 islands. Covering an area of 133,000 square miles, it is the largest structure on earth to have been made by living organisms, and can be seen from outer space.
호주의 대보초는 세계에서 가장 큰 산호계이다. 이 자연적인 구조는 호주 Queensland 주의 해안에서 가까운 곳에 위치해 있고, 2,900개의 개별 산호초들과 900개의 섬들로 이루어져 있다. 133,000 제곱 마일(약 344,400 제곱 킬로미터)의 지역에 걸쳐 있으며, 그것은 지구상에서 생물체에 의해 만들어진 가장 큰 구조이고, 우주에서도 보인다.

68) The reefs are composed of billions of tiny organisms known as "coral polyps" that have built up over time. The formation stretches more than 1,600 miles from the Torres Strait in the north to the area between Lady Elliot and Fraser Islands in the south.
그 산호초들은 시간이 흐르며 점점 축적되어 온 "산호충"이라고 알려져 있는 수십억 개의 작은 생물체들로 구성되어 있다. 이 형성물은 북쪽의 Torres 해협에서 남쪽의 Lady Elliot 섬과 Fraser 섬 사이에 있는 지역까지 1,600마일(약 2,575 킬로미터) 이상 펼쳐져 있다.

The reef was formed through a long and complex process. 69) It began to take shape between 58 and 48 million years ago when the Coral Sea Basin was developing. When the Australian continent reached its present location, sea levels began to change, and the coral reefs grew more quickly. They began to flourish in the favorable sea temperatures and levels of sunlight that resulted from the shift. However, changing climate cycles and the resulting changes in sea levels caused the reefs to grow in spurts and then periodically lie dormant and even decline. 70) Scientists believe that the present Great Barrier Reef was formed about 20,000 years ago when new coral polyps started growing over the remains of the old reef.
그 산호초는 길고 복잡한 과정을 통해 형성되었다. 그것은 산호 해역 분지가 발달하고 있던 때인 5천8백만년 전에서 4천8백만년 전 사이에 형태를 갖추기 시작하였다. 호주 대륙이 지금의 위치에 다다랐을 때, 해수면이 변하기 시작했고 산호초들이 더 빠르게 자랐다. 산호초들은 그 변화로 인해 적합해진 해수 온도와 일조량 속에서 잘 자라기 시작했다. 그러나, 변하는 기후 주기와 그 결과로 초래된 해수면의 변화로 인해 산호초들은 갑자기 증가했다가 주기적으로 성장을 멈췄고, 심지어 감소하였다. 과학자들은 현재 호주의 대보초가 그 오래된 산호초의 잔해 위로 새로운 산호충이 자라기 시작했던 때인 약 2만년 전에 형성되었다고 생각한다.

Today, 71) the Great Barrier Reef harbors a wide variety of species, many of which are endemic to the reef system and currently endangered. The reef has 30 species of whales, dolphins, and porpoises. Six species of endangered sea turtles breed in the reef, including two which have developed into distinct populations in the northern and southern parts.
오늘 날, 호주의 대보초는 다양한 종들의 서식지가 되고 있는데, 이들 중 다수가 그 산호계 태생이며, 현재는 멸종될 위기에 처해있다. 그 산호초는 30종에 달하는 고래, 돌고래 및 쥐 돌고래를 보유하고 있다. 북부와 남부지역에서 독특한 개체군으로 진화한 2종을 포함하여 멸종 위기에 처한 6종의 바다 거북이들이 그 산호초에서 번식을 하고 있다.

Around two million people visit the Great Barrier Reef yearly. The site is protected by an Australian national park that regulates human activities such as fishing and tourism in the area. While the government attempts to control the impact of tourism, 71) the reef's rich biodiversity remains under constant threat from illegal fishing and other harmful human activities.
연간 약 2백만 명에 달하는 사람들이 호주의 대보초를 방문한다. 이 곳은 낚시나 관광 같은 인간의 활동들을 규제하는 호주 국립 공원에 의해 보호를 받는다. 정부가 관광산업의 영향을 통제하려고 노력하고 있으나, 산호초의 풍부한 생물의 다양성은 불법 낚시 및 그 외 인간의 해로운 활동들로 인해 지속적인 위협을 받고 있는 상태이다.

TEST 1

어휘
coral **n.** 산호
reef **n.** 암초
individual **adj.** 개별의, 각각의
organism **n.** 생물체, 유기체
be composed of **phr v.** ~로 구성되어 있다
tiny **adj.** 매우 작은
formation **n.** 형성, 형성물
stretch **v.** 펼쳐지다
complex **adj.** 복잡한
continent **n.** 대륙
flourish **v.** 잘 자라다, 번창하다
favorable **adj.** 좋은, 적합한
temperature **n.** 온도
climate cycle **n.** 기후 주기
in spurts **phr.** 빠른 속도로 많이
periodically **ad.** 주기적으로
dormant **adj.** 성장하지 않는, 활동을 하지 않는
decline **v.** 감소하다
harbor **v.** (동물 등의) 서식지가 되다
a variety of **phr.** 다양한
endangered **adj.** 위험에 처한
distinct **adj.** 구별되는
population **n.** 개체군
impact **n.** 영향
biodiversity **n.** 생물의 다양성
remain **v.** 계속 ~하다
threat **n.** 위협
illegal **adj.** 불법의
harmful **adj.** 해로운

67. 주제
이 기사의 주제는 무엇인가?

(a) 해안 섬의 형성 방법
(b) 유기체가 자연 구조를 생성하는 방법
(c) 세계 자연의 경이로움 중 하나
(d) 오스트레일리아 고유의 토착 야생 동물

해설 해당 기사는 호주의 대보초의 위치 및 크기(첫 번째 문단), 구성 요소(두 번째 문단), 형성 과정(세 번째 문단), 서식하는 동물(네 번째 문단), 현 상태(마지막 문단)에 대해 전반적으로 설명하고 있다. 지구에서 생명체에 의해 만들어진 가장 큰 구조, 즉 신비로운 자연 현상에 대한 기사라고 할 수 있으므로, 정답은 (c)이다.

정답 (c)

어휘
wonder **n.** 경이로운 것, 불가사의

68. 세부사항
어떻게 산호초가 형성되는가?

(a) 아주 작은 생물체들의 축적으로 인해
(b) 인간의 활동을 통제함으로써
(c) 기후의 변화를 통해
(d) 바다의 형성을 통해

해설 두 번째 문단의 첫 번째 문장을 보면, 산호초들은 시간이 흐르며 점점 축적되어 온 "산호충"이라고 알려져 있는 수십억 개의 작은 생물체들로 구성되어 있다고(The reefs are composed of billions of tiny organisms known as "coral polyps" that have built up over time.) 하였으므로, 정답은 (a)이다.

정답 (a)

어휘
buildup **n.** 축적, 증가

69. 특정정보

수백만 년 전 호주의 대보초 형성에 있어서 도움이 되지 않았던 것은 무엇인가?

(a) 적합한 수온
(b) 산호층 감소
(c) 호주 대륙의 이동
(d) 산호 해역 분지의 형성

해설 세 번째 문단을 보면, 대보초는 산호 해역 분지가 발달하고 있던 때인 5천8백만년 전과 4천8백만년 전 사이에 형태를 갖추기 시작했다고(It began to take shape between 58 and 48 million years ago when the Coral Sea Basin was developing.) 하였으므로 (d)는 간접적으로 도움이 되었다고 할 수 있다. 또한 호주 대륙이 현재의 위치에 다다랐을 때, 해수면이 변하기 시작했고 산호초들이 더 빠르게 자랐으며(When the Australian continent reached its present location, sea levels began to change, and the coral reefs grew more quickly.), 그 변화로 인해 적합해진 해수 온도와 일조량 속에서 잘 자라기 시작했다고(They began to flourish in the favorable sea temperatures and levels of sunlight that resulted from the shift.) 하였으므로, (c)와 (a) 역시 대보초 형성에 도움을 준 것이 맞다. 그러나 해수면이 낮아진 것이 대보초 형성에 도움을 주었다는 언급은 없었으므로, 정답은 (b)이다.

정답 (b)

어휘
drift **n.** (서서히 일어나는) 이동

70. 추론

현재 산호초의 발달에 대해 어떤 것이 사실인가?

(a) 수백만 년 동안 자라오고 있다.
(b) 지속적으로 바다 쪽으로 움직인다.
(c) 성장하는 것을 멈추었다.
(d) 상대적으로 새로운 형성물이다.

해설 네 번째 문단의 마지막 문장을 보면, 과학자들이 현재 호주의 대보초가 오래된 산호초의 잔해 위로 새로운 산호충이 자라기 시작했던 때인 약 2만년 전에 형성되었다고 생각한다고(Scientists believe that the present Great Barrier Reef was formed about 20,000 years ago when new coral polyps started growing over the remains of the old reef.) 하였으므로, 현재의 산호초는 수백만 년 전의 산호초보다 상대적으로 새롭게 형성된 것임을 추론할 수 있다. 따라서 정답은 (d)이다.

정답 (d)

어휘
constantly **ad.** 지속적으로
relatively **ad.** 상대적으로

71. 추론

이 글에 따르면, 호주의 대보초는 왜 보호되어야 하는가?

(a) 그것은 이 지역에 자생하는 많은 동물들의 서식지이다.
(b) 그것은 수입을 창출하는 관광지이다.
(c) 그것은 어부에게 생계수단을 제공한다.
(d) 그것은 기후 변화를 통제하는데 도움을 준다.

해설 네 번째 문단의 첫 번째 문장을 보면, 호주의 대보초는 다양한 종들을 보호하고 있는데, 이들 중 다수가 그 산호계 태생이라고(The Great Barrier Reef harbors a wide variety of species, many of which are endemic to the reef system) 하였고, 다섯 번째 문단의 마지막 문장에서 산호초의 풍부한 생물의 다양성이 불법 낚시 및 그 외 인간의 해로운 활동들로 인해 계속 위협받고 있다고(The reef's rich biodiversity remains under constant threat from illegal fishing and other harmful human activities.) 하였으므로, 대보초가 다양한 동물들의 유일한 서식지이기 때문에 보호되어야 한다는 것을 추론할 수 있다. 따라서 정답은 (a)이다.

정답 (a)

어휘
generate **v.** 창출하다, 발생시키다
tourist destination **n.** 관광지
livelihood **n.** 생계

TEST 1

72. 동의어

해당 구절의 문맥 상, flourish은(는) ________ 을(를) 의미한다.

(a) (꽃이) 피다
(b) 잘 자라다
(c) 형성하다
(d) 감소하다

해설 해당 단어가 포함된 부분은 산호초들이 적합한 해수 온도와 일조량 속에서 '잘 자라기' 시작했다는 것을 의미하므로, 정답은 (b)이다.

정답 (b)

73. 동의어

해당 구절의 문맥 상, harbors은(는) ________ 을(를) 의미한다.

(a) 번식하다
(b) 추방하다
(c) 정박하다
(d) 보호하다

해설 해당 단어가 포함된 부분은 호주의 대보초가 다양한 종들의 '서식지가 되고 있다'는 것을 의미한다. 이는 ' 쉴 곳을 제공하다, 보호하다'라고도 표현될 수 있으므로, 정답은 (d)이다.

정답 (d)

Part 4 Q. 74-80

February 12, 2018
2018년 2월 12일

Mr. Edward Palmer
Hotel Manager
Blue Sapphire Hotel

Mr. Edward Palmer
호텔 지배인
블루 사파이어 호텔

Dear Mr. Palmer:
Palmer씨께:

74, 78) Please be reminded of your outstanding balance for the landscaping work we completed for Blue Sapphire Hotel. 75) When you asked for a discounted 'cash price' for the work, we agreed provided that full payment would be made the day it was completed. However, since you were out of the office on the day of completion, we could not collect the payment on that day. As you requested over the telephone, we left the invoice with your assistant, hoping that the payment would be made the next day. More than a week has passed, and our office hasn't received your payment as of this writing.
저희가 블루 사파이어 호텔을 위해 완료했던 조경 작업에 대한 미지급 잔금에 대해 기억해주시기 바랍니다. 귀하께서 그 작업에 대해 할인된 '현금가'를 요청하셨을 때, 저희는 작업이 끝나는 당일 전액이 납입되는 조건으로 동의하였습니다. 그러나, 완료 당일 귀하께서 사무실에 계시지 않았기에 저희는 대금을 받을 수 없었습니다. 귀하께서 전화상으로 요청하신 대로, 저희는 대금이 그 다음날 지불되길 바라며 귀하의 비서에게 그 송장을 맡겼습니다. 일주일 이상이 지났고, 저희 사무실은 이 글을 쓰는 순간에도 귀하의 대금을 받지 못했습니다.

We are happy to offer a variety of payment plans to our clients, including a discounted cash price. However, we do ask our clients to honor the terms of their contracts punctually so we can continue to offer all clients excellent service. Unfortunately, 76, 77) the delay in your payment is affecting our cash flow and preventing us from completing a commission for another valued client. I'm sure you understand how failing to meet the expectations of our other customers could be detrimental to our business.
저희는 고객들에게 할인된 현금가를 포함하여 다양한 결제 방식을 제공하는 것을 기쁘게 생각합니다. 그러나, 저희가 모든 고객들에게 훌륭한 서비스를 계속 제공할 수 있도록, 고객들에게 계약조건을 정해진 기간까지 이행해 달라고 꼭 요청합니다. 불행히도, 귀하의 대금 지급 지연이 저희의 현금 유동성에 영향을 미치고 있고 또 다른 소중한 고객의 의뢰를 완료하지 못하게 하고 있습니다. 다른 고객들의 기대에 부응하지 못하는 것이 얼마나 저희 사업에 해가 될 수 있는지 귀하께서도 아실 거라 확신합니다.

74, 78) We would like to make a request for the immediate payment of the completed work mentioned above. I have attached an invoice for $80,500.00 for the service completed on February 4, 2018. 78) As a sign of good faith, we are waiving applicable late payment penalties if you will comply with our request no later than Wednesday, February 24th.
상기 언급된 작업 완료 건에 대한 즉각적인 대금 납부를 요청 드립니다. 2018년 2월 4일에 완료된 작업에 대한 80,500달러의 송장을 첨부했습니다. 성의의 표시로, 귀하께서 2월 24일 수요일까지 저희의 요청에 따라 주신다면 해당되는 연체료를 면제해드리겠습니다.

If you have any question regarding this matter, please contact me at 312-752-3489 or e-mail me at staten@diamond_landscaping.com. 78) We thank you in advance for your kind cooperation.
이 사안과 관련하여 문의가 있으시면, 312-752-3489로 연락 주시거나 staten@diamond_landscaping.com로 이메일 주시기 바랍니다. 친절한 협조에 미리 감사드립니다.

Sincerely, 진심을 담아,
Abigail Staten
Finance Officer
Diamond Landscaping Co.

어휘
remind **v.** (~해야 할 것을) 상기시키다, 알려주다
outstanding **adj.** 미지급된, 미해결된
balance **n.** 지불 잔액, 잔금
landscaping **n.** 조경
provided **conj.** ~하는 조건 하에, 만약 ~라면
invoice **n.** 송장
honor **v.** (약속 등을) 이행하다
terms **n.** (계약, 지불 등의) 조건
delay **n.** 지연
cash flow **n.** 현금 유동성
commission **n.** (예술 관련) 의뢰
meet **v.** (요구, 기대 등을) 충족시키다
expectation **n.** 기대
detrimental **adj.** 유해한
immediate **adj.** 즉각적인
waive **v.** (특정한 경우에 규칙 등을) 적용하지 않다, 포기하다
applicable **adj.** 해당되는
regarding **prep.** ~에 대하여
in advance **phr.** 미리, 사전에
cooperation **n.** 협조

74. 세부사항
Abigail Staten이 왜 Edward Palmer 에게 편지를 썼는가?

(a) 회사의 서비스를 홍보하기 위해
(b) 회사의 재정 문제에 대해 이야기하기 위해
(c) 의무에 대해 상기시키기 위해
(d) 작업에 대해 선지급을 요청하기 위해

해설 첫 번째 문단을 보면, Abigail Staten이 Edward Palmer에게 본인의 회사에서 완료한 블루 사파이어 호텔 조경 작업에 대한 미지급 잔고를 기억해 달라고(Please be reminded of your outstanding balance for the landscaping work we completed for Blue Sapphire Hotel.) 하며, 세 번째 문단 첫째줄에서 즉시 대금을 납부해 달라고 요청하고(We would like to make a request for the immediate payment) 있으므로, 정답은 (c)이다.

정답 (c)

어휘
financial **adj.** 재정상의
obligation **n.** 의무
advanced payment **n.** 선불, 선지급

75. 세부사항
Palmer는 언제 그의 지불을 제출하기로 되어 있었는가?

(a) 합의가 이루어지기 전에
(b) 작업이 완료된 후 일주일 후
(c) 프로젝트 종료 다음 날
(d) 작업이 끝난 날

해설 첫 번째 문단의 두 번째 문장을 보면, Palmer가 그 작업에 대해 할인된 '현금가'를 요청했을 때, 작업이 끝나는 당일 전액이 납입되는 조건으로 동의했다고 (When you asked for a discounted 'cash price' for the work, we agreed provided that full payment would be made the day it was completed.) 말하고 있으므로, 정답은 (d)이다.

정답 (d)

어휘
fulfill **v.** 이행하다
agreement **n.** 계약
interfere **v.** 방해하다
commitment **n.** 책무

76. 세부사항

Palmer가 계약을 이행하지 못하는 것이 Staten의 회사에 어떤 영향을 끼치고 있는가?

(a) 회사의 다른 약속을 방해하고 있다.
(b) 고객이 회사와의 접촉을 취소하고 있다.
(c) 이로 인해 그 회사는 신규 고객을 잃었다.
(d) 회사는 더 이상 할인을 제공할 수 없다.

해설 두 번째 문단을 보면, Palmer의 대금 지급 지연이 현금 유동성에 영향을 미치고 있고 또 다른 소중한 고객의 의뢰를 완료하지 못하게 하고 있다고(the delay in your payment is affecting our cash flow and preventing us from completing a commission for another valued client.) 말하고 있으므로, 정답은 (a)이다.

정답 (a)

어휘
charge **v.** (요금 등을) 청구하다
installment **n.** 할부, 할부금

77. 추론

Diamind Landscaping이 현금 지불 계획을 제안하는 이유는 무엇인가?

(a) 연체료를 부과할 수 있어야 하기 때문에
(b) 다른 프로젝트에 대한 자금을 준비해야 하기 때문에
(c) 분할 지불을 피하기 위해
(d) 회사의 현금 부족 방지를 위해

해설 두 번째 문단의 마지막 문장을 보면, 대금 지급 지연이 이 회사의 현금 유동성에 영향을 미치고 있고 또 다른 소중한 고객의 의뢰를 완료하지 못하게 하고 있으며, 다른 고객들의 기대에 부응하지 못하는 것이 이 사업에 얼마나 해가 될 수 있는지 아실 거라 확신한다는(the delay in your payment is affecting our cash flow and preventing us from completing a commission for another valued client. I'm sure you understand how failing to meet the expectations of our other customers could be detrimental to our business.) 것을 말하고 있으므로, 다른 프로젝트에 대한 자금을 준비해야한다는 것을 추측할 수 있다. 따라서 정답은 (b)이다.

정답 (b)

어휘
settle **v.** 지불하다, 정산하다
extend **v.** 연장하다

78. 추론

이 편지에 따르면, 잔액이 신속하게 지불되지 않을 시 발생할 수 있는 상황으로 가장 적합한 것은 무엇인가?

(a) Staten은 또 다른 편지를 쓸 것이다.
(b) Staten의 회사는 문을 닫을 것이다.
(c) 잔금에 연체료가 추가 될 것이다.
(d) 지불 기간이 연장될 것이다.

해설 성의의 표시로, 요청에 응해준다면 해당 연체료를 면제해준다는 것을(As a sign of good faith, we are waiving applicable late payment penalties if you will comply with our request no later than Wednesday, February 24th.) 통해 이후에 지불하게 되면 연체료를 더해서 지불해야 한다는 것을 추측할 수 있다. 따라서 정답은 (c)이다.

정답 (c)

어휘
courteous **adj.** 공손한
firm **adj.** 단호한
desperate **adj.** 간절한, 절망적인

79. 동의어

해당 구절의 문맥 상, outstanding은(는) ______을(를) 의미한다.

(a) 미납된
(b) 처리된
(c) 훌륭한
(d) 과도한

해설 해당 단어가 포함된 부분은 조경 작업에 대해 '미지급된' 잔고를 기억해달라는 것을 의미하므로, 정답은 (a)이다.

정답 (a)

80. 동의어

해당 구절의 문맥 상, waiving은(는) ________을(를) 의미한다.

(a) 강요하다
(b) 포기하다
(c) 봉사하다
(d) 기대하다

해설 해당 단어가 포함된 부분은 해당되는 연체료를 '면제해준다(청구를 포기한다)'는 것을 의미하므로, 정답은 (b)이다.

정답 (b)

Chapter 3

Reading & Vocabulary

02 독해 모의고사 2회

53	(d)	54	(b)	55	(c)	56	(a)	57	(b)
58	(a)	59	(a)	60	(a)	61	(c)	62	(b)
63	(d)	64	(a)	65	(d)	66	(b)	67	(d)
68	(b)	69	(a)	70	(c)	71	(d)	72	(a)
73	(c)	74	(c)	75	(b)	76	(b)	77	(d)
78	(a)	79	(a)	80	(b)				

Part 1 Q. 53-59

HANS CHRISTIAN ANDERSEN
한스 크리스티안 안데르센

53) Hans Christian Andersen was a Danish writer and poet who is best known for his children's stories. These include the popular stories "The Little Mermaid," "The Emperor's New Clothes," and "The Snow Queen." Many of his stories and poems have been translated into several languages and adapted into films, plays, ballets, and animated movies.
Hans Christian Andersen은 동화로 잘 알려진 덴마크 작가이자 시인이었다. 그의 동화는 유명한 이야기인 "The Little Mermaid," "The Emperor's New Clothes," 그리고 "The Snow Queen"을 포함한다. 그의 이야기와 시들 중 많은 작품들이 다양한 언어로 번역되었고, 영화, 연극, 발레 및 만화 영화로 각색되었다.

Born on April 2, 1805, in Odense, Denmark, Andersen was the only child of Hans Andersen, a shoemaker, and Anne Marie Anders, a laundry worker. Despite being poor, his father made sure to take Andersen to the local playhouse. 54) After his father's death, the 14-year-old Andersen traveled to Copenhagen to pursue an acting career in the Royal Danish Theater. Under the patronage of Jonas Collin, the theater's director, he attended grammar school in Slagelse, then a school in Elsinore until 1827, and finally the University of Copenhagen in 1828.
1805년 4월 2일에 덴마크의 Odense 에서 태어난 Anderson은 제화공인 Hans Andersen과 세탁부인 Anne Marie Anders의 유일한 자식이었다. 가난했음에도 불구하고, 그의 아버지는 Andersen을 꼭 동네 극장에 데려갔다. 그의 아버지가 사망한 후, 14살의 Anderson은 Royal Danish Theater에서 연기 경력을 쌓기 위해 코펜하겐으로 갔다. 극장의 감독인 Jonas Collin의 후원 아래, 그는 Slagelse 에 있는 중등학교에 다녔고, 이후 1827년까지는 Elsinore에 있는 학교에 다녔으며, 마침내 1828년에 Copenhagen 대학교에 가게 되었다.

In 1829, Andersen earned some success when he published a short story titled "A Journey on Foot from Holmen's Canal to the East Point of Amager," an account of a character's walking trip. 55, 57) He received a grant from King Frederick VI for travel expenses and went on a 16-month tour through Germany, Switzerland, Italy, and France. 57) This trip started Andersen's lifelong fondness for travel. In 1835, he published his first successful novel, "The Improvisatore," which was largely based on his experiences in Italy.
1829년, Andersen은 "A Journey on Foot from Holmen's Canal to the East Point of Amager"이라는 제목의 단편 소설을 출판하여 성공을 거두었다. 그는 덴마크 국왕인 Frederick 6세로부터 여행 경비 명목으로 보조금을 받았고, 독일, 스위스, 이탈리아 그리고 프랑스까지 16개월 동안 여행을 계속했다. 이 여행은 Andersen이 평생 여행을 좋아하게 된 계기가 되었다. 1835년에 그는 성공적인 첫 장편 소설인 "The Improvisatore"를 출판했고, 이 책은 주로 이탈리아에서의 그의 경험에 기반을 두고 있었다.

56) 1835 was also the year that Andersen published his first book of fairy tales, "Tales, Told for Children," which included "The Tinderbox" and "The Princess and the Pea." More children's stories were published in 1836 and 1837, completing his first volume. He completed his second volume in 1842 and newer collections appeared in the succeeding years.
1835년은 Andersen이 그의 첫 번째 동화책인 "Tales, Told for Children"을 출판한 해이기도 했다. 이 동화책은 "The Tinderbox"와 "The Princess and the Pea"를 포함했다. 더 많은 동화가 1836년과 1837년에 출판되었고, 이는 그의 첫 번째 동화집을 완성시켰다. 그는 1842년에 두 번째 동화집을 완성했고, 추후 몇 년 동안 새 모음집들이 등장했다.

His appeal across cultures was so strong that his stories began to be translated into English as

TEST 2

early as 1846. His books have become timeless favorites and are still being published around the world. In recent decades, Hollywood songs and a Disney cartoon have helped to ensure that Andersen's stories remain popular.
다른 문화 전반에 걸친 그의 호소력이 너무 강했기 때문에, 그의 이야기는 이미 1846년에 영어로 번역되기 시작했다. 그의 책들은 세월이 흘러도 변함없이 사랑받는 작품이 되었고, 여전히 전 세계에 출판되고 있다. 최근 수십 년 동안, 할리우드 노래와 디즈니 만화는 Andersen의 이야기들이 인기를 유지하는데 도움을 주었다.

In 1872, Andersen fell from his bed, incurring an injury from which he never fully recovered. He died on August 4, 1875, in Copenhagen. The Danish government had recognized Hans Christian Andersen as a national treasure even before his death. And in Denmark, International Children's Book Day is celebrated on his birthday.
1872년에 Andersen은 침대에서 떨어졌고, 이는 그가 결코 완치할 수 없었던 부상을 초래했다. 그는 1875년 8월 4일에 코펜하겐에서 사망했다. 덴마크 정부는 Hans Christian Andersen이 사망하기 전 이미 그를 국보로 인정했다. 그래서 덴마크에서는 그의 생일에 세계 동화책의 날을 기념한다.

어휘
adapt **v.** 각색하다
playhouse **n.** 극장
pursue **v.** 추구하다
career **n.** 직업, 경력
account **n.** 설명, 이야기
grant **n.** 보조금
complete **v.** 완성하다
volume **n.** 책, 권
succeeding **adj.** 계속되는, 다음의
appeal **n.** 매력, 호소력
favorite **n.** (가장) 좋아하는 것
ensure **v.** (반드시) ~하게 하다
incur **v.** 초래하다
injury **n.** 부상
recognize **v.** 인정하다
celebrate **v.** 기념하다, 축하하다

53. 세부사항

Hans Christian Andersen은 무엇으로 가장 유명한가?

(a) 그의 문화적 호소력
(b) 그의 여행
(c) 그의 불행한 죽음
(d) 그의 동화

해설 첫 번째 문단의 첫 번째 문장에서 그가 동화로 잘 알려진 덴마크 작가이자 시인이었다고(Hans Christian Andersen was a Danish writer and poet who is best known for his children's stories.) 하였으므로, 정답은 (d)이다.

정답 (d)

어휘
unfortunate **adj.** 불행한
fairy tale **n.** 동화, 우화

54. 세부사항

Andersen이 연기를 하기 위해 코펜하겐에 가기로 결정했던 때는 언제인가?

(a) 대학을 마친 후
(b) 아버지가 사망한 후
(c) 덴마크 정부의 인정을 받은 후
(d) 이탈리아를 방문한 후

해설 두 번째 문단의 세 번째 문장을 보면, 14살에 아버지가 사망한 후 Royal Danish Theater에서 연기 경력을 쌓기 위해 코펜하겐으로 갔다고(After his father's death at the age of fourteen, Andersen traveled to Copenhagen to pursue an acting career in the Royal Danish Theater.) 하였으므로, 정답은 (b)이다.

정답 (b)

어휘
pass away **phr v.** 사망하다

55. 세부사항

기사에 따르면, Andersen은 어떻게 그의 여행 자금 일부를 댈 수 있었는가?

(a) 어머니의 돈 사용하기
(b) 자신의 작품 판매하기
(c) 보조금 받기
(d) 아버지로부터의 선물 받기

해설 세 번째 문단의 두 번째 문장을 보면, 그가 Frederick 6세로부터 여행 경비 명목으로 보조금을 받았고, 독일, 스위스, 이탈리아 그리고 프랑스까지 16개월 동안 여행을 계속했다고(He received a grant from King Frederick VI for travel expenses and went on a 16-month tour through Germany, Switzerland, Italy, and France.) 하였으므로, 정답은 (c)이다.

정답 (c)

어휘
work **n.** 작품

56. 특정정보

1835년 그의 첫 번째 소설 이외에 Andersen이 출판했던 작품은 무엇인가?

(a) 첫 번째 동화집을 출판했다.
(b) 시집을 출판했다.
(c) 여행 전기를 출판했다.
(d) 동요 모음집을 출판했다.

해설 네 번째 문단의 첫 번째 문장을 보면, 1835년은 Andersen이 그의 첫 번째 동화책인 "Tales, Told for Children"을 출판한 해(1835 was also the year that Andersen published his first book of fairy tales, "Tales, Told for Children")라고 하였으므로, 정답은 (a)이다.

정답 (a)

어휘
memoir **n.** 회고록, 전기
compilation **n.** 모음집

57. 추론

Andersen이 성년을 대부분 어떻게 보냈을 것 같은가?

(a) Royal Danish Theater에서 연기를 하며 보냈다.
(b) 여러 장소를 탐험하고 글을 쓰며 보냈다.
(c) 화려한 파티를 개최하며 보냈다.
(d) 생계를 유지하기 위해 애쓰며 보냈다.

해설 세 번째 문단을 보면, Frederick 6세로부터 여행 경비 명목으로 받은 보조금으로 16개월 동안 여행을 다녔다고(He received a grant from King Frederick VI for travel expenses and went on a 16-month tour through Germany, Switzerland, Italy, and France.) 하였고, 이 여행은 Andersen이 평생 여행을 좋아하게 된 계기가 되었다고(This trip started Andersen's lifelong fondness for travel.) 하였으므로, 성인이 된 후 여행을 자주 했을 것이라는 것을 추론할 수 있다. 또한 1835년에 그는 성공적인 첫 장편 소설인 "The Improvisatore"를 출판했고, 이 책은 주로 이탈리아에서의 그의 경험에 기반을 두고 있었다고(In 1835, he published his first successful novel, "The Improvisatore," which was largely based on his experiences in Italy.) 하였으므로, 정답은 (b)이다.

정답 (d)

어휘
explore **v.** 탐험하다
extravagant **adj.** 화려한, 사치스러운
struggle **v.** 허덕이다, 애쓰다

58. 동의어

해당 구절의 문맥 상, patronage은(는) ______을(를) 의미한다.

(a) 후원
(b) 지도력
(c) 우정
(d) 보호

해설 해당 단어가 포함된 부분은 극장의 감독인 Jonas Collin의 '후원' 아래 Andersen이 학교를 다녔다는 것을 의미하므로, 정답은 (a)이다.

정답 (a)

TEST 2

59. 동의어

해당 구절의 문맥 상, timeless은(는) ______을(를) 의미한다.

(a) 변함없는
(b) 잊기 쉬운
(c) 지속되는
(d) 불멸의

해설 해당 단어가 포함된 부분은 Andersen의 책들이 '세월이 흘러도 변함없이' 사랑받는 작품이 되었다는 것을 의미하므로, 정답은 (a)이다.

정답 (a)

Part 2 Q. 60-66

HITLER'S PAINTING COLLECTION DISCOVERED IN A CONVENT
수녀원에서 발견된 히틀러의 그림 수집품

60) A collection of paintings belonging to Adolf Hitler was discovered in a convent in the town of Doskany, north of Prague. *The Telegraph* reported that 60) Jiri Kuchar, a historian from Czechoslovakia, unearthed the collection. The body of artistic works includes a massive canvas called *Memories of Stalingrad* that shows wounded German soldiers taking shelter in a trench. 61) The painting is said to have been one of Hitler's favorites, which experts see as surprising because Hitler suffered one of his greatest defeats in the battle of Stalingrad during World War II.
Adolf Hitler의 소유였던 그림 소장품은 프라하 북부 Doskany 마을의 한 수녀원에서 발견되었다. <The Telegraph>는 체코슬로바키아 출신의 역사학자인 Jiri Kuchar가 그의 소장품을 발굴했다고 보도했다. 이 다수의 예술 작품 중에는 참호로 피신한 독일 부상 군인들을 그린 <Memories of Stalingrad>라고 불리는 거대한 유화가 포함되어 있다. 이 그림은 Hitler가 가장 좋아하는 그림 중 하나라고 전해지는데, 전문가들은 이를 놀라워한다. 왜냐하면 Hitler가 2차 세계대전 동안 크게 패했던 전투 중 하나가 스탈린그라드에서 벌어졌던 전투였기 때문이다.

60, 62) Adolf Hitler was known for ordering German forces to plunder museums and other art establishments for expensive works of art and to hide them. 63) Robert M. Edsel, author of "*Rescuing da Vinci*", tells of how American soldiers recovered thousands of lost artworks during the Second World War. Some of the artworks Hitler's forces stole were priceless paintings and sculptures by masters such as Michelangelo, Edgar Degas, Paul Cézanne, and Vincent Van Gogh. The German dictator himself was known to be a frustrated artist and architect.
Adolf Hitler는 독일군에게 값비싼 예술작품이 있는 박물관 및 다른 미술관을 약탈하여 작품을 숨겨 놓으라고 명령한 것으로 알려져 있다. "Rescuing da Vinci"의 작가인 Robert M.Edsel은 2차 세계대전 동안 손실된 수천 개의 예술작품을 미군이 어떻게 되찾았는지 말해준다. Hitler의 군대가 훔쳤던 예술 작품 중 몇 가지는 Michelangelo, Edgar Degas, Paul Cézanne, and Vincent Van Gogh와 같은 거장들이 작업한 귀중한 그림과 조각상이다. 이 독일 출신의 독재자는 성공하지 못한 예술가이자 건축가로 알려져 있었다.

60) Hitler was reported to have ordered the collection discovered by Kuchar to be hidden in a monastery in southern Bohemia. This collection was found by American forces during the war. However, nobody knows how exactly the paintings later disappeared and ended up in the convent in Prague. The Czech historian has only discovered seven of the paintings in the collection and reports that nine more paintings are still missing.
Hitler는 Kuchar가 발견한 이 수집품을 보헤미아 남부에 있는 수도원에 숨기라고 명령했던 것으로 전해진다. 이 수집품은 전쟁 중에 미군에 의해 발견되었다. 그러나, 정확히 어떻게 그 그림들이 사라졌다가 결국 프라하에 있는 수도원에서 발견되었는지는 아무도 모른다. 체코의 역사학자는 이 수집품에서 단지 7점의 그림을 발견했으며, 이외에 9점의 그림이 여전히 행방불명이라고 전한다.

Art experts predict that the collection could be auctioned for about $2.6 million, but historians believe that the collection's historical value is a lot more. The convent in Doskany, however, has declared that it is not willing to auction off the collection and intends to keep it. Meanwhile, Kuchar is still searching for the remaining paintings, but said it will be difficult to find them. 64) Some institutions, whose artworks may have belonged to the original collection, may not want to be associated with Hitler's notorious acts during World War II, and presumably might wish to remain silent about them.
예술 전문가들은 이 수집품이 약 260만 달러에 경매로 부쳐질 것이라고 예측하지만, 역사학자들은 이 수집품의 역사적 가치가 더 크다고 생각한다. 그러나 Doskany 의 수녀원은 이 수집품을 경매하고 싶지 않으며 보관하려 한다고 공표했다. 한편, Kuchar는 여전히 나머지 그림들을 찾고 있지만, 그림들을 찾는 게 어려울 것이라고 말했다. 원래 수집품의 일부였을지도 모르는 예술 작품을 소유한 몇몇 기관들은 2차 세계대전 동안 Hitler가 저지른 악명 높은 행위와 연루되는 것을 원하지 않기 때문에, 아마 침묵을 지키고 싶어 할 것이다.

어휘
convent **n.** 수녀원
massive **adj.** 거대한
shelter **n.** 피신, 피난처
defeat **n.** 패배
establishment **n.** 기관
priceless **adj.** 귀중한, 값을 매길 수 없는
dictator **n.** 독재자
frustrated **adj.** 좌절한, 성공하지 못한
monastery **n.** 수도원
missing **adj.** 없어진, 행방불명의
predict **v.** 예측하다
declare **v.** 공표하다
associated **adj.** 연관된
presumably **ad.** 아마도

60. 세부사항
Jiri Kuchar가 발견한 것은 무엇인가?

(a) 도난을 당한 그림 수집품
(b) 유명한 Michelangelo의 조각상
(c) Van Gogh의 귀중한 걸작
(d) da Vinci의 *Mona Lisa*

해설 첫 번째 문단의 첫 번째 및 두 번째 문장을 보면, Adolf Hitler의 소유였던 그림 수집품이 프라하 북쪽에 있는 Doskany 마을의 한 수녀원에서 발견되었다고(A collection of paintings belonging to Adolf Hitler has been discovered in a convent in the town of Doskany, north of Prague.) 하였고, 체코슬로바키아 출신의 역사학자인 Jiri Kuchar가 그 수집품을 찾아냈다고(Jiri Kuchar, a historian from Czechoslovakia, unearthed the collection.) 하였다. 그리고 나서 두 번째 문단의 첫 번째 문장에서 Adolf Hitler가 독일군에게 값비싼 예술작품이 있는 박물관 및 다른 미술관을 약탈하여 작품들을 숨겨놓으라고 명령한 것으로 알려져 있다고(Adolf Hitler was known for ordering German forces to plunder museums and other art establishments for expensive works of art and to hide them) 하였고, 세 번째 문단의 첫 번째 문장을 보면 Kuchar가 발견한 수집품은 보헤미아 남부에 있는 수도원에 숨기라고 명령했던 것으로 전해진다고(Hitler was reported to have ordered the collection discovered by Kuchar to be hidden in a monastery in southern Bohemia.) 하였으므로, 정답은 (a)이다.

정답 (a)

어휘
masterpiece **n.** 걸작, 명작

TEST 2

61. 추론

Hitler가 *Memories of Stalingrad*를 좋아하는 것이 왜 놀라운 것일까?

(a) 2차 세계대전에서 패배한 것을 떠올리게 할 것이다.
(b) 실패한 예술가로서 더 좌절감을 느끼게 할 것이다.
(c) 전쟁 중에 패했던 전투를 떠올리게 할 것이다.
(d) 전시 중 저질렀던 약탈 범죄를 떠올리게 할 것이다.

해설 첫 번째 문단의 마지막 문장을 보면, Memories of Stalingrad는 Hitler가 가장 좋아하는 그림 중 하나라고 전해지는데, 전문가들은 이를 놀라워한다며 (The painting is said to have been one of Hitler's favorites, which experts see as surprising) 이는 Hitler가 2차 세계대전 동안 크게 패했던 전투들 중 하나가 스탈린그라드에서 벌어졌던 전투였기 때문이라고(because Hitler suffered one of his greatest defeats in the battle of Stalingrad during World War II.) 하였으므로, 정답은 (c)이다.

정답 (c)

어휘
looting **n.** 약탈

62. 추론

독일군들이 귀중한 예술품을 모으게 된 동기는 무엇인가?

(a) 예술작품에 강한 관심을 가지고 있어서
(b) 그들의 독재자의 명령을 받아서
(c) 개인의 부를 위해 판매하고자 해서
(d) 미국인에게서 무언가를 약탈하기 위해서

해설 두 번째 문단의 첫 번째 문장을 보면, Adolf Hitler가 독일군에게 값비싼 예술작품이 있는 박물관 및 다른 미술관을 약탈하여 작품들을 숨겨 놓으라고 명령한 것으로 알려져 있다고(Adolf Hitler was known for ordering German forces to plunder museums and other art establishments for expensive works of art and to hide them.) 하였으므로, 적군에게 도난을 당하지 않도록 보호한 것이 아니라 Hitler가 그들의 예술작품을 약탈했다는 것을 알 수 있다. 따라서 정답은 (b)이다.

정답 (b)

어휘
precious **adj.** 귀중한
protect **v.** 보호하다
war effort **n.**전쟁 물자

63. 세부사항

전쟁 중 도난 당했던 다수의 작품을 되찾은 사람은 누구인가?

(a) Jiri Kuchar
(b) Robert M. Edsel
(c) 러시아군
(d) 미군

해설 두 번째 문단의 두 번째 문장을 보면, "Rescuing da Vinci"의 작가인 Robert M.Edsel이 2차 세계대전 동안 손실된 수천 개의 예술작품들을 미군이 어떻게 되찾았는지 말해준다고(Robert M. Edsel, author of "Rescuing da Vinci," tells of how American soldiers recovered thousands of lost artworks during the Second World War.) 하였으므로, 정답은 (d)이다.

정답 (d)

64. 추론

이 기사에 따르면, Kuchar가 행방불명 된 그림을 찾기 어려운 이유는 무엇인가?

(a) 소유주들이 그림의 출처를 수치스러워 할 수도 있다.
(b) 그림이 잘 숨겨져 있다.
(c) 독일인들이 전리품 포기를 거부한다.
(d) 수녀원이 수집품을 보관하고자 한다.

해설 네 번째 문단의 마지막 문장을 보면, 원래 수집품의 일부였을지도 모르는 예술 작품을 소유한 몇몇 기관들은 2차 세계대전 동안 Hitler가 저지른 악명 높은 행위와 연루되는 것을 원하지 않기 때문에, 아마 침묵을 지키고 싶어 할 것이라고(Some institutions, whose artworks may have belonged to the original collection, may not want to be associated with Hitler's notorious acts during World War II, and presumably might wish to remain silent about them.) 하였으므로, 소유주들이 그림의 출처에 대해 수치스러워 할 수도 있다는 것을 추론할 수 있다. 따라서 정답은 (a)이다.

정답 (a)

어휘
ashamed **adj.** 수치스러워 하는
refuse **v.** 거부하다
surrender **v.** 포기하다, 항복하다

65. 동의어
해당 구절의 문맥 상, plunder은(는) ________ 을(를) 의미한다.

(a) 검색하다
(b) 주다
(c) 파괴하다
(d) 도둑질하다

해설 해당 단어가 포함된 부분은 Hitler가 독일군에게 값비싼 예술작품이 있는 박물관 및 다른 미술관을 '약탈하라고' 명령했다는 것을 의미한다. 이는 '도둑질하라고' 명령했다고도 표현할 수 있으므로, 정답은 (d)이다.

정답 (d)

66. 동의어
해당 구절의 문맥 상, notorious은(는) ________ 을(를) 의미한다.

(a) 유명한
(b) 악명 높은
(c) 유죄의
(d) 인기 없는

해설 해당 단어가 포함된 부분은 몇몇 기관들이 2차 세계대전 동안 Hitler가 저지른 '악명 높은' 행위와 연루되는 것을 원하지 않는다는 것을 의미하므로, 정답은 (b)이다.

정답 (b)

Part 3 Q. 67-73

THE TASMANIAN DEVIL
태즈메이니아산 주머니곰

The Tasmanian devil, commonly called a "devil," is a fierce, meat-eating animal that lives on the Australian island of Tasmania. Being a marsupial like the kangaroo, the Tasmanian devil gives birth very early, and the underdeveloped young continue growing in the mother's pouch. [71] The animal is known for its bad temper after which it was named. It will go into an uncontrollable rage when threatened by a predator, fighting for a mate, or defending its food.
소위 "악마"라고 불리는 태즈메이니아산 주머니곰은 호주의 태즈메이니아 섬에 서식하는 사나운 육식 동물이다. 캥거루처럼 유대목 동물인 태즈메이니아산 주머니곰은 매우 이른 시기에 출산하며, 미숙한 새끼는 계속해서 어미의 주머니 속에서 자란다. 이 동물은 고약한 성질로 유명한데, 이를 따라 이름이 지어졌다. 천적에게 위협당할 때, 짝을 구하기 위해 싸울 때, 혹은 음식을 지키려고 할 때 걷잡을 수 없이 난폭해진다.

[67] The Tasmanian devil is about the same size as a small dog and has a muscular build, large head, and black fur. It also has long front legs and short back legs, giving it an unusual gait. [67] Other traits that contribute to the animal being called a devil include its unpleasant odor, and the loud screeching sound it makes. It is also known for its keen smell, sharp teeth, and muscular jaw that can deliver a very powerful bite.
태즈메이니아 데블 주머니곰은 소형견과 크기가 비슷하며, 근육질의 몸, 큰 머리, 그리고 검은색 털을 가지고 있다. 또한 앞 다리가 길고 뒷다리가 짧아 걸음걸이가 특이하다. 이 동물을 악마라고 불리게 하는 또 다른 특성에는 불쾌한 냄새와 크게 꽥꽥대는 소리가 있다. 또한 예리한 후각, 날카로운 이빨, 그리고 무는 힘을 굉장히 강력하게 만들어주는 근육질의 턱으로 유명하다.

[68] Tasmanian devils typically feed on smaller animals such as snakes, birds, and insects, while ignoring fruits and vegetation. They are at their most rowdy and temperamental when fighting for the right to feed on a large carcass. Devils mostly hunt at night and spend their days alone in hollow logs, caves, or burrows. They use their long whiskers, strong sense of smell, and excellent sight to avoid predators and find food. They will eat almost anything they can catch and consume everything - even hair, organs, and bones.
태즈메이니아산 주머니곰은 과일과 초목은 무시하는 반면에 뱀, 새, 그리고 곤충과 같은 더 작은 동물들을 주로 먹는다. 그들은 덩치가 큰 동물의 시체를 먹기 위해 싸울 때 가장 소란스럽고 괴팍해진다. 주머니곰들은 주로 밤에 사냥하며 낮에는 빈 통나무, 동굴, 혹은 굴에서 혼자 시간을 보낸다. 그들은 긴 수염, 강력한 후각 그리고 훌륭한 시각을 사용하여 천적을 피하고 먹이를 찾는다. 잡을 수 있는 것은 거의 다 먹고 심지어 머리카락, 장기, 그리고 뼈까지 모두 먹는다.

Tasmanian devils are not monogamous animals, and males will mate with more than one female. [69] Males compete violently for females, and then guard their partners from other male devils. The annual mating period lasts about three weeks and the female devil gives birth 18 days later. A female gives birth to 20 to 30 young devils during each mating season. However, the mother has only four nipples in its pouch, so only a few babies survive.

TEST 2

태즈메이니아산 주머니곰은 일부일처의 동물이 아니어서 수컷들은 한 마리 이상의 암컷과 짝짓기를 할 것이다. 수컷들은 암컷들을 차지하기 위해 맹렬히 경쟁하고, 다른 수컷 주머니곰들로부터 짝을 보호한다. 매년 짝짓기 철은 약 3주 정도 지속되고, 암컷 주머니곰들은 18일 이후에 출산한다. 매 짝짓기 철마다 암컷은 20~30마리 정도의 새끼를 낳는다. 그러나 어미는 주머니에 젖꼭지가 4개밖에 없어 단지 몇 마리의 새끼만 살아남는다.

Once plentiful throughout Australia, Tasmanian devils are now found only on the island state of Tasmania. 70) Biologists believe their extinction on mainland Australia was caused by the introduction of Asian dogs.

한 때 호주 전역에 걸쳐 많았지만, 태즈메이니아산 주머니곰은 현재 태즈메이니아주 섬에서만 발견된다. 생물학자들은 이들이 호주 대륙에서 멸종된 것은 아시아 견종들이 도입되었기 때문이라고 생각한다.

어휘

fierce **adj.** 사나운
marsupial **n.** 유대목 동물, 유대류
underdeveloped **adj.** 미숙한
temper **n.** 성질, 기질
threaten **v.** 위협하다
predator **n.** 천적, 포식자
gait **n.** 걸음걸이
trait **n.** 특성
contribute to **phr v.** ~의 원인이 되다, ~에 기여하다
odor **n.** 냄새, 악취
screech **v.** 꽥 하는 소리를 내다
keen **adj.** 예리한
temperamental **adj.** 괴팍한
carcass **n.** (큰 동물의) 시체
organ **n.** 장기
monogamous **adj.** 일부일처의
extinction **n.** 멸종

67. 사실확인

다음 중 태즈메이니아산 주머니곰의 특징이 아닌 것은 무엇인가?

(a) 긴 앞다리가 있다.
(b) 크고 불쾌한 소리를 낸다.
(c) 악취가 난다.
(d) 털이 갈색이다.

해설 두 번째 문단의 첫 번째 문장을 보면, 태즈메이니아산 주머니곰은 소형견과 크기가 비슷하며, 근육질의 몸, 큰 머리, 그리고 검은색 털을 가지고 있다고(The Tasmanian devil is about the same size as a small dog with a muscular build, large head, and black fur.) 하였으므로, 털이 갈색이라는 것은 사실이 아니다. 따라서 정답은 (d)이다.
이어지는 문장에서 긴 앞다리와 짧은 뒷다리를 가지고 있다고(It also has long front legs and short back legs) 하였으므로 (a)는 사실이며, 주머니곰을 악마라고 불리게 하는 또 다른 특성에는 불쾌한 냄새와 크게 꽥꽥대는 소리가 있다고(Other traits that contribute to the animal being called a devil include their unpleasant odor, and the loud screeching) 하였으므로, (b)와 (c) 역시 사실이다.

정답 (d)

어휘

foul **adj.** 더러운, 악취 나는

68. 특정정보

주머니곰이 주로 먹는 먹이는 무엇인가?

(a) 주로 물고기를 먹는다.
(b) 주로 작은 동물을 먹는다.
(c) 주로 과일을 먹는다.
(d) 주로 어린 태즈메이니아산 주머니곰을 잡아먹는다.

해설 세 번째 문단의 첫 번째 문장을 보면, 태즈메이니아산 주머니곰은 과일과 초목은 무시하는 반면에 뱀, 새, 그리고 곤충과 같은 더 작은 동물들을 주로 먹는다고(Tasmanian devils typically feed on smaller animals such as snakes, birds, and insects, while ignoring fruits and vegetation.) 하였으므로, 정답은 (b)이다.

정답 (b)

69. 세부사항
일 년 중 특정 시기에 수컷들은 왜 더 공격적으로 변하는가?

(a) 암컷들의 주목을 끌기 위해
(b) 짝에게 줄 먹이를 얻기 위해
(c) 새끼를 보호하기 위해
(d) 더 큰 천적에 맞서 방어하기 위해

해설 네 번째 문단의 두 번째 및 세 번째 문장을 보면, 수컷들은 암컷들을 차지하기 위해 맹렬히 경쟁하고, 다른 수컷 주머니곰들로부터 짝을 보호한다고(Males compete violently for females, and then guard their partners from other male devils.) 하였고, 이 짝짓기 철이 매년 약 3주 정도 지속된다고(The annual mating period lasts about three weeks) 하였으므로, 정답은 (a)이다.

정답 (a)

어휘
attention **n.** 주목, 주의
offspring **n.** 새끼, 자식

70. 특정정보
호주 대륙에서 주머니곰의 멸종을 야기한 것은 무엇인가?

(a) 서식지 파괴
(b) 인구수 증가
(c) 견종 도입
(d) 서로를 향한 공격적 행동

해설 다섯 번째 문단의 마지막 문장을 보면, 생물학자들은 주머니곰이 호주 대륙에서 멸종된 것이 아시아 견종들이 도입되었기 때문이라고 생각한다고(Biologists believe their extinction on mainland Australia was caused by the introduction of Asian dogs.) 하였으므로, 정답은 (c)이다.

정답 (c)

어휘
destruction **n.** 파괴

71. 추론
태즈메이니아산 주머니곰이 좋은 애완동물이 될 수 없는 이유는 무엇일까?

(a) 굉장히 크기 때문에
(b) 많은 보살핌을 필요로 하기 때문에
(c) 많이 먹는 경향이 있기 때문에
(d) 굉장히 공격적인 동물이기 때문에

해설 첫 번째 문단의 세 번째 문장을 보면, 이 동물이 괴팍한 성질로 유명하다고(The animal is known for its bad temper) 하였으므로, 매우 공격적인 동물이라 애완동물로는 적합하지 않다는 것을 추론할 수 있다. 따라서 정답은 (d)이다.

정답 (d)

어휘
demand **v.** 필요로 하다
attention **n.** 보살핌, 주의
aggressive **adj.** 공격적인

72. 동의어
해당 구절의 문맥 상, rowdy은(는) ________을(를) 의미한다.

(a) 난동을 부리는
(b) 연약한
(c) 무례한
(d) 평화로운

해설 해당 단어가 포함된 부분은 덩치가 큰 동물의 시체를 먹기 위해 싸울 때 주머니곰이 가장 '소란스럽고' 괴팍해진다는 것을 의미한다. 이는 '난동을 부리고'라고도 표현될 수 있으므로, 정답은 (a)이다.

정답 (a)

73. 동의어 | 해당 구절의 문맥 상, plentiful은(는) ______을(를) 의미한다.

(a) 과밀한
(b) 부족한
(c) 풍부한
(d) 거대한

해설 해당 단어가 포함된 부분은 주머니곰이 한 때 호주 전역에 걸쳐 '많았다'는 것을 의미한다. 이는 '풍부했다'라고도 표현될 수 있으므로, 정답은 (c)이다.

정답 (c)

Part 4 Q. 74-80

Ms. Mary Modest:
Financial Manager
Saundex Financial
Ms. Mary Modest:
재무 관리자
Saundex Financial

Dear Ms. Modest:
Modest씨께:

First, let me start by saying that I'm very happy to work for Saundex Financial and eager to continue contributing to its profitability under your management. I have learned and grown so much under your guidance that I've come up with new ideas for the company. Please allow me then to mention an opportunity for greater profits.
우선 저는 Saundex Financial에서 근무하는 것이 매우 행복하고 귀하의 관리 하에 회사의 수익성에 지속적으로 기여하길 간절히 바란다는 점을 말씀드립니다. 귀하의 지도 아래 굉장히 많이 배우고 성장하였기에 회사를 위한 새로운 아이디어를 생각해냈습니다. 더 많은 수익을 낼 수 있는 기회에 대해 말씀드리는 것을 허락해주시기 바랍니다.

I'm confident that you will agree that 74) my efforts as your salesman have been effective in bringing in greater profits for Saundex. 75, 76) My sales in the past year more or less came in at $425,000, surpassing the $250,000 goal we had anticipated at our year-end meeting twelve months ago. 74) I believe, however, that I can be even more productive for the company as your Sales Manager.
Saundex가 더 큰 이익을 올리는데 회사의 영업사원으로서 제가 들인 노력이 굉장히 효과적이었다는 것에 동의하실 거라고 자부합니다. 지난해 제 영업실적은 거의 42만 5천 달러에 달하며, 이는 12개월 전 연말 회의 때 기대했던 목표 금액인 25만 달러를 뛰어넘는 금액입니다. 그러나 저는 영업부장이 된다면 회사를 위해 생산성을 훨씬 더 높일 수 있다고 생각합니다.

Having had four years of experience selling our financial portfolio, I've gained a clear idea about our customers' needs and how to meet them. I know ways to increase sales dramatically and gear our sales team to do precisely that. As Sales Manager, 77) I truly believe that we can procure an excess of $10,000,000 in sales by the end of a two-year period, generating a level of profits we have never attained before.
4년 동안 회사의 재무 포트폴리오를 판매해오며, 고객의 니즈와 이를 충족시킬 방법에 대한 명확한 생각을 갖게 되었습니다. 저는 매출을 대폭 증가시키고 영업부가 이를 정확하게 해낼 수 있게 만드는 방법을 알고 있습니다. 영업부장으로서 저는 우리가 2년이라는 기간이 끝날 때까지 1,000만 달러 이상의 매출을 올릴 수 있을 것이라고 진심으로 믿어 의심치 않습니다. 이는 예전에는 결코 달성하지 못했던 수준의 수익을 창출하는 것입니다.

I know you are a very busy person, but 78) you also have a reputation for being fair and approachable. If you can find the time to meet with me at your convenience, I would be very happy to discuss this matter in whole and share my ideas with you. 78) I would very much appreciate your thoughts on this professional proposal.
귀하께서 굉장히 바쁘신 분이신 건 알지만, 공정하고 다가가기 쉬운 분이라는 평판도 있는 것으로 알고 있습니다. 편하신 시간에 저를 만나 주실 수 있다면, 이 사안에 대해 전반적으로 논의하고 제 아이디어를 공유하고 싶습니다. 이 업무 관련 제안에 대해 귀하의 의견을 말씀해주신다면 매우 감사하겠습니다.

Cordially,
Richard Felt
Sales Associate
Saundex Financial

진심을 담아,
Richard Felt
판매 사원
Saundex Financial

어휘
be eager to **phr v.** ~를 간절히 바라다
profitable **adj.** 수익성이 있는
effective **adj.** 효과적인
productive **adj.** 생산적인
dramatically **ad.** 대폭으로, 극적으로
gear **v.** 준비하다
generate **v.** 창출하다
attain **v.** 달성하다
reputation **n.** 명성, 평판
approachable **adj.** 다가가기 쉬운
appreciate **v.** 감사하다, 환영하다
Sales Associate **n.** 영업 사원

74. 주제/목적

Richard Felt가 Mary Modest에게 편지를 쓴 목적은 무엇인가?

(a) 실적 부족에 대해 사과하기 위해
(b) Modest씨에게 매출 증가에 대해 보고하기 위해
(c) 영업부장으로 승진하려는 제안서를 논의하기 위해
(d) 회사의 영업부장으로서 사임하기 위해

해설 두 번째 문단을 보면, Richard Felt는 Saundex가 더 큰 이익을 올리는데 회사의 영업사원으로서 본인이 들인 노력이 굉장히 효과적이었다고(My efforts as your salesman have been effective in bringing in greater profits for Saundex.) 하며 영업부장이 된다면 회사를 위해 생산성을 훨씬 더 높일 수 있다고 생각한다고(I believe, however, that I can be even more productive for the company as your Sales Manager.) 말하고 있으므로, 영업부장으로 승진하기 위해 해당 편지를 쓰는 것을 알 수 있다. 따라서 정답은 (c)이다.

정답 (c)

어휘
lack **n.** 부족
performance **n.** 성과, 실적
promote **v.** 승진하다
resign **v.** 사임하다

75. 추론

Felt의 영업 실적에 대해서 뭐라고 할 수 있는가?

(a) 판매 할당을 채우는데 4년이 걸렸다.
(b) 요구 받은 것보다 더 많은 수익을 가져왔다.
(c) 지난해부터 할당을 채우지 못하고 있다.
(d) 잘 해오고 있기 때문에 할당을 더 높게 설정하고 있다.

해설 두 번째 문단의 두 번째 문장을 보면, 지난해 본인의 영업실적이 거의 42만 5천 달러에 달하며, 이는 12개월 전 연말 회의 때 기대했던 목표 금액인 25만 달러를 뛰어넘는 금액이라고(My sales in the past year more or less came in at $425,000, surpassing the $250,000 goal we had anticipated at our year-end meeting twelve months ago.) 말하고 있으므로, 요구 받은 것보다 더 많은 수익을 가져왔다는 것을 추론할 수 있다. 따라서 정답은 (b)이다.

정답 (b)

어휘
sales quota **n.** 판매 할당

76. 특정정보

지난해에 Felt는 할당량을 대략 얼마나 초과했는가?

(a) 25만 달러
(b) 17만 5천 달러
(c) 42만 5천 달러
(d) 천만 달러

해설 두 번째 문단의 두 번째 문장을 보면, 지난해 본인의 영업실적이 거의 42만 5천 달러에 달하며, 이는 12개월 전 연말 회의 때 기대했던 목표 금액인 25만 달러를 뛰어넘는 금액이라고(My sales in the past year more or less came in at $425,000, surpassing the $250,000 goal we had anticipated at our year-end meeting twelve months ago.) 말하고 있으므로, Felt가 달성한 금액인 42만 5천 달러에서 예산했던 금액인 25만 달러를 감하면 17만 5천 달러가 된다. 따라서 정답은 (b)이다.

정답 (b)

어휘
exceed **v.** 초과하다
approximately **ad.** 대략적으로

77. 사실확인

다음 중 사실이 아닌 것은 무엇인가?

(a) Felt는 영업부가 더 좋은 성과를 낼 수 있도록 본인이 동기를 부여할 수 있다고 생각한다.
(b) Felt는 회사에서 4년 동안 경력을 쌓아왔다.
(c) Felt는 본인의 제안이 받아들여지면 생산성이 더 높아질 거라고 생각한다.
(d) Felt는 1년 후 천만 달러를 넘는 매출액을 달성할 수 있을 거라고 생각한다.

해설 세 번째 문단의 세 번째 문장을 보면, Felt는 회사가 2년이라는 기간이 끝날 때까지 1,000만 달러 이상의 매출을 올릴 수 있을 것이라 믿어 의심치 않는다고(I truly believe that we can procure an excess of $10,000,000 in sales by the end of a two-year period) 말하고 있다. 따라서 정답은 (d)이다.

정답 (d)

어휘
motivate **v.** 동기를 부여하다
suggestion **n.** 제안
achieve **v.** 달성하다

TEST 2

78. 추론
이 편지는 Modest에게 어떤 영향을 미칠 것 같은가?

(a) 그녀는 Felt의 제안을 고려할 것이다.
(b) 그녀는 Felt의 편지를 무시할 것이다.
(c) 그녀는 Felt가 현재 직위를 유지하도록 할 것이다.
(d) 그녀는 Felt에게 1년 더 기다리라고 부탁할 것이다.

해설 마지막 문단을 보면, Felt는 Modest가 공정하고 다가가기 쉬운 사람이라는 평판도 있다고 하며(You also have a reputation for being fair and approachable.) 업무 관련 제안에 대해 의견을 말해 준다면 매우 감사할 것이라고(I would very much appreciate your thoughts on this professional proposal.) 말하고 있으므로, Modest가 Felt의 제안을 고려할 가능성이 있다는 것을 추론할 수 있다. 따라서 정답은 (a)이다.
정답 (a)

어휘
retain v. 유지하다, ~한 상태로 계속 고용하다

79. 동의어
해당 구절의 문맥 상, anticipated은(는) ________을(를) 의미한다.

(a) 기대된
(b) 기다린
(c) 추측된
(d) 실현된

해설 해당 단어가 포함된 부분은 회의 때 '기대했던' 목표 금액보다 Felt가 더 많은 수익을 올렸다는 것을 의미하므로, 정답은 (a)이다.
정답 (a)

80. 동의어
해당 구절의 문맥 상, procure은(는) ________을(를) 의미한다.

(a) 구매하다
(b) 수입을 올리다
(c) 관리하다
(d) 수행하다

해설 해당 단어가 포함된 부분은 것을 특정 매출액을 '확보할' 수 있다는 것을 의미하므로, 이는 '수입을 올릴 수 있다'라고도 표현될 수 있다. 따라서 정답은 (b)이다.
정답 (b)

Chapter 3

Reading & Vocabulary

03 독해 모의고사 3회

53	(a)	54	(b)	55	(b)	56	(d)	57	(c)
58	(d)	59	(a)	60	(a)	61	(c)	62	(b)
63	(d)	64	(c)	65	(b)	66	(d)	67	(b)
68	(a)	69	(c)	70	(d)	71	(c)	72	(b)
73	(c)	74	(d)	75	(c)	76	(c)	77	(d)
78	(a)	79	(b)	80	(a)				

Part 1 Q. 53-59

CHRISTOPHER NOLAN
크리스토퍼 놀란

Christopher Nolan is an award-winning British-American director and screenwriter. 53) Best known for their intricate plots and unusual narrative structures, several of Nolan's releases were huge box office hits, particularly *Inception* and *The Dark Knight trilogy.*
Christopher Nolan 은 수상 경력이 있는 영국계 미국인 감독이자 극작가이다. 복잡한 구성과 독특한 서사 구조로 유명한 Nolan의 최근 작 중 몇 편은 크게 흥행했고, 특히 <Inception>과 <The Dark Knight> 3부작이 그러했다.

Nolan was born in London, England, on July 30, 1970. His father was a British copywriter, and his mother was an American flight attendant. 54) He developed an interest in filmmaking at the age of seven when he shot a home movie using his father's Super 8 film camera. In 1989, he entered University College London to study English literature. His interest in filmmaking continued, however, and he joined the school's film society, serving as its president for two years.
Nolan은 1970년 7월 30일에 영국의 런던에서 태어났다. 그의 아버지는 영국 카피라이터였고, 어머니는 미국 승무원이었다. 아버지의 Super 8 필름 카메라를 사용하여 홈 비디오를 찍었던 7살 때, 그는 영화 제작에 흥미를 키웠다. 1989

년에, 그는 칼리지 런던 대학교에 입학하여 영문학을 공부했다. 그러나 영화 제작에 대한 그의 관심은 계속 되었고, 학교의 영화 동아리에 가입하여 2년간 대표 역할을 했다.

55) After graduating in 1993, Nolan worked by producing training videos for companies while making short films in his spare time. His first full-length movie, *Following*, was released in 1998. Made with the help of friends from his college film society, this low-budget, black-and-white thriller tells the story of a writer who becomes obsessed with stalking strangers. The film was well-received in several film festivals across the world, and served as Nolan's "calling card" as a writer-director.
1993년에 졸업한 후, Nolan은 기업을 위한 교육 비디오를 제작하는 일을 하며, 여가 시간에는 단편 영화를 제작했다. 그의 첫 번째 장편 영화인 <Following>은 1998년에 개봉했다. 대학교 영화 동아리 친구들의 도움으로 제작된 이 저예산 흑백 스릴러 영화는 타인을 스토킹하는 데에 집착하게 된 작가의 이야기를 다룬다. 이 영화는 전 세계 여러 영화제에서 좋은 평을 받았으며, 작가이자 감독으로서 Nolan의 "명함" 역할을 하게 되었다.

The success of *Following* attracted the attention of Newmarket Films, which acquired and produced Nolan's screenplay and next movie, *Memento*. This development launched his mainstream career. The independent film is based on a short story by Nolan's younger brother, Jonathan, and 56) featured select sequences in a non-chronological order, essentially telling the story backwards. *Memento* was praised by critics, and nominated for Best Screenplay by both the Golden Globes and the Academy Awards.
<Following>의 성공은 Newmarket Films의 관심을 끌었고, 이 회사는 Nolan의 영화 대본이자 다음 영화인 <Memento>를 사들여 제작하였다. 이 영화 제작으로 그의 주요 경력이 시작되었다. 이 독립영화는 Nolan의 동생인 Jonathan의 단편 소설에 기반을 두었고, 기본적으로 줄거리를 거꾸로 전개하며, 시간을 거스르는 순서로 엄선된 시퀀스를 특징으로 삼는다. <Memento>는 비평가들의 찬사를 받았고, Golden Globes와 Academy Awards 모두에서 최고의 각본상 후보로 올랐다.

Christopher Nolan's biggest break came when he directed *The Dark Knight* trilogy, a big-budget Hollywood adaptation of the Batman comic books. *Batman Begins*, the first of the series, pleased fans and critics alike when it was released in 2005. Its sequel, 57) *The Dark Knight*, opened in 2008 and became the first movie to earn over $500 million in two days. Before completing the trilogy with *The Dark Knight Rises*, Nolan wrote and directed the critically acclaimed blockbuster *Inception*, which won four Academy Awards in 2011.
Christopher Nolan의 가장 큰 성공 기회는 할리우드에서 큰 예산을 들여 Batman만화를 각색한 <The Dark Knight>3부작을 감독했을 때 왔다. 시리즈의 첫 번째 영화인 <Batman Begins>는 2005년에 개봉했을 때 팬과 비평가 모두를 만족시켰다. 속편인 <The Dark Knight>는 2008년에 공개되었고, 이틀 만에 5억 달러 이상의 수익을 올린 첫 번째 영화가 되었다. <The Dark Knight Rises>로 3부작을 완성하기 전에, Nolan은 비평가들의 극찬을 받은 블록버스터 <Inception>의 각본을 쓰고 감독까지 했는데, 이 영화는 2011년에 네 개의 Academy Awards를 수상했다.

Christopher Nolan's complex storytelling and vivid visual style have made him a major figure in both independent and mainstream cinema. He has continued to be an important Hollywood figure, exploring genres such as science fiction and spy thrillers in his films.
Christopher Nolan의 복잡한 이야기 방식과 강렬한 영상 스타일은 독립 및 주류 영화계에서 그를 주요 인물로 만들어 놓았다. 그는 영화에서 SF 및 스파이 스릴러와 같은 장르를 탐구하면서 중요한 할리우드 인물로 계속 활동 해왔다.

어휘
award-winning **adj.** 상을 받은
intricate **adj.** 복잡한
narrative structure **n.** 서사 구조
trilogy **n.** 3부작
serve **v.** ~ 역할을 하다
release **v.** 발표하다
well-received **adj.** 좋은 평을 받은
acquire **v.** 얻다, 인수하다
feature **v.** ~를 특징으로 삼다
select **adj.** 엄선된
sequence **n.** (영화 장면 등의) 연속
praise **v.** 칭찬하다
adaptation **n.** 각색
vivid **adj.** 선명한

TEST 3

53. 세부사항
Christopher Nolan의 영화는 무엇으로 가장 유명한가?

(a) 복잡한 줄거리
(b) 저렴한 제작비용
(c) 단순한 서사 기법
(d) 만화 각색을 토대로 한 것

해설 첫 번째 문단의 두 번째 문장을 보면, 복잡한 구성과 독특한 서사 구조로 유명한 Nolan의 최근 작 중 몇 편이 크게 흥행했다고(Best known for their intricate plots and unusual narrative structures, several of Nolan's recent releases were huge box office hits) 하였으므로, 정답은 (a)이다.

정답 (a)

어휘
complex **adj.** 복잡한

54. 세부사항
Christopher Nolan이 처음 영화 제작에 참여한 것은 언제인가?

(a) 영화 단체에 가입하였을 때
(b) 어렸을 때 홈 비디오를 만들었을 때
(c) 취미로 영화 제작을 시작했을 때
(d) 대학교를 졸업했을 때

해설 두 번째 문단의 세 번째 문장을 보면, 그가 아버지의 Super 8 필름 카메라를 사용하여 홈 비디오를 찍었던 7살 때 영화 제작에 흥미를 키웠다고(He developed an interest in filmmaking at the age of seven when he shot a home movie using his father's Super 8 film camera.) 하였으므로, 정답은 (b)이다.

정답 (b)

어휘
involve **v.** 참여시키다, 수반하다

55. 세부사항
기사에 따르면, Nolan이 대학교를 졸업한 후 즉시 했던 일은 무엇인가?

(a) 여러 가지 단편 영화를 발표했다.
(b) 회사용 교육 비디오를 제작했다.
(c) 첫 장편 영화 제작을 시작했다.
(d) 대학교 영화 동아리를 지휘했다.

해설 세 번째 문단의 첫 번째 문장을 보면, 그가 1993년에 졸업한 후에 기업을 위한 교육 비디오를 제작하는 일을 하며, 여가 시간에는 단편 영화를 제작했다고(After graduating in 1993, Nolan worked by producing training videos for companies while making short films in his spare time.) 하였으므로, 정답은 (b)이다.

정답 (b)

어휘
supervise **v.** 지휘하다, 지도하다

56. 특정정보
다음 중 영화 Memento를 특별하게 만드는 점은 무엇인가?

(a) 제한된 예산으로 제작되었다.
(b) 전부 흑백으로 촬영되었다.
(c) 대학교 친구들과의 합작품이다.
(d) 보통의 사건 순서를 따르지 않는다.

해설 네 번째 문단의 세 번째 문장을 보면, Memento는 기본적으로 줄거리를 반대로 이야기하며 시간을 거스르는 순서로 엄선된 시퀀스를 특징으로 삼는다고(featured select sequences in a non-chronological order, essentially telling the story backwards.) 하였으므로, 정답은 (d)이다.

정답 (d)

어휘
distinctive **adj.** 독특한, 눈에 띄는
collaboration **n.** 공동작업

57. 추론

기사에 따르면, 2008년에 개봉한 The Dark Knight에 대해서 뭐라고 말할 수 있는가?

(a) Batman 시리즈의 마지막 작품이다.
(b) Nolan이 처음 만화책을 각색한 것이다.
(c) 영화 흥행 기록을 깨트렸다.
(d) Nolan이 많은 상을 받게 해주었다.

해설 다섯 번째 문단의 세 번째 문장을 보면, *The Dark Knight*가 2008년에 공개되었고, 이틀 만에 5억 이상의 수익을 올린 첫 번째 영화가 되었다고(The Dark Knight, opened in 2008 and became the first movie to earn over $500 million in two days.) 하였으므로, 기존의 영화 흥행 기록을 깨트렸다는 것을 추론할 수 있다. 따라서 정답은 (c)이다.

정답 (c)

어휘
box office record **n.** 박스 오피스 기록, 영화 흥행 기록

58. 동의어

해당 구절의 문맥 상, developed은(는) ________을(를) 의미한다.

(a) 지었다
(b) 거절했다
(c) 높였다
(d) 얻었다

해설 해당 단어가 포함된 부분은 Nolan이 7살 때 영화 제작에 흥미를 '키웠다'는 것을 의미한다. 이는 흥미를 '얻었다'라고도 표현할 수 있으므로, 정답은 (d)이다.

정답 (d)

59. 동의어

해당 구절의 문맥 상, acclaimed은(는) ________을(를) 의미한다.

(a) 찬사를 받은
(b) 지탄을 받은
(c) 환영 받지 못하는
(d) 소유하는

해설 해당 단어가 포함된 부분은 2011년에 Nolan이 비평가들의 '극찬을 받은' 영화 Inception의 각본을 쓰고 감독했다는 것을 의미한다. 이는 '찬사를 받은 영화'라고도 표현할 수 있으므로, 정답은 (a)이다.

정답 (a)

Part 2 Q. 60-66

GLOBAL WARMING MAY SHRINK FISH
지구온난화가 물고기의 크기를 줄어들게 할지도 모른다

The size and body weight of much of the world's fish population could decrease by as much as 24% in the next 40 years. This finding from a study conducted by scientists at the University of British Columbia was published in the journal Natural Climate Change. The study demonstrates that the rising temperature of ocean water due to global climate change is causing a decrease in its oxygen levels. 60, 64) One result of this oxygen depletion is the inability of fish to develop into full-sized adults, 64) threatening one of the world's major food sources.

향후 40년간 전 세계의 어류 개체군 중 다수의 크기와 무게가 24%만큼 줄어들 수 있다. British Columbia 대학교의 과학자들이 실시한 연구의 결과가 학술지 Natural Climate Change에 게재되었다. 이 연구는 지구 기후 변화로 인해 해수의 온도가 올라가는 것이 산소량 감소를 야기하고 있다는 것을 보여준다. 산소 결핍의 결과 중 하나는 물고기가 성체 크기로 자라는 게 불가능해지는 것이고, 이는 세계 주요 식량원 중 하나를 위협하게 될 것이다.

The researchers designed a computer model to learn how global warming would affect more than 600 species of fish in different parts of the world. The study suggests that the average size of an adult fish in over 75% of the world's fish species can be expected to shrink by the year 2050. Those that would be most affected are the ones from the Indian Ocean, showing a potential decrease in average size by 24%. 61) Because oxygen levels also decrease with depth in oceans, deep-sea fish will be the most vulnerable, including popularly harvested food sources like cod, haddock, and halibut.

연구진은 지구 온난화가 전 세계 다양한 곳에 있는 600여 종의 물고기에게 어떤 영향을 미치는지 알아내기 위해 컴퓨터 모델을 고안했다. 이 연구는 전 세계 어종의 75%가 넘는 종의 성어 평균 크기가 2050년까지 줄어들 것으로 예상된다는 점을 시사한다. 가장 영향을 많이 받는 것은 인도양에 사는 물고기이며, 평균 크기가 24% 감소할 것으로 보인다. 수심이 깊어질수록 산소량이 감소하기 때문에, 대구, 해덕, 넙치와 같이 일반적으로 수확되는 식량원을 포함한 심해어가 가장 취약한 개체가 될 것이다.

The newly warmed water would also stimulate an increase in many species' metabolism. 62) Any in-

TEST 3

crease in a fish's basal metabolic rate, the rate an animal uses energy while awake and at rest, will consequently force it to consume more oxygen just to maintain normal bodily functions. This will contribute further to the depletion of the life-giving gas in the ocean and prevent other fish from growing properly.
또한 최근에 따뜻해진 해수는 많은 어종의 신진대사 증가를 촉진시킬 것이다. 동물이 깨어 있을 때와 휴식을 취할 때 사용하는 에너지 비율인 물고기의 기초 신진대사율이 증가하는 것은 결과적으로 정상 생체 기능을 유지하기 위해서 어쩔 수 없이 더 많은 산소를 소모하게끔 만들 것이다. 이는 더 나아가 바다에서 생물을 살아있게 해주는 기체가 고갈되는 원인이 될 것이고, 다른 물고기가 제대로 자라는 것을 막을 것이다.

The study further predicts that species will eventually relocate to colder waters where oxygen is more abundant. Like any organism, fish have adapted over time to thrive in their specific environments. As the oxygen levels change in their current habitats, fish will move toward areas where the gas levels are closer to those of their ideal environments. 63) The larger the fish is, the colder the water it will relocate to. Populations of the biggest fish will most likely move closest to the North and South Poles where oxygen is most plentiful.
이 연구는 더 나아가 결국 산소가 더 풍부한, 더 찬물로 어종이 이동할 것이라고 예측한다. 모든 생물처럼, 물고기는 자신만의 특정한 환경에서 잘 자라기 위해 시간이 흐르면서 적응해왔다. 현재 서식지의 산소량이 변화하면, 물고기는 이상적인 환경의 산소량과 더 가까운 양의 산소가 있는 곳으로 이동할 것이다. 물고기가 더 클수록, 이동해가는 물의 온도는 더 낮아진다. 가장 큰 물고기의 개체군이 산소가 가장 풍부한 북극이나 남극에 제일 가깝게 갈 가능성이 크다.

어휘
population **n.** 개체군, 인구
conduct **v.** (수행)하다
publish **n.** 게재하다
demonstrate **v.** 보여주다, 입증하다
depletion **n.** 고갈
shrink **v.** 줄어들게 하다
stimulate **v.** 자극하다, 촉진하다
metabolism **n.** 신진대사
consequently **ad.** 결과적으로
bodily function **n.** 생체 기능
consume **v.** 소모하다
contribute to **phr v.** ~에 기여하다, ~의 원인이 되다
relocate **v.** 이동하다
abundant **ad.** 풍부한
organism **n.** 생명체, 유기체
specific **adj.** 특정한
plentiful **adj.** 풍부한

60. 특정정보
바다의 물고기 크기가 줄어드는 직접적인 요인은 무엇인가?

(a) 감소하는 수중 산소 공급량
(b) 바다의 어종 수 증가
(c) 지구 대기의 온난화
(d) 해수면 온도의 상승

해설 산소 결핍으로 인한 결과 중 하나는 물고기가 성체 크기로 자라는 게 불가능해지는 것이라고(One result of this oxygen depletion is the inability of fish to develop into full-sized adults) 하였으므로, 정답은 (a)이다.

정답 (a)

어휘
atmosphere **n.** 대기

61. 세부사항

대구나 넙치 같은 물고기가 지구 온난화로 가장 안 좋은 영향을 받는 이유는 무엇인가?

(a) 그들은 보통 인간에게 잡아 먹힌다.
(b) 그들은 번식 속도가 가장 느리다.
(c) 그들은 바다 깊은 곳에서 산다.
(d) 그들은 신진대사가 매우 느리다.

해설 두 번째 문단의 마지막 문장을 보면, 수심이 깊어질수록 산소량이 감소하기 때문에(Because oxygen levels also decrease with depth in oceans), 대구, 해덕, 넙치와 같이 일반적으로 수확되는 식량원을 포함한 심해어가 가장 취약한 개체가 될 것이라고(deep-sea fish will be the most vulnerable, including popularly harvested food sources like cod, haddock, and halibut.) 하였으므로, 정답은 (c)이다.

정답 (c)

어휘
reproduce **v.** 번식하다

62. 세부사항

신진대사율 증가는 물고기의 행동에 어떻게 영향을 미치는가?

(a) 물고기가 소모 가능한 산소를 저장하게 만든다.
(b) 물고기가 산소를 더 많이 사용하게 만든다.
(c) 물고기가 더 들썩이게끔 유도한다.
(d) 물고기가 이동하게끔 유도한다.

해설 세 번째 문단의 두 번째 문장을 보면, 물고기의 기초 신진대사율이 증가하는 것은 결과적으로 정상 생체 기능을 유지하기 위해서 어쩔 수 없이 더 많은 산소를 소모하게끔 만들 것이라고(Any increase in a fish's basal metabolic rate will consequently force it to consume more oxygen just to maintain normal bodily functions.) 하였으므로, 정답은 (b)이다.

정답 (b)

63. 추론

기사에 따르면, 작은 물고기는 차가운 물의 어느 부분으로 이동할 것 같은가?

(a) 인도양의 차갑고 수심이 깊은 곳까지
(b) 어부가 도달할 수 없는 차가운 물까지
(c) 큰 물고기처럼 북극과 남극에 가까운 곳
(d) 큰 물고기보다는 북극과 남극에서 더 떨어진 곳

해설 마지막 문단의 끝에서 두 문장을 보면, 물고기가 더 클수록 이동해가는 물의 온도는 더 낮아진다고(The larger the fish is, the colder the water it will relocate to.) 하며, 가장 큰 물고기의 개체군이 산소가 가장 풍부한 북극이나 남극에 제일 가깝게 갈 가능성이 크다고(Populations of the biggest fish will most likely move closest to the North and South Poles where oxygen is most plentiful.) 하였으므로, 작은 물고기는 큰 물고기보다는 북극과 남극에서 더 떨어진 곳으로 이동할 것이라고 추론할 수 있다. 따라서 정답은 (d)이다.

정답 (d)

어휘
reach **v.** 닿다, 도달하다

64. 추론

이 기사에서 다루고 있는 주요 걱정거리는 무엇인 것 같은가?

(a) 바다 생태계의 파괴
(b) 기후 변화의 해로운 영향
(c) 다가올 주요 식량원 부족
(d) 먼 바다로 이동하는 물고기

해설 첫 번째 문단의 마지막 문장을 보면, 산소 결핍으로 인한 결과 중 하나는 물고기가 성체 크기로 자라는 게 불가능해지는 것이라고(One result of this oxygen depletion is the inability of fish to develop into full-sized adults) 하며, 이것이 세계 주요 식량원 중 하나를 위협하게 될 거라고(threatening one of the world's major food sources) 하였으므로, 다가올 식량원 부족을 걱정하고 있다는 것을 알 수 있다. 따라서 정답은 (c)이다.

정답 (c)

어휘
destruction **n.** 파괴
looming **adj.** (안 좋은 일이) 서서히 다가오는

TEST 3

65. 동의어
해당 구절의 문맥 상, vulnerable은(는) ________을(를) 의미한다.

(a) 관대한
(b) 민감한
(c) 면역성이 있는
(d) 위험한

해설 해당 단어가 포함된 부분은 심해어가 산소 부족에 가장 '취약한' 개체라는 것을 의미한다. 이는 산소 부족에 '민감한' 개체라고도 표현할 수 있으므로, 정답은 (b)이다.
정답 (b)

66. 동의어
해당 구절의 문맥 상, adapted은(는) ________을(를) 의미한다.

(a) 이동했다
(b) 거절했다
(c) 복사했다
(d) 적응했다

해설 해당 단어가 포함된 부분은 물고기가 시간이 흐르면서 자신의 환경에 '적응해왔다'는 것을 의미하므로, 정답은 (d)이다.
정답 (d)

Part 3 Q. 67-73

TRUFFLES
송로버섯

Truffles are a type of mushroom that grows underground. 67) They are typically found around certain types of trees on whose roots they rely upon for nourishment. They vary in size and come in two colors: black and white. 67) Because of their irregularly round shape, truffles usually resemble the chocolate confection that bears the same name. Sought after for their 67) earthy and pungent taste, truffles have been valued since ancient times, especially by the early Greeks and Romans. Today, truffles are highly prized in international haute cuisine, or high cuisine.
송로 버섯은 지하에서 자라는 버섯의 한 종류이다. 그들은 자양분을 얻기 위해 자신들이 필요로 하는 뿌리를 가지고 있는 특정 종류의 나무 근처에서 보통 발견된다. 그들의 크기는 다양하고, 검은색과 백색, 이렇게 두 가지 색을 띤다. 불규칙한 둥근 모양 때문에, 송로 버섯은 일반적으로 같은 이름을 지닌 초콜릿 과자와 닮았다. 흙내가 나고 톡 쏘는 맛이 좋아 고대부터 특히 고대 그리스인과 로마인에게 귀하게 여겨져 왔다. 오늘날, 송로 버섯은 세계 각국의 고급 요리 또는 고급 요리에서 높은 평가를 받고 있다.

Truffles are so rare that they have been dubbed the "Diamonds of the Kitchen." They can only be harvested during certain times of the year, usually between September and May. They are also not easy to harvest; truffles can grow at depths of one-meter underground, and 68) it is usually difficult to determine which trees harbor them. 68, 69) Specially-trained dogs and "truffle pigs" are normally used to sniff out mature truffles. All of these factors make truffles so expensive—one pound costs as much as $1,000—that the delicacy is normally served only in posh restaurants.
송로 버섯은 굉장히 희귀해서 "주방의 다이아몬드"라는 별명으로 불리고 있다. 그들은 특정 시기에만 수확될 수 있는데, 보통 9월과 5월 사이이다. 수확하는 것도 쉽지 않은데, 왜냐하면 송로 버섯은 지하 1미터 깊이에서 자랄 수 있고, 어떤 나무가 집이 되어주는지 알아내는 것이 대개 어렵기 때문이다. 다 자란 송로 버섯을 후각으로 찾아내기 위해 특별 훈련을 받은 개와 "송로버섯 돼지"가 주로 사용된다. 이 모든 요인들이 송로 버섯을 너무 비싸게 — 1파운드(약 0.454kg) 당 1,000달러 — 만들기 때문에, 이 진미는 고급 레스토랑에서만 제공된다.

The two most well-known types of truffles are the black Perigord truffle, found in Perigord, France, and the white Alba Madonna truffle that is native to Piedmont, Italy. The black truffle is less costly than its white counterpart. It has a more refined flavor which has been described as "syrupy sweet." On the other hand, the white truffle has a flavor that hints of garlic and a musky aroma. 70) Black truffles are best for cooking into sauces, creams, and stews. White truffles, however, are best served raw to retain their intense flavor and aroma.
가장 잘 알려진 송로 버섯 두 종류는 프랑스의 Perigord 에서 발견되는 흑색 Perigord 송로버섯과 이탈리아의 Piedmont 태생인 백색 Alba Madonna 송로버섯이다. 흑색 송로 버섯은 백색 송로버섯보다 덜 비싸다. 그것은 "시럽 같은 단맛"으로 묘사되는 더 정제된 맛을 지니고 있다. 반면에, 백색 송로 버섯은 마늘과 사향 냄새를 약간 풍기는 맛을 지닌다. 흑색 송로 버섯은 소스, 크림, 그리고 스튜를 요리하기에 가장 좋다. 그러나 백색 송로 버섯은 강렬한 맛과 향을 유지하기 위해 날것으로 제공되는 게 가장 좋다.

71) Truffles go well with simple dishes like omelets, pastas, and salads. They are either shaved over

or mixed into these dishes. Recently, truffle oil, which is basically olive oil infused with a small amount of either black or white truffles, has been introduced to the market as a more affordable substitute for truffles. It is also used to reproduce the essence of truffles in cooking.
송로 버섯은 오믈렛, 파스타 및 샐러드와 같은 단순한 요리에 잘 어울린다. 그들은 이런 요리 위에 얇게 깎여 뿌려지거나 혹은 안에 섞인 채로 제공된다. 최근에는 송로버섯 대체품으로 가격이 더 적당한 송로버섯 기름이 시장에 출시되었는데, 이 기름은 주로 소량의 흑색 또는 백색 송로 버섯과 함께 우려낸 올리브유이다. 이것은 요리에 송로버섯의 맛의 정수를 재현하기 위해서도 사용된다.

어휘
typically **adj.** 일반적으로, 보통
nourishment **n.** 자양분
vary **v.** 다양하다
irregularly **ad.** 불규칙적으로
confection **n.** 당과 제품
earthy **adj.** 흙 같은
pungent **adj.** 톡 쏘는
prize **v.** 귀하게 여기다
dub **v.** ~라는 별명으로 부르다
determine **v.** 알아내다
delicacy **n.** 진미, 별미
counterpart **n.** 상대, 대응관계에 있는 것
refined **adj.** 정제된
retain **v.** 유지하다
intense **adj.** 강렬한
affordable **adj.** 적당한, 알맞은
infuse **v.** 우리다, 주입하다

67. 사실확인
다음 중 송로버섯의 특징이 아닌 것은 무엇인가?
(a) 나무의 뿌리에서 자란다.
(b) 비싼 사탕으로 만들어진다.
(c) 다양한 크기와 모양이 있다.
(d) 강한 맛을 지닌다.

해설 첫 번째 문단을 보면, 송로 버섯은 자양분을 얻기 위해 자신들이 필요로 하는 뿌리를 가지고 있는 특정 종류의 나무 근처에서 보통 발견된다고(They are typically found around certain types of trees on whose roots they rely upon for nourishment.) 하며, 크기가 다양하고(They vary in size), 불규칙적으로 둥근 모양을(irregularly round shape) 띠며, 흙내가 나고 톡 쏘는 맛을(earthy and pungent taste) 지니고 있다고 하였으므로, (a), (c), (d)는 사실이다. 그러나 비싼 사탕으로 만들어진다는 내용은 언급되지 않았으므로, 정답은 (b)이다.
정답 (b)

어휘
spicy **adj.** 강렬한

68. 세부사항 | 이 글에 따르면, 송로 버섯은 왜 고가인가?
(a) 찾기 어렵기 때문에
(b) 재배될 수 없기 때문에
(c) 붙어 자라는 나무가 희귀하기 때문에
(d) 예측 가능한 수확 시기가 없기 때문에

해설 두 번째 문단의 세 번째 및 네 번째 문장을 보면, 어떤 나무가 송로버섯의 집이 되어주는지 알아내는 것이 대개 어렵다고(it is usually difficult to determine which trees harbor them.) 하며, 다 자란 송로버섯을 후각으로 찾아내기 위해 특별 훈련을 받은 개와 "송로버섯 돼지"가 주로 사용되고(Specially-trained dogs and "truffle pigs" are normally used to sniff out mature truffles.), 이러한 모든 요소가 송로버섯을 굉장히 비싸게 만든다고(All of these factors make truffles so expensive.) 하였으므로, 정답은 (a)이다.
정답 (a)

TEST 3

69. 추론
송로버섯을 찾기 위해 개와 돼지가 사용되는 이유는 무엇일 것 같은가?

(a) 땅을 깊게 팔 수 있다.
(b) 어떤 나무를 찾아야 하는지 안다.
(c) 뛰어난 후각을 지니고 있다.
(d) 훈련하기 쉽다.

해설 두 번째 문단의 네 번째 문장을 보면, 다 자란 송로버섯을 후각으로 찾아내기 위해 특별 훈련을 받은 개와 "송로버섯 돼지"가 보통 사용된다고(Specially-trained dogs and "truffle pigs" are normally used to sniff out mature truffles) 하였으므로, 개와 돼지가 뛰어난 후각을 지니고 있기 때문에 버섯을 찾는 데 사용한다는 것을 추론할 수 있다. 따라서 정답은 (c)이다.

정답 (c)

어휘
sense of smell **n.** 후각

70. 세부사항
색이 다른 것 이외에, 백색 송로 버섯은 흑색 송로 버섯과 어떻게 다른가?

(a) 더 순한 맛을 지닌다.
(b) 프랑스에서만 발견된다.
(c) 덜 비싸다.
(d) 요리되지 않았을 때 맛이 더 좋다.

해설 세 번째 문단의 마지막 두 문장을 보면, 흑색 송로버섯은 소스, 크림, 그리고 스튜를 요리하기에 가장 좋지만(Black truffles are best for cooking into sauces, creams, and stews.), 백색 송로 버섯은 강렬한 맛과 향을 유지하기 위해 날것으로 제공되는 게 가장 좋다고(White truffles, however, are best served raw to retain their intense flavor and aroma.) 하였으므로, 정답은 (d)이다.

정답 (d)

어휘
mild **adj.** 순한

71. 추론
기사에 따르면, 송로 버섯이 제공되는 방식에 대해 가장 사실인 것 같은 것은 무엇인가?

(a) 일반 식당에서 제공된다.
(b) 향신료를 사용하지 않고 제공될 수 있다.
(c) 주 요리로 제공되지 않는다.
(d) 보통 날 것으로 제공된다.

해설 마지막 문단의 첫 번째 및 두 번째 문장을 보면, 송로 버섯은 오믈렛, 파스타 및 샐러드와 같은 단순한 요리에 잘 어울린다고(Truffles go well with simple dishes like omelets, pastas, and salads.) 하며, 이런 요리 위에 깎인 채로 혹은 안에 섞인 채로 제공된다고(They are either shaved over or mixed into these dishes.) 하였으므로, 송로 버섯이 주 요리로는 제공되지 않는다는 것을 추론할 수 있다. 따라서 정답은 (c)이다.

정답 (c)

어휘
ordinary **adj.** 보통의,

72. 동의어
해당 구절의 문맥 상, posh은(는) __________ 을(를) 의미한다.

(a) 속물적인
(b) 호화로운
(c) 현대적인
(d) 보통의

해설 해당 단어가 포함된 부분은 송로 버섯이 보통 '호화로운' 레스토랑에서만 제공된다는 것을 의미하므로, 정답은 (b)이다.

정답 (b)

73. 동의어 | 해당 구절의 문맥 상, substitute은(는) _____ 을(를) 의미한다.

(a) 부가물
(b) 보충물
(c) 대체물
(d) 선호도

해설 해당 단어가 포함된 부분은 송로버섯 '대체품'으로 가격이 더 적당한 송로버섯 기름이 시장에 출시되었다는 것을 의미하므로, 정답은 (c)이다.

정답 (c)

Part 4 Q. 74-80

Walter Jackson
8750 Roosevelt St.
San Diego, CA

Walter Jackson
캘리포니아 주 샌디에고
루즈벨트 가 8750번지

74) I am pleased to inform you that Collins University's School of Law has admitted you to its Juris Doctor degree program for next semester. You are among the select students whose academic achievements, diverse talents, and strong character qualify them for the program. We believe that you will contribute significantly to the academic rigor that characterizes our school.
Collins 대학교 법과 대학원에서 다음 학기 귀하의 법무 박사 과정 입학을 허락했다는 것을 알리게 되어 기쁩니다. 귀하는 해당 과정에 적합한 학업 성취, 다양한 재능, 그리고 강인한 성격을 지니고 있는 엄선된 학생 중 한 명입니다. 저희는 학교의 특징이 되는 학업 가중치에 귀하가 지대한 공헌을 할 것이라 생각합니다.

75, 78) To reserve your place at Collins University, please submit an initial deposit of 10% of your tuition fee along with a completed copy of the confirmation form enclosed with this letter. The deadline for confirming your participation in next semester's program is May 1, but we would appreciate hearing from you sooner. Please note that the initial deposit is non-refundable.
Collins 대학교에 입학하기 위해서, 이 편지와 같이 완성된 확인서 사본과 등록금의 10%에 해당하는 초기 예치금을 함께 동봉해서 제출해주십시오. 다음 학기 과정 참여 확정 마감일은 5월 1일이지만, 그보다 전에 귀하로부터 소식을 듣기를 고대하겠습니다. 초기 예치금은 환불이 불가능하다는 점 유념하여 주시기 바랍니다.

76) Your enrollment is subject to the condition that you present an official transcript of records verifying the completion of your bachelor's degree. 78) Please prepare two notarized copies of your transcript(s), including the final grades for all courses taken, for our evaluation. 77) Once we have reviewed your grades, we will send updates within the next few weeks about your scholarship and student loan options.
귀하의 등록은 학사 학위 수료를 증명하는 공식 기록 사본을 제시해야 합니다. 당사가 평가할 수 있도록 최종 학점을 포함한 모든 과정의 학점을 공증된 사본 2부를 준비해 주시기 바랍니다. 귀하의 성적을 검토한 후, 향후 몇 주 이내에 귀하의 장학금 및 학자금 대출 옵션에 대한 업데이트를 보내드리겠습니다.

Along with this letter are admissions materials and brochures for you to peruse. 78) Please go over the enclosed information sheet which highlights the deposit process and other important information. If you have any questions or concerns after reading this letter, you may contact our office at 799-9995, or send us an email at admissions@collinsuniversity.edu.
이 편지와 함께 입학 관련 자료들과 책자를 보내드리니, 숙독하여 주십시오. 예치금 입금 과정과 다른 중요 정보를 표시해놓은 동봉된 안내서를 검토해보십시오. 이 편지를 읽은 후 질문이나 걱정거리가 있다면, 저희 사무실에 555-0199로 전화하거나, 이메일을 보내주시기 바랍니다.

We are looking forward to your attendance at Collins University.
귀하의 Collins 대학교 입학을 기대하겠습니다.

Sincerely,
Samantha Goodman
Dean of Admissiona
Collins University

진심으로
Samantha Goodman
입학 처장
Collins 대학교

TEST 3

어휘
admit **v.** 입학을 허가하다
select **adj.** 엄선된
achievement **n.** 성취
diverse **adj.** 다양한
qualify **v.** 자격을 주다, 적합하게 하다
contribute to **phr v.** ~에 공헌하다
significantly **adv.** 크게
vigor **n.** 활력, 활기
deposit **n.** 예치금, 보증금
confirmation form **n.** 확인서
appreciate **v.** 고마워하다, 환영하다
be subject to **phr v.** ~에 달려있다
completion **n.** 완료
notarized **adj.** 공증된
transcript **n.** 성적표
evaluation **n.** 평가, 감정
material **n.** 자료
highlight **v.** 강조하다, 표시하다

74. 주제/목적

Samantha Goodman이 Walter Jackson에게 편지를 쓴 주 목적은 무엇인가?

(a) 등록금을 납부하라고 요청하기 위해
(b) 지원 자격 요건에 대해 안내하기 위해
(c) 대학교 등록을 유도하기 위해
(d) 대학교 합격을 알리기 위해

해설 첫 번째 문단의 첫 번째 문장을 보면, Collins 대학교 법과 대학원에서 Walter Jackson의 다음 학기 법무 박사 과정 입학을 허락했다는 것을 알리게 되어 기쁘다고(I am pleased to inform you that Collins University's School of Law has admitted you to its Juris Doctor degree program for next semester.) 말하고 있으므로, 정답은 (d)이다.

정답 (d)

어휘
requirement **n.** 자격 요건

75. 세부사항

편지에 따르면, Jackson은 왜 초기 예치금을 납부해야 하는가?

(a) 학사 학위를 받기 위해
(b) 성적표를 받기 위해
(c) 대학교에 등록하겠다는 의향을 확인 시켜주기 위해
(d) 재정 지원을 받을 자격을 갖추기 위해

해설 두 번째 문단의 첫 번째 문장을 보면, Collins 대학교에 자리를 확보하고 싶다면, 등록금의 10%에 해당하는 초기 예치금과 함께 제출해달라고(To reserve your place at Collins University, please submit a 10% initial deposit of your tuition fee.) 말하고 있으므로, 정답은 (c) 이다.

정답 (c)

어휘
acquire **v.** 얻다
eligible **adj.** ~을 할 수 있는

76. 추론

Jackson이 성적표를 제출하지 않으면 어떤 일이 벌어질 수 있는가?

(a) 장학금 수혜 자격이 되지 않을 것이다.
(b) 다른 학교에 지원할 수 없을 것이다.
(c) 대학교 입학 자리가 취소될 것이다.
(d) 초기 예치금이 환불될 것이다.

해설 세 번째 문단의 첫 번째 문장을 보면, 등록 여부는 학사 학위를 마쳤다는 것을 입증하는 공식 성적 기록을 제시한다는 조건에 달려있다고(Your enrollment is subject to the condition that you present an official transcript of records verifying the completion of your bachelor's degree.) 말하고 있으므로, 성적표를 제출하지 않을 시 입학이 불가능해질 수 있음을 추론할 수 있다. 따라서 정답은 (c)이다.

정답 (c)

어휘
slot **n.** 자리

77. 추론

Goodman이 Jackson의 성적표가 필요한 이유는 무엇일 것 같은가?

(a) 그가 법무 박사 과정에 적합한지 확인하기 위해
(b) 그가 대학교 입학을 취소하는 것을 방지하기 위해
(c) 그가 고등학교 수업을 마쳤다는 것을 입증하기 위해
(d) 그가 어떤 종류의 지원을 받을 자격이 있는지 결정하기 위해

해설 세 번째 문단의 마지막 문장을 보면, 몇 주 이내에 Jackson이 학비 지원 관련 소식을 받게 될 것이라고(Once we have reviewed your grades, we will send updates within the next few weeks about your scholarship and student loan options.)말하고 있으므로, 장학금 지원 여부를 판단하기 위해 성적표를 요구한다는 것을 추론할 수 있다. 따라서 정답은 (d)이다.

정답 (d)

어휘
qualify **v.** 자격을 갖추다, 자격을 주다
determine **v.** 알아내다, 결정하다
back out phr **v.** (하기로 했던 것을) 취소하다, 빠지다

78. 특정정보

다음 중 Jackson이 편지를 읽은 후 요청 받은 사항이 아닌 것은?

(a) 입학처에 전화하기
(b) 동봉된 자료 읽기
(c) 학교 성적표 준비하기
(d) 등록금 예치금 보내기

해설 우선 두 번째 문단의 첫 번째 문장을 보면, Collins 대학교에 자리를 확보하고 싶다면, 등록금의 10%에 해당하는 초기 예치금과 함께 제출해달라고(To reserve your place at Collins University, please submit a 10% initial deposit of your tuition fee.) 말하고 있으므로, (d)는 요청 받은 사항이 맞다. 그리고 세 번째 문단의 두 번째 문장에서 공증된 성적표 2부를 준비해달라고(Please prepare two notarized copies of your transcript(s).) 요청하고 있고, 네 번째 문단의 두 번째 문장에서 동봉된 안내서를 검토해달라고(Please go over the enclosed information sheet) 말하고 있으므로, (b)와 (c) 역시 요청 받은 사항이다. 그러나 전화를 달라고 직접적으로 요청하지는 않았으므로, 정답은 (a)이다.

정답 (a)

어휘
require **v.** 요청하다

79. 동의어

해당 구절의 문맥 상, characterizes은(는) ________을(를) 의미한다.

(a) 지정하다
(b) 정의하다
(c) 구별하다
(d) 묘사하다

해설 해당 단어가 포함된 부분은 학교의 '특징이 되는' 학업 가중치에 귀하가 지대한 공헌을 할 것이라는 것을 의미하므로, 정답은 (b)이다.

정답 (b)

80. 동의어

해당 구절의 문맥 상, peruse은(는) ________을(를) 의미한다.

(a) 검토하다
(b) 생략하다
(c) 집중하다
(d) 고려하다

해설 해당 단어가 포함된 부분은 입학 관련 자료 및 책자를 보내니 '숙독하여' 달라는 것을 의미한다. 이는 '검토하다'라고도 표현할 수 있으므로, 정답은 (a)이다.

정답 (a)

TEST 3